The Book of Ben Sira
in Modern Research

Beihefte zur Zeitschrift für die alttestamentliche Wissenschaft

Herausgegeben von
Otto Kaiser

Band 255

Walter de Gruyter · Berlin · New York
1997

The Book of Ben Sira
in Modern Research

Proceedings of the
First International Ben Sira Conference
28 – 31 July 1996
Soesterberg, Netherlands

Edited by Pancratius C. Beentjes

Walter de Gruyter · Berlin · New York
1997

∞ Printed on acid-free paper which falls within the guidelines of the ANSI
to ensure permanence and durability

Library of Congress Cataloging-in-Publication Data

International Ben Sira Conference (1st : 1996 : Soesterberg, Netherlands)
    The book of Ben Sira in modern research : proceedings of the first
International Ben Sira Conference, 28–31 July 1996, Soesterberg, Netherlands /edited by Pancratius C. Beentjes.
        p.   cm. – (Beihefte zur Zeitschrift für die alttestament-
liche Wissenschaft, ISSN 0934-2575 ; Bd. 255)
    Includes bibliographical references.
    ISBN 3-11-015673-3
    1. Bible. O. T. Apocrypha. Ecclesiasticus – Criticism, interpreta-
tion, etc. – Congresses. I. Beentjes, Pancratius Cornelis. II. Title.
III. Series: Beihefte zur Zeitschrift für die alttestamentliche Wissenschaft ; 255,
BS1765.2.I58   1997
229'.406–dc21   97-34015
                                                                    CIP

Die Deutsche Bibliothek – Cataloging-in-Publication Data

[Zeitschrift für die alttestamentliche Wissenschaft / Beihefte]
Beihefte zur Zeitschrift für die alttestamentliche Wissenschaft. – Berlin ;
New York : de Gruyter
    Früher Schriftenreihe
    Reihe Beihefte zu: Zeitschrift für die alttestamentliche Wissenschaft
    Bd. 255. The book of Ben Sira in modern research. – 1997
The book of Ben Sira in modern research : proceedings of the First
International Ben Sira Conference, 28–31 July 1996, Soesterberg, Nether-
lands / ed. by Pancratius C. Beentjes. – Berlin ; New York : de Gruy-
ter, 1997
    (Beihefte zur Zeitschrift für die alttestamentliche Wissenschaft ; Bd.
    255)
    ISBN 3-11-015673-3

ISSN 0934-2575

Printed in Germany
Printing: Werner Hildebrand, Berlin
Binding: Lüderitz & Bauer-GmbH, Berlin

Introduction

The year 1996 commemorated the centenary of a major event, namely the discovery in the Cairo genizah of some Hebrew fragments that turned out to be the Hebrew text of the Book of Ben Sira (Ecclesiasticus) given up as lost for many centuries. The first couple of decades after these discoveries were almost exclusively devoted to text-critical research of the recovered Hebrew Ben Sira manuscripts originating from the 11th or 12th Century.

The discovery at Masada in April 1964 of a substantial portion of a Hebrew Ben Sira Scroll that has been set in the first half of the 1st Century BCE brought another revolution in Ben Sira research. For these very old Scroll fragments were solid proof of the reliability of the text-critical state of the mediaeval manuscripts, as brought to light between 1896 and 1931. Since the late 1960s, a shift in Ben Sira research has been visible. Some excellent monographs were published in which the Book of Ben Sira was more and more studied from theological, cultural and literal perspectives.[1] The publication by Gerhard von Rad of his *Weisheit in Israel* (1970) was a further impulse to the renewed scholarly attention to Ben Sira. So in the early 1980s, it became extremely popular: about 600 publications on the Book of Ben Sira have been published since 1980.

---

[1] See, for instance, J. Haspecker, *Gottesfurcht bei Jesus Sirach* (AnBib 30) Rome 1967; J. Hadot, *Penchant mauvais et volonté libre dans la Sagesse de Ben Sira (L'Ecclésiastique)* Bruxelles 1970; J. Marböck, *Weisheit im Wandel. Untersuchungen zur Weisheitstheologie bei ben Sira* (BBB 37) Bonn 1971; Th. Middendorp, *Die Stellung Jesus Ben Siras zwischen Judentum und Hellenismus*, Leiden 1973; O. Rickenbacher, *Weisheitsperikopen bei Ben Sira* (OBO 1) Freiburg/Schw. 1973; G.L. Prato, *Il Problema della teodicea in Ben Sira* (AnBib 65) Rome 1975; H. Stadelmann, *Ben Sira als Schriftgelehrter* (WUNT 2. Reihe, Band 6) Tübingen 1980; P.C. Beentjes, *Jesus Sirach en Tenach*, Nieuwegein 1981.

Over all these years, Ben Sira scholars had only met one other incidentally. An excellent opportunity, however, to organize an international meeting of Ben Sira experts was offered by the commemoration
of the 1896 discoveries of the first Hebrew Ben Sira genizah fragments.
So at the end of July 1996 the 'First International Ben Sira Conference'
was held at Soesterberg in the Netherlands. The present volume contains the Proceedings of this meeting. At the risk of not doing justice to
the depth of research invested in the individual papers and the variety
of opinions, some points of interest should be emphasized.

The history and rivalry beween scholars at the end of the 1890s is
outlined by Dr. Stefan Reif, Director of the Taylor-Schechter Genizah
Collection at Cambridge University Library. Many facts about to the
British scholarly environment at the end of the 19th Century shed light
on the personalities of scholars involved in the discovery and identification of the mediaeval Ben Sira manuscripts, their relationships and
the human elements functioning at the centre of scholarly enterprise.

Professor F.V. Reiterer, Director of the 'Ben Sira Forschungsprojekt'
of the Paris-Lodron University of Salzburg (Austria) reviews the
themes and main points of the 600 or so publications about the Book of
Ben Sira that have been published since 1980. Two much discussed
topics of Ben Sira research, namely the structure of the book and its redaction history, are treated in a separate chapter by Professor Johannes
Marböck (Graz, Austria). As there is a real lack of research into both
form and structure of the Book of Ben Sira, Marböck's contribution is
well suited as a starting point for further inves-tigations into this very
complicated subject. The analysis by Professor Núria Calduch-Benages
(Rome) of the 'trial motive' in the Book of Ben Sira surprisingly shows
that Sir 2,1-6 contains a programmatic occurrence of this motive, which
is worked out in various ways and contexts througout the book. In all
instances, testing is part of the search for Wisdom, which in any way is
a major element in the book's structure.

According to Dr. Claudia Camp (Fort Worth, Texas), Ben Sira's
adoption of the female personification of Wisdom is part of his gender
ideology. Not only has Ben Sira linked Wisdom to Torah and cult, but
also anchored Wisdom, Torah, and cult to the ideology of 'honor and
shame'. Not only Chapters 23-26, but also the priestly imagery in
Chapter 50 highlight the cultic need for control of the feminine.

On priests, there is a vivid debate among scholars whether Ben Sira be considered a priest or not. In a stimulating contribution, Dr. Benjamin Wright (Bethlehem, Penn., USA) advances an intriguing theory relating to some works (1 Enoch, Aramaic Levi), roughly contemporary to Ben Sira, that were criticizing the Jerusalem priesthood. He points out some passages in the Book of Ben Sira (e.g. 3,21-24; 34,1-8; 43,2-5) opposing these contemporary works.

Two distinguished Ben Sira scholars demonstrate that a careful reading of Ben Sira texts should always be the basis for a fruitful exegetical investigation. Professor Alexander Di Lella (Washington DC, USA) shows that Sir 1,11-30 is to be read as an elegantly crafted poem that must go back to a rhetorically well structured Hebrew parent text. Professor Maurice Gilbert (Namur, Belgium) offers a thorough analysis of Sir 10,19-11,6, a pericope that has been studied intensively (H.-P. Rüger, A.A. Di Lella, G.L. Prato, and A. Minissale). Evidence is adduced that this poem on 'the wisdom of the poor' is a well structured diptych describing the right way to be honoured, which is the fear of God and Wisdom.

The significance of the Hebrew Ben Sira texts and fragments discovered in the Judaean Desert (Qumran and Masada) cannot be underestimated, as those texts are crucial to the textual history of the Book of Ben Sira. The contribution of Dr. Corrado Martone (Turin, Italy) is a fine example of how a careful reading and reconstruction of those texts can help towards a better understanding of Ben Sira.

Professor Pancratius Beentjes (Utrecht, Netherlands) reflects on the considerations in his decision to publish a new text edition of all extant Hebrew Ben Sira manuscripts together with a synopsis of all parallel Hebrew Ben Sira texts. During the compilation of this synopsis a textual phenomenon showed up, namely a consonantal interchange, that had never been systematically described nor analysed for the Hebrew Ben Sira manuscripts. It could probably shed some new light upon the manufacture of the mediaeval Ben Sira manuscripts and their provenance.

Of course I like to thank all the sponsors of the 'First International Ben Sira Conference':
'Katholieke Theologische Universiteit Utrecht' (KTU)
'Koninklijke Nederlandse Akademie van Wetenschappen' (KNAW)
'Stichting voor Filosofie en Theologie' (SFT)

'Nederlandse Onderzoekschool voor Theologie en Religiewetenschappen' (NOSTER)
'Wetenschappelijk Onderwijsfonds Radboudstichting'
'Stichting Sormani Fonds'
'Mr. Paul De Gruyter Stichting'
'Maatschappij tot Nut der Israelieten in Nederland'.
    I am also indebted to J. Christopher Rigg (Bennekom, Netherlands) for correcting the texts of the authors who are not native speakers of English.
    Finally, let me thank Professor Dr. Otto Kaiser, editor of *Beihefte zur Zeitschrift für die allttestamentliche Wissenschaft*, and Publishing House Walter de Gruyter, Berlin, for accepting the proceedings of the Ben Sira conference in the series.

Nieuwegein, Netherlands   P.C. Beentjes
June 1997

Contents

X   Contents

The Discovery of the Cambridge
Genizah Fragments of Ben Sira:
Scholars and Texts

By Stefan C. Reif

It is now over twenty years since I took over the curatorship of the Genizah Collection at Cambridge University Library and developed a project to conserve, research and publish those remarkable fragments that were somewhat unceremoniously dubbed by their discoverer, Solomon Schechter, "a hoard of Hebrew manuscripts".[1] That project has ranged from the esoteric to the mundane, both in the nature of the items that it has treated and in the manner in which it has publicised their content. A conscious attempt has been made not only to exploit the scholarly riches of the world's most precious and variegated source of medieval hebraica and judaica but also to promote its historical importance among lay people as well as specialists. With those ends in mind, I have constantly made reference to the exciting tale that began with a trip to the Near East by two devout Scotswomen, encompassed an outstanding piece of detective work on the part of a red-headed Rumanian rabbi in Cambridge, and climaxed with the reconstruction of the long-lost Hebrew text of a work composed by Simeon ben Jeshua ben Eleazar, better known simply as Ben Sira, some twenty-two hundred years ago in the Holy Land.[2] In the process of doing so, I have be-

---

1   "A Hoard of Hebrew Manuscripts" is the title of the article published in his *Studies in Judaism* II (Philadelphia 1908) 1-30, that originally appeared in two parts in the *Times* and the *Jewish Chronicle*; see A. Oko, *Solomon Schechter M.A., Litt.D.: A Bibliography* (Cambridge 1938) 30-31.

2   S.C. Reif, *A Guide to the Taylor-Schechter Genizah Collection* (Cambridge 21979); *Published Material from the Cambridge Genizah Collections. A Bibliography 1896-1980* (Genizah Series 6, Cambridge 1988); "Jenkinson and Schechter at Cambridge: An Expanded and Updated Assessment", *Transactions of the Jewish Historical Society of England* 32 (1993) 279-316;

come acquainted with manuscripts and theories, encountered colourful personalities, and come upon items of correspondence that undoubtedly warranted further attention. It has become progressively more obvious to me, as the degree of information and documentation has steadily increased, that the whole topic warranted closer attention and that a careful examination of the evidence would permit the further revelation of stirring sets of events and intriguing *dramatis personae*. That I have now finally succumbed to the allure of such data and applied myself more seriously than before to its content and significance is much to the credit of the organiser of the conference at which this paper was delivered and as a result of which this volume came into being. It is a pleasure to record my deep gratitude to Professor Beentjes for inviting me to participate and thereby encouraging me to set down my understanding of the topic that stands at the head of this essay.

The reason for the special attention currently being given to Ben Sira is of course the occurrence of the hundredth anniversary of the discovery of the first Genizah fragment of its Hebrew text. Before proceeding to further consideration of that significant development, and of its numerous and no less important ramifications, it is of substantial relevance to our treatment to offer a few remarks, by way of preface, on the changing face of scholarly method. Among our academic predecessors of a hundred years ago, there was considerable reluctance to address the ordinary in the assessment of history. The ultimate aim was the pursuit of absolute truth and to that end the preference was for the grand notion and the ideological trend over what were regarded as the more ephemeral aspects of human endeavour. Major works of literature, dominant national figures and momentous events were the stuff of history and to retain their aura of superiority they and those who wrote about them required to be isolated from the vulgar, the mundane and the personal. A century or so later, scholars, in the natural sciences no less than in the humanities, are much more conscious of the subjective element intrinsic to their researches and are wary of expressing anything in absolute

---

"William Robertson Smith in relation to Hebraists and Jews at Christ's College Cambridge", *William Robertson Smith: Essays in Reassessment* (ed. W. Johnstone) (Sheffield 1995) 210-24; "One Hundred Years of Genizah Research at Cambridge", *Jewish Book Annual* 53 (1995-96) 7-28; *Hebrew Manuscripts at Cambridge University Library: A Description and Introduction* (Cambridge 1996).

terms. Partly as a consequence, they are more at home with the humanity of history than with its grander sweeps. Testimonies to the petty incident, details of the underprivileged group and remnants of the unconventional text are given a status once denied them and there is an almost voyeuristic obsession with individuals, their lives and their motivations.[3]

Today's intense interest in both the most obscure contents of the Genizah Collection itself and in the people associated over the years with its discovery and exploitation is to a considerable degree due to such changes in scholarly outlook. What Schechter and his colleagues set aside in their day as unimportant today attracts fresh attention, whether it is economic data, printed matter or magical charms. *Wissenschaftsgeschichte* is also now a flourishing science and it is widely felt that enthusiasm for an academic subject must also entail a fascination with those who have promoted it. Here too, it has become as important to know about the personal involvement as it is to be *au fait* with the technical data. All of which brings us to the subject of this presentation, the intention of which is not only to put on record the part played by Cambridge in the recovery of the Hebrew text of Ben Sira (or, if you prefer, Ecclesiasticus), but also to convey further information about the personalities involved, their relationships and possible motivations, and the manner in which the human element functions at the centre of the scholarly enterprise. Through the judicious examination of manuscript as well as printed material, particularly that which has previously received little or no attention, it should become obvious that scholarship, no matter how detached and clinical it perceives itself to be, always remains a human and not an angelic activity. As the Babylonian rabbis of some sixteen hundred years ago put it, *qin'at soferim tarbeh ḥokhmah*, or, translated into contemporary terminology, "the competitive element leads to an increase in productivity".[4]

It hardly requires to be stated that Schechter's identification of the first Genizah fragment of the Hebrew Ben Sira in 1896 did not occur in a scholarly vacuum. It is consequently necessary to trace the earlier in-

---

3   S.C. Reif, "Jewish Liturgy in the Second Temple Period: Some Methodological Considerations", *Proceedings of the Eleventh World Congress of Jewish Studies* (Division C, I; Jerusalem 1994) 1-8.

4   The saying is cited by the fourth century Babylonian rabbis, Joseph and Dimi, as recorded in b. BB 21a and 22a.

terest expressed in that book on the part of scholars in England and
thereby to establish the context in which the issue of the nature of its
original language had become a burning one. The two major figures involved were Solomon Schechter[5] and David Samuel Margoliouth[6] and
some facts about the personalities and backgrounds of these two scholars, and how they compared, must now be in order. Schechter was
raised in a Rumanian hasidic family in the strained financial circumstances that were typical of Eastern European Jewry. He received an
intensive rabbinic education in *yeshivot* but was also early inspired by
the broader and more historical approach of some of his teachers. He
was able to indulge that interest at rabbinical seminaries in Vienna and
Berlin, before making his way to London as the private tutor of the
scholarly philanthropist, Claude Montefiore,[7] and then to Cambridge in
1890 as the Lecturer, and subsequently Reader in Talmudic and Rabbinic Literature. Though intellectually brilliant, enthusiastic and crea-
tive, he remained physically unkempt and socially unpolished, always
the outsider in frustrated pursuit of somewhere he could call his spiritual home. Having in his earlier years adopted a critical stance towards
hasidism, he warmed again towards a number of its elements as he
matured. He was powerfully committed to traditional Judaism, both as
an ideology and a way of life, an early supporter of Zionism, and an
outstanding interpreter, editor and defender of rabbinic texts. He had
little patience for the Christian biblical critics of his day.[8]

Margoliouth, for his part, originated from a Jewish family that took a
singularly different route from Eastern to Western European culture.
His father, Ezekiel, and another relative, Moses, were converted to
Anglican Christianity and became active missionaries among the Jews,
with a considerable reputation among those anxious to bring the

---

5   For biographical details (1847-1915), see N. Bentwich, *Solomon Schechter: A
     Biography* (Philadelphia ²1940); Reif, "Jenkinson and Schechter"; and Oko,
     Solomon Schechter.
6   For biographical details, see G. Murray, "David Samuel Margoliouth 1858-
     1940", *Proceedings of the British Academy* 36 (London 1940) 389-97.
7   Bentwich, *Schechter*, 47-49; E. Kessler, *An English Jew: The Life and Writ-
     .ings of Claude Montefiore* (London 1989).
8   S. Schechter, "Higher Criticism – Higher Anti-Semitism", *Seminary Addresses
     and Other Papers* (Cincinnati 1915) 35-39.

Church's message to the chosen people.[9] David won a scholarship to the English public school, Winchester College, and carried off an assortment of university prizes as a student of classics at New College, Oxford, before turning his attention to oriental studies and winning election to the Laudian Chair of Arabic in 1889. With a deep voice, an "exotic and vivid appearance" and an outstanding linguistic ability, Margoliouth was one of the great Oxford characters of his day. In matters academic he delighted in adopting sceptical positions, such as when he denied the authenticity of the Elephantine Papyri and of pre-Islamic Arabic poetry, but in the ecclesiastical context he remained thoroughly conservative. It would appear that not until his late years did he feel any special sympathy for the people from whom his family had stemmed.[10]

Given his interest in dating rabbinic language and literature and in establishing its chronological relationship to the latest books of the Hebrew Bible, it is not surprising to find that one of Schechter's first publications after his appointment at Cambridge, and indeed an early contribution to the newly published *Jewish Quarterly Review*, was an article on Ben Sira. Since talmudic and midrashic texts cite Hebrew verses from that work, it was obviously important to him to list, analyse and annotate these so that they could better be assessed in the context of "solving the great Sirach difficulties". Encouraged and assisted by Montefiore, Schechter also provided translations of the relevant texts, as well as demonstrating impressive erudition in his detailed end-notes. Clearly he had at the back of his mind that he might at some later stage be able to argue for, if not prove an authentic Jewish transmission of the Hebrew text of Ben Sira, and he saw in the rabbinic texts a stage in that possible transmission.[11]

There can be little doubt about what constituted the immediate inspiration for his study. The inaugural lecture of the newly appointed Laudian Professor of Arabic in the University of Oxford had been published in the previous year and had dealt with none other than Ecclesi-

---

9   W. T. Gidney, *The History of the London Society for Promoting Christianity among the Jews, from 1809 to 1908* (London 1908) 16-17, 216, 247, 281, 399, 534-35 and 626.

10 Murray, "Margoliouth", 389, 392-93, and 395-96.

11 Schechter, "The Quotations from Ecclesiasticus in Rabbinic Literature", *JQR* 3 (1891) 682-706, with the passage about the difficulties on 685.

asticus. Since the holder of the chair was required to lecture on the Semitic languages ('Arabic, Chaldee and Syriac'), Margoliouth thought it singularly apt to continue the work he had begun in his Kennicott Prize Dissertation of 1887 and to tackle the matter of the original Hebrew of Ben Sira. Having examined all the versions, he concluded that the most reliable evidence was to be found in the Greek and Syriac versions and proceeded to reconstruct a specimen Hebrew text based on their renderings. He was obviously of the view that the rabbinic testimony was of little consequence and indeed took the opportunity of a sideways swipe at the "whole Rabbinic farrago" and of including a theologically tendentious statement about the "grave of the Old-Hebrew and the old-Israel".[12] Hebraists were not generally impressed with Margoliouth's reconstruction and a controversy got under way between him and the leading semiticists, T. K. Cheyne, S. R. Driver and A. Neubauer, as recorded in the columns of the *Expositor*.[13] For Schechter the matter appears to have called not only for a discussion concerning Semitic languages but also for a scholarly crusade (if that term may be used in this context!) in defence of Jewish literary traditions. It was insufficient for him to claim that the Greek and Syriac versions were unlikely candidates for the role of authentic transmitters; more than that, they were no less than "defaced caricatures of the real work of Sirach".[14]

The battle lines had been drawn and the skirmishes continued for five years. Only then was a new weapon discovered that had the potential to settle the matter once and for all and, paradox of all paradoxes, it was a woman who brought it to England and thus contributed to the debate about the kind of language in which a great literary misogynist had written Ecclesiasticus. Indeed, the credit must go not to one woman but to two, Mrs Agnes Smith Lewis and Mrs Margaret Dunlop Gibson. Born as twins in the little town of Irvine on the Ayrshire coast of Scotland, some 25 miles south-west of Glasgow, they were unfortunately bereft of their mother after only three weeks but somehow, through the devotion of their father, the lawyer, John Smith, the interest of the local Presbyterian minister, William Robertson, and their boarding school

---

12   D. S. Margoliouth, *An Essay on the Place of Ecclesiasticus in Semitic Literature* (Oxford 1890), especially 21.
13   *Expositor* 4/1 (1890) 295-320, 381-91.
14   Schechter, "Hebrew Manuscripts", 26.

at Birkenhead, Agnes and Margaret received a sound education in religion, literature and languages. Such an education, combined with a huge
fortune fortuitously inherited by their father from an American cousin
and bequeathed to them by him in 1866, provided the inspiration and
the means for the private study of the Classical and Semitic languages
and for trips to the Near East that resulted in the acquisition of many
exciting manuscripts. The remarkable partnership of these two formi-
dable women and their exclusive devotion to each other were only
briefly interrupted by the marriage of Margaret to the ailing clergyman,
James Young Gibson, in 1883, and of Agnes to the obsessive academic,
Samuel Savage Lewis, in 1888, neither husband surviving more than
about two years in the happy state. On settling in Cambridge, Mrs
Lewis and Mrs Gibson, though disadvantaged and marginalised by their
gender and their religious noconformism in central University circles,
became pillars of the Presbyterian community and close friends of
many of the less conventional and more liberal dons in the city.[15]

Thus it was that their scholarly reputations became interdependent
for a short but important period with that of Schechter. Having in the
spring of 1896 brought home a haul of manuscripts from Jerusalem, the
plain of Sharon and Cairo, they were able to call on the services of the
Reader in Talmudic to help them identify items that were written in a
form of Hebrew unfamiliar to them from their Old Testament studies.
Schechter examined the fragments in their dining-room and quickly
identified one as a vellum leaf of the Palestinian Talmud, itself a significant find, given the paucity of manuscript sources for that work. It
was, however, another "scrap of paper" that attracted his closer attention and that he immediately wished to take with him for further study
and for possible publication. Within a matter of hours he had communi-
cated the result of his research to his women friends by way of telegram
and letter, the texts of each conveying a palpable sense of excitement.[16]
Although he expressly requested them to keep the matter confidential,
he himself could not control his enthusiasm and spread the word among
colleagues at the University Library.[17] Mrs Lewis immediately wrote

---

15   A. W. Price, *The Ladies of Castlebrae* (Gloucester 1985). Born in 1843, Mar-
     garet died in 1920 and Agnes in 1926.
[16] A photograph of that letter has been included in this volume.
17   A. S. Lewis, *In the Shadow of Sinai: A Story of Travel and Research from
     1895 to 1897* (Cambridge 1898) 172-78.

with the news to the *Athenaeum* and the *Academy* and Schechter published the text in the July issue of the *Expositor*.[18] What he had identified was a Hebrew text of parts of Ecclesiasticus 39-40 and he was
convinced that it represented a reliable witness to the original language
of the book. Now surely, he must have thought, the scholarly controversy had been settled in his favour. Little did he realise then that Margoliouth would not be convinced even when seriously challenged by
Nöldeke and that the opposing view would not finally be refuted until
discoveries by Yigael Yadin at Masada in 1964.[19]

Schechter himself has little to say about which precise scholarly
quest inspired him to undertake a trip to Cairo in the winter of 1896-97
in search of manuscripts.[20] Undoubtedly, the medieval Hebrew fragments that had been purchased by the Library from Rabbi Solomon
Wertheimer of Jerusalem or presented to it by the Reverend Greville
Chester in the previous three years, and the fact that some of them had
been written in Cairo, had made him think about the possibilities of
further discoveries. It is equally likely that the success of the Anglo-
Jewish lawyer, Elkan Nathan Adler, in bringing home a sack of palaeographical treasures from the Egyptian capital a year before had not
gone unnoticed.[21] Surely, however, Schechter's excitement about the
Ben Sira fragment brought to him by Mrs Lewis was a major factor in
his decision to travel East in pursuit of the source of such a precious
item and in the expectation of discovering many more like it. With the
advice, encouragement and financial assistance of the philosemitic
Master of St John's College, Charles Taylor[22], and the support of Jewish and non-Jewish colleagues, our Rumanian rabbinic hero made his

---

18 *Athenaeum* 3577 (16 May 1896) 652; *Academy* 1254 (16 May 1896) 405; *Ex-
    positor* 5/4 (1896) 1-15.
19 D. S. Margoliouth, *Expositor* 5/4 (1896) 140-51; T. Nöldeke, *Expositor* 5/5
    (1897) 347-64; Y. Yadin, "The Ben Sira Scroll from Masada", *ErIsr* 8 (1967),
    Hebrew section, 1-45.
20 Schechter, "Hebrew Manuscripts", 3.
21 Lewis, *Shadow of Sinai*, 176; E. N. Adler, "The Hebrew Treasures of Eng-
    land", *Transactions of the Jewish Historical Society of England* 8 (1918) 16;
    Reif, "One Hundred Years of Genizah Research", 9-10; see also note 43 be-
    low.
22 *Eagle* 30 (1908-9) 64-85 and 197-204; *Dictionary of National Biography
    Supplement 1901-11* (London 1912) 480-82; and *Who Was Who 1897-1915*
    (London ⁶1988) 513.

way to Cairo and, having befriended Chief Rabbi Aaron Raphael Ben Shim'on, was virtually given the keys to the Ben Ezra Synagogue and to the manuscript riches that its Genizah contained.[23] He had come upon a veritable *embarras de richesse* and could hardly believe that so many thousands of items were in his hands and that such a variety of subjects were represented among the fragments. Since there was certainly no time to examine the contents, he removed what we now know to have been 140,000 of them to Cambridge, doubtless eager to locate a goodly proportion of Ben Sira texts among them, and to confirm his reputation as the Cambridge scholar who had restored its Hebrew text.

Two Oxford scholars at the Bodleian Library had other plans. Adolf Neubauer, expert in Jewish studies, and Arthur Cowley, erudite semiticist, had, within five weeks of Mrs Lewis's letter appearing in the *Athenaeum*, located another nine leaves of the same manuscript of Ecclesiasticus.[24] It is possible that they were already working on such a project but more probable that Mrs Lewis was right when she later wrote that it was "natural to think" that it was her letter of 13 May, published on 16 May, that had been "of some assistance in guiding Messrs Neubauer and Cowley to this important result".[25] While Schechter was planning his trip to Cairo, his academic competitors in "the other place" were losing no time in forging ahead in the scholarly race by preparing their texts for publication.

Their volume, published by the University of Oxford "at the Clarendon Press" was in the bookshops by January, 1897[26], while Schechter was still ferreting around the various Cairo synagogues and checking whether they had any treasures to compare with those of the Ben Ezra.

---

23 On the Egyptian Chief Rabbi and background, see J. M. Landau, *Jews in Nineteenth-Century Egypt* (New York and London 1969), especially 99-110 and 238.

24 For biographical details of Neubauer (1831-1907) and Cowley (1861-1931), see *Dictionary of National Biography Second Supplement* (London 1912) 5-7; *Who Was Who 1897-1915* (London [6]1988) 382; Dictionary of National Biography 1931-1940 (London 1949) 194-95; *Who Was Who 1929-1940* (London 1941) 297.

25 Lewis, *Shadow of Sinai*, 175.

26 A. E. Cowley and A. Neubauer, *The original Hebrew of a Portion of Ecclesiasticus (XXXIX.15 to XLIX.11), together with the Early Versions and an English Translation, followed by the Quotations from Ben Sira in Rabbinical Literature* (Oxford 1897).

Those *au fait* with the subject of Ben Sira in the previous few years will
have found familiar aspects to the Cowley-Neubauer edition of what
the title-page confidently cites as "the original Hebrew". The history of
the work in Jewish literature is again summarised and its quotations in
rabbinic literature are re-examined. English translations are once more
provided and there are discussions on both the nature of the Hebrew
language and the place of the ancient versions in the book's literary
history. The Lewis-Schechter fragment is included in the edition but the
introduction covers much ground before it actually makes reference to
that discovery on its fourth page, at which point it is also noted that
Schechter's edition has been corrected by the writers. Even then there is
something of a reluctance to set matters in an accurate chronological
perspective. Far from clearly stating that they were inspired by Lewis
and Schechter, the editors follow up their paragraph about Cambridge
developments by reporting that "almost simultaneously the Bodleian
Library acquired, through Professor Sayce, a box of Hebrew and Arabic
fragments" among which they had found other texts of Ben Sira.
Schechter's personal and professional relations with Neubauer had
never been quite as disastrous as those of his Cambridge predecessor S.
M. Schiller-Szinessy[27] but they had nevertheless always been strained.
News of Neubauer's work on Ben Sira could hardly have cheered
Schechter up and he is on record during his 1897 visit to Cairo as having described his Oxford rival in German as a *"Lump"*, that is, nothing
better than a scoundrel.[28] What then was his response to the situation
on his return to Cambridge in the spring of that year? He was already
aware that what he had retrieved from the Ben Ezra synagogue would
grant him immortality in Jewish scholarship and that no one individual
or generation would ever be able to quarry more than a small proportion of the collection's rich seams of new knowledge.[29] He could nevertheless make a start on this massive challenge to scientific Jewish study

27   R. Loewe, "Solomon Marcus Schiller-Szinessy, 1820-1890: First Reader in
      Talmudic and Rabbinic Literature at Cambridge", *Transactions of the Jewish
      Historical Society of England* 31 (1968) 161-62.
28   Reif, "Jenkinson and Schechter", 293 and notes 52-53. The letter from
      Schechter to his wife was written on 12 January 1897 and is in his correspon-
      dence housed at the Jewish Theological Seminary of America's New York li-
      brary, archive 101.21.
29   Schechter, "Hebrew Manuscripts", 29-30.

and he consequently set about the systematic sorting of the fragments, assisted by a team of Cambridge scholars, each with a particular expertise. Mrs Lewis and Mrs Gibson dealt with the Syriac; Charles Taylor with post-biblical hebraica and with palimpsests; Francis Burkitt, soon to be University Lecturer in Palaeography and later Norrisian Professor of Divinity, with Greek items; Hartwig Hirschfeld, from Jews' College and University College in London, with the Arabic; and Herman Leonard Pass, a young Jewish student who converted to Christianity and served in the Church, with the Hebrew Bible.[30]

The University Librarian, Francis Jenkinson, a kindly and scholarly classicist with a broad love of learning and of special collections, was of great practical assistance, as well as a source of sound advice. He was involved in arranging Schechter's trips abroad and having manuscripts copied for him. He opened the Library for Schechter at unusual times and kept order among the fragments, arranging for their careful conservation according to the technical knowledge of the day. He helped Schechter to deal with public matters and showed tolerance and understanding when his Jewish colleague tended to be irascible and impatient.[31] The five years during which Schechter applied himself with boundless energy and enthusiasm to the Genizah material were undoubtedly the most academically productive and significant in his whole life. There is hardly an area of Hebrew, Jewish and general Semitic studies that was not illuminated during his day and that has not continued to derive benefit from his work in the century since then.

But had his passion for Ben Sira been replaced by these wider interests? There is evidence to the contrary and various indications that it still stood at the centre of much of his activity. When he sent his precious haul ahead of himself to Cambridge, he wrote to Jenkinson anxiously requesting that the material continue to be regarded as his private property and not be made available to other scholars until he had dealt with it.[32] Clearly his underlying fear was that an academic rival might

---

30   Reif, "One Hundred Years of Genizah Research", 11-13.
31   Reif, "Jenkinson and Schechter", 291-92 and 297-304.
32   The letter was written from the Hotel Metropole in Cairo on 12 January 1897 and sent "c/o Cook's Agency". It bears the classmark Add.6463.3416 at Cambridge University Library and is reproduced in the newsletter of the Genizah Research Unit at that Library, *Genizah Fragments* 32 (October 1996) as well as in this conference volume.

again steal a march on him. And if the Ben Sira connection is not specifically deducible from that letter, it most certainly is in the report of
his Cairo adventure, published in the *Times* in August, 1897. here he refers to the Lewis and "Oxford" finds of Ecclesiasticus, and expresses
the hope that his recent acquisitions "will yield more remains of these
semi-sacred volumes".[33] It may even be the case that when he wrote
these words, he had already discovered more leaves of the same manuscript since both Taylor and Jenkinson refer to the occurrence of such
discoveries having taken place earlier that summer. It is not insignifi-
cant that they are both very careful about chronicling the precise dates
of virtually all Schechter's subsequent successes in locating Ben Sira
manuscripts. The whole Cambridge team, having once been upstaged,
was not again ready to permit any possibility of doubt about precedence
in such matters. The atmosphere of excitement is best conveyed in
Jenkinson's diaries and in the records of correspondence between him
and Schechter. In one instance, he records that Schechter "nearly went
off his head" and in others there is evidence that the impatience of his
Jewish colleague to prepare his new finds for the press, to have them
conserved, and to ensure that he had checked the collection for every
possible Ben Sira item, had led to some friction between the two, especially when Schechter had on one occasion rudely burst into the University Librarian's room.[34] When Jenkinson's brother-in-law was writing his biography some thirty years later, he remembered Schechter for
having damaged his health by working in the dust of all the fragments
and for having recovered the Hebrew Ecclesiasticus.[35]

Indeed, by the time that Schechter and Taylor published their edition
of 1899, another eleven leaves had been uncovered in Cambridge, and
additional material was available from the Taylor-Schechter collection
for the joint Oxford-Cambridge facsimile edition of 1901, all sorted
into three distinct manuscripts, referred to as A, B and C.[36] In their edi-

---

33 Schechter, "Hebrew Manuscripts", 10.
34 Letters from Schechter to Jenkinson, 17 and 19 June 1898, housed at Cam-
    bridge University Library, Add.6463.3903 and .3908, summarised in Reif,
    "Jenkinson and Schechter", 300.
35 H.F. Stewart, *Francis Jenkinson: Fellow of Trinity College Cambridge and
    University Librarian: A Memoir* (Cambridge 1926) 85.
36 S. Schechter and C. Taylor, *The Wisdom of Ben Sira: Portions of the Book
    Ecclesiasticus from Hebrew Manuscripts in the Cairo Genizah Collection pre-
    sented to the University of Cambridge by the Editors* (Cambridge 1899); *Fac-*

tion, Taylor and Schechter attempted to regain the lead in the scholarly race by each making a major contribution to forwarding the debate. In Taylor's own words, "the discoverer is responsible for the Text, the Notes on the Text, and the Introduction; and the present writer for the Translation and Footnotes and the Appendix, which contains discussions of some passages extracted from the folios edited by Messrs Cowley and Neubauer".[37] The personal and institutional rivalry between the two ancient English universities and their dons that underlies much of the Ben Sira story is further exemplified in a remark made by Schechter in a letter to Jenkinson. He offers his estimate that "the matters I brought from Cairo contain many valuable things which make our Library as important for Hebrew literature as Oxford at least".[38] That would explain Jenkinson's response to Cowley when the latter wrote on 17 August, 1899, requesting permission to collate the newly discovered fragments of Ecclesiasticus. His notation on the letter records that he simply indicated to Cowley that the relevant fragments were "still in Dr Schechter's possession" despite the fact that the Collection had been officially presented to the University of Cambridge by then.[39] That Schechter was perfectly within his rights to hold on to such possession is clear from the sixth condition of the agreement between the donors and the recipients of the Taylor-Schechter Collection, viz. "that the fragments of Ecclesiasticus and those with Greek writing remain in the possession of the donors until they have brought out complete editions of them".[40]

Meanwhile, scholars outside Oxford and Cambridge were also keen to jump on the Ben Sira bandwagon. George Margoliouth, a relative of David Samuel and nephew of Moses, and also a convert to Christianity, had been educated in Germany, Oxford and Cambridge (where he was Tyrwhitt scholar in 1891) and ordained by the Church of England before being appointed at the British Museum to be responsible for the Hebrew, Syriac and Ethiopic manuscripts and ultimately proving him-

---

similes of the Fragments hitherto recovered of the Book of Ecclesiasticus in Hebrew (Oxford and Cambridge 1901).

37   Taylor, *Wisdom*, VI.

38   Letter from Schechter to Jenkinson dated 12 January 1897; see note 31 above.

39   The letter is among the Jenkinson correspondence at Cambridge University Library, Add.6463.428.

40   *Cambridge University Reporter* 1215 (14 June 1898) 968-69.

self no mean or narrow semiticist.[41] He found two more leaves of MS
B at the British Museum in the spring of 1899 and hastened to announce the fact to the press and to publish the text with a brief introduction in the *Jewish Quarterly Review*.[42] Since the text fitted exactly
between some of Schechter's finds, Jenkinson thought it mean of him
not to hand over the information to Schechter for inclusion in his edition and branded Margoliouth "a self-advertising tramp" for his efforts![43] Two other manuscript collectors and researchers, who could
claim to have been involved with the Genizah material for at least as
long as Schechter, if not longer, were Elkan Nathan Adler, brother of
Chief Rabbi Hermann, and Moses Gaster, religious leader of the Se-
fardi community in England.[44] Adler located two more leaves of MS A
among the fragments that he had brought from the Ben Ezra Synagogue
in January, 1896, and Gaster identified a leaf of MS C in his private
collection. Both discoveries were published in the *Jewish Quarterly
Review*, adding to the evidence for the authenticity of the Jewish
transmission of the Hebrew.[45] That authenticity was not established beyond doubt in the mind of the Paris rabbi and college lecturer, the
knowledgeable and productive scholar, Israel Lévi. He had various
changes of mind in the course of the 1890s but was apparently won
over when he himself came upon fragments of MSS C and D and was
able to publish them in the *Revue des Etudes Juives* in 1900.[46] By the
time he published his edition of Ben Sira in 1904, he felt able to declare

---

[41]   For biographical details of George Margoliouth (1853-1924), see *Who Was
       Who 1916-1928* (London 1929) 540. The date of death given in the *Encyclo-
       paedia Judaica* vol. 11, 966 requires correction.

[42]   *Times*, 4 April 1899; *JQR* 12 (1899) 1-33.

[43]   Letter from Jenkinson to Robert Proctor, 10 April 1899, housed at Cambridge
       University Library, Add.6464.390.

[44]   For biographical details of Adler (1861-1946), see E. Levine, "Elkan Nathan
       Adler: In Memoriam", *Jewish Historical Society of England Miscellanies* 5
       (1948) 117-27 and *EncJud* 2 275-76. For those of Gaster (1856-1939), see the
       contributions of B. Schindler, M. Schwarzfeld, S.L. Bensusan and N. Cartojan
       in *Occident and Orient. Gaster Anniversary Volume* (eds. B. Schindler and A.
       Marmorstein) (London 1936) xv-xviii, 1-36 and B. Schindler, *Gaster Centen-
       ary Publication* (London 1958).

[45]   *JQR 12* (1900) 466-80, 688-702.

[46]   *REJ* 40 (1900) 1-30; see also note 47 below.

that "the fact remains nevertheless that the body of the book is really the original, the very work of Ben Sira".[47]

In Budapest, the renowned figure of *the Wissenschaft des Judentums*, Wilhelm Bacher, was earlier convinced and took the opportunity of calling Lévi to task for his doubts and of demonstrating what he regarded as the "untenableness" of D. S. Margoliouth's arguments, which he described as rising "like a soap bubble...only to burst after a short brilliancy".[48] Such exchanges were mild in comparison with the insults and criticism levelled at each other by Margoliouth and Schechter in various publications, especially the *Expository Times*. In what were often vituperative and personal comments, they denigrated each other's scholarship and record of publication, made mutual accusations about unscholarly styles of debate, and threatened (without being able to bring themselves to carrying out the threat) to withdraw from the debate.[49] By the early years of the new century, Schechter's position had become the dominant one and his colleague, Israel Abrahams, who was to succeed him later at Cambridge, was certainly one of his supporters. English gentleman that he was, Abrahams felt the need to record his dissatisfaction with the whole style of at least one aspect of the Ben Sira debate. As he expressed it, "a protest must be entered against the tone in which one prominent controversialist is conducting the discussion".[50] For his part, Jenkinson assisted Schechter by looking over his letters to the press on the subject and deriving pleasure from the discomfiture they brought to Margoliouth.[51]

By the time that Schechter left Cambridge to head the Jewish Theological Seminary in New York in 1902, his initial search of the Cambridge Genizah material had been completed and he had found, or inspired the discovery of a substantial part of the Hebrew Ecclesiasticus. The contribution of Cambridge to that process of reconstruction was not destined to increase for about half a century. In the University Li-

---

47 I. Lévi, *The Hebrew Text of the Book of Ecclesiasticus Edited with Brief Notes and a Selected Glossary* (SSS 3 Leiden 1904) XI.

48 *JQR* 12 (1900) 106, publishing a communication from Budapest in June 1899.

49 Examples may be found in *ExpTim* of September 1899, 568, and of January-February 1900, 287; see also Oko, 34-36 and 52 and Margoliouth's contributions to *JQR* 12 (1900) and 13 (1901).

50 *JQR* 12 (1900) 172.

51 Reif, "Jenkinson and Schechter" (note 2 above) 303; Jenkinson's diary entry for 4 July 1899, Add.7422 at Cambridge University Library.

brary, Ernest Worman took over responsibility for the Genizah Collection but he died a premature death in 1909,[52] leaving a situation in which 30,000 fragments had received attention and the remaining 110,000 somehow came to be regarded as of no particular significance to scholarship. For almost thirty years the Library employed only one orientalist, himself actually an indologist, to take charge of all matters touching upon language and literature from Casablanca to Yokohama, including the Genizah manuscripts. During that period, scholars from outside Cambridge used the finds from the Ben Ezra Synagogue to make a major impact on such fields as Jewish history in the medieval orient, the transmission of biblical texts and translations, and the Hebrew poetry of the Middle Ages, but the feverish activity of Schechter's day within the Library became a thing of the past.[53]

That situation changed again for the better during the 1950s. The appointment of two promising young librarians just before the Second World War had augured well for the future and a number of developments after the War laid the foundations for further discoveries among the items so peremptorily dismissed a few decades earlier. Jewish scholars were gradually returning to their normal activities after the terrible events of the thirties and forties and the creation of the State of Israel had given an impetus to Jewish studies. Copies of Hebrew manuscripts from around the world were systematically being copied for a new microfilm institute in Jerusalem and researchers at the Institute of Jewish Studies of the Hebrew University were again pursuing active research projects on major collections of hebraica. The excitement engendered by the discovery of the Dead Sea Scrolls had also led to further interest in the search for manuscripts in general and copies of early Jewish literature in particular, and Cambridge's lecturer in Rabbinics, Dr J. L. Teicher, was a controversial and ardent student of medieval Hebrew texts. At Cambridge University Library, where a new Librarian had been elected, those returning from the War were again available to assist readers and the oriental staff had been strengthened by the appointment of a keen, scholarly and charming young woman, Susan

---

52   *Ernest James Worman 1871-1909* (Cambridge 1910), containing six tributes by friends and colleagues.
53   Reif, "One Hundred Years of Genizah Research", 13-20.

Skilliter, who had just completed a degree in oriental languages, after an earlier spell of work as a junior in the Library.[54]

Thus it was that in the summer of 1954, the distinguished arabist, Professor Shelomo Dov Goitein, from the Hebrew University of Jerusalem, came to be asked by the Librarian, H. R. Creswick, whether there was any serious scholarly value in the 110,000 fragments that had been earlier set aside as unimportant. His examination of the material and his reply in the enthusiastic affirmative set off a chain of events that even the genial Miss Skilliter and her helpful colleague, Don Crane, found it difficult to cope with. Goitein stressed that the neglected items were every bit as important as those that had received close attention for almost sixty years and proved it by pointing to some exciting examples of new discoveries that could be made among them.[55] The word was quickly spread in the international world of scientific learning and the erstwhile trickle of scholars that had made its way to Cambridge, soon turned into a stream and later threatened to become a torrent. There is no doubt that knowledge and understanding of numerous fields of medieval Hebrew and Jewish studies advanced by leaps and bounds as a result of their research activities and the contents of the "New Series" born out of Goitein's wise observations quickly came to be regarded with as much respect as its predecessor.[56]

But the process of creating the New Series (containing over 42,000 items) was by no means all sweetness and light. That part of the precious cache was "still in much the same primitive state as it was when it arrived in large crates from Cairo".[57] Since no librarian was exclusively responsible for the Genizah Collection or qualified enough to identify and classify its contents, it was left to visiting scholars to remove items from crates and suggest how and where they might be placed. This was not always done in the most professional manner, not every scholar adhered to his field of specialisation, and differences of opinion led even to the changing of classmarks. What is more, individual academics even took to adopting an astonishingly proprietorial approach to some of the crates by writing their names on the lids. Among

54   Reif, "One Hundred Years of Genizah Research", 20-22.
55   S.D. Goitein, "Involvement in Geniza Research", *Religion in a Religious Age* (ed. S.D. Goitein) (Cambridge Mass. 1974) 139-46.
56   Reif, "One Hundred Years of Genizah Research", 22-24.
57   *Cambridge University Reporter* 4290 (14 March 1962) 1162.

the most active of the Jewish scholars were Yefim Schirmann, Shalom Spiegel and Nehemiah Allony and much as they contributed handsomely to the furtherance of Jewish studies, they were at the same time a cause of much frustration to the librarians. As it was reported at the time, "the energetic activity of a few devoted visitors...although undoubtedly of the utmost value, interrupts the normal working procedure" and there were times when the inadequacy of the Manuscripts Reading Room was "exasperating both to the staff and to the public".[58]

This background explains a great deal about the discovery of the next fragments of the Hebrew Ben Sira. Though undoubtedly more expert – indeed a world authority – in the field of medieval Hebrew poetry[59], Schirmann was well enough acquainted with earlier Hebrew literature to recognise leaves of Ecclesiasticus when he saw them and was certainly unable to resist the temptation to edit the finds himself. During his visits in 1957 and 1959 he was dedicatedly sorting material in the crates and creating boxes of them for the New Series (primarily for his work on poetry) when he came across two folios of MS B and another two of MS C. He was at the time editor of the Israeli periodical *Tarbiz* and he was able to publish texts of these in that publication within a few months of their discovery.[60] For reasons that should already be apparent, the sound library principle of not changing classmarks was overturned by the desire to give the fragments more prominence by adding them to that part of the Collection that already had many of the major treasures found in Schechter's day and some inevitable confusion ensued.[61] Nor were all Schirmann's readings and re-

---

58 *Cambridge University Reporter* 4254 (7 June 1961) 1810 and 4290 (14 March 1962) 1162.

59 For biographical details of Schirmann (1904-1981), *see EncJud* vol. 14, 968-69 and *Hayyim (Jefim) Schirmann Jubilee Volume* (eds. S. Abramson and A. Mirsky) (Hebrew; Jerusalem 1970) 413-27. The major work resulting from his research at Cambridge in those years was his Hebrew volume *New Poems from the Genizah* (Jerusalem 1965).

60 *Tarbiz* 27 (1957-58) 440-43 and 29 (1959-60) 125-34. The first text was included, with his notes, in the second edition of Segal's *Seper ben Sira Ha-Shalem* (Jerusalem ²1958) 375-78, with a statement by Segal in the preface expressing the supposition that there would be further finds in Cambridge.

61 E.g. what is now T-S 12.871 was formerly T-S NS 193.107 and what is now T-S 12.867 was formerly T-S NS 194.114. For details of all the Cambridge Genizah fragments, see the appendix to this article.

constructions beyond doubt and it was to the benefit of Ben Sira research when the American Catholic scholar, Alexander Di Lella, who had ploughed a fairly lonely furrow when writing on the subject for his doctoral dissertation, visited Cambridge in 1963, re-edited the texts with fresh transcriptions and plates, and drew wider attention to their significance.[62]

By the summer of 1974, the internal Library situation had totally changed. There was specific responsibility for the Genizah Collection and a Genizah Research Unit had been established to co-ordinate all the work on the fragments. A fully comprehensive programme of conservation, microfilming, research and publication was under way and a team of young scholars, financed by successful fund-raising efforts, would from that time onwards contribute impressively to Genizah research as well as progressing in their own academic careers as a result. During that and the subsequent year, a joint research initiative with the Israel Academy of Sciences and Humanities brought a number of scholars to Cambridge University Library to join me in completing the sorting of the New Series and in undertaking similar work on the remaining 68,000 items, then given the title of the Additional Series.[63] The first two who donned overalls and began to sift through the crates were Professors Israel Yeivin and Ezra Fleischer of the Hebrew University of Jerusalem and it was the former whose eagle eye identified two more fragments of what he thought, and I soon confirmed to be Ben Sira manuscripts. The pieces were conserved and given classmarks and, Yeivin and I having decided that I would ultimately prepare them for publication, I made some introductory notes and consigned these to a file for later expansion. Following the new principle of making nothing available in unconserved state, and everything accessible to readers after conservation, they were then added to the Collection open to consultation by any visiting scholar.[64]

Early in 1982, the Library was visited by the head of the rabbinical seminary in Budapest, Alexander (Sándor) Scheiber, who, despite the considerable difficulties of operating as a scholar of Jewish studies under the Communist regime, had throughout his career published nu-

---

62   A. Di Lella, *Bib* 45 (1964) 153-67.

63   Reif, "One Hundred Years of Genizah Research", 26-27.

64   They were placed in binder T-S AS 213 under the general heading of Miscellaneous and Unidentified.

merous Genizah fragments of various types in generally brief articles, some of them in Hungarian.[65] On examining the new material in the Additional Series, Scheiber independently identified one of the Ben Sira fragments and expressed interest in publishing it. Rather than unnecessarily duplicating scholarly effort, Yeivin and I agreed to pass on the information we had about both fragments so that Scheiber could make them widely available. He did so in the obscure Hungarian periodical *Magyar Könyvszemle* and, in a somewhat hasty fashion, identified one as part of MS C and the other as part of MS D, the so-called Rothschild MS of Paris.[66] Once again, the fragments enjoyed the benefit of a more precise treatment by Di Lella who visited Cambridge in 1987 and subsequently produced improved editions, correcting some readings and identifying the second manuscript not as D but as a new MS, to which he gave the name F.[67]

There may be other Ben Sira items lurking among the smaller and less legible contents of some of the Additional Series binders but that remains a matter for future researchers. The story of the scholars and the texts at Cambridge appears to have been told in its entirety and undoubtedly reveals the degree to which the human element plays more than a small part in scholarly activities.

By way of conclusion, I have to report an interesting development that occurred only two weeks before this paper was delivered at the Ben Sira Conference held in Soesterberg. For years it has been the ambition of all Genizah scholars to see the subject of their research given at least equal attention with the Dead Sea Scrolls not only by specialists but also in the wider world.[68] Similarly, those with deep interests in Ben Sira have felt that it deserved recognition as a most important part of Hebrew literature. In a letter from the Israel Postal Authority dated 14 July 1996, I have been informed of the Israel Philatelic Service's intention of issuing a stamp that marks the centenary of the Genizah as well

---

65 Many of these articles appear in the collection entitled *Geniza Studies* and published in Hildesheim in 1981.

66 *Magyar Könyvszemle* 98 (1982) 179-85; *Genizah Fragments* 3 (April 1982) 4.

67 Di Lella, *Bib* 69 (1988) 226-38.

68 For the relevance of the Genizah material to the study of the Judaean scrolls, see my entry "Genizah" in the forthcoming *Encyclopedia of the Dead Sea Scrolls*, being edited by J. C. VanderKam and L. H. Schiffman for Oxford University Press in New York.

as the fiftieth anniversary of the finding of the Dead Sea Scrolls. And the choice of manuscript with which to illustrate the issue ? – A fragment of one of the Genizah texts of the Hebrew Ben Sira of course!

Letter from Solomon Schlechter to Agnes Lewis identifying the first Genizah fragment of the Hebrew Ben Sira, 13 May 1896:

"Dear Miss Lewis,

I think we have reason to congratulate ... ourselves. For the ... fragment I took with me represents a piece *of the original Hebrew of Ecclesiasticus*. It is the first time that such a thing was discovered. Please do not speak yet about the matter till tomorrow. I will come to you tomorrow about 11 p.m. and talk over the matter with you how to make the matter known.
In haste and geat excitement.

Yours sincerely
    S. Schlechter"

An Inventory of Cambridge Ben Sira Genizah MSS

Classmark	Folios	Content	MS	Discovery
12.863	2	3:6 – 5:10 +		
		14:11 – 16:26	A	Schechter
12.864	2	5:10 – 7:29 +		
		11:34 – 14:11	A	Schechter
12.871[69]		10:19 – 11:10	B	Schirmann
NS 38a.1	1	15:1 – 16:7	B	Schirmann
16.312	2	30:11 – 31:11	B	Schechter
		37:27 – 38:27		
16.313	2	32:1 – 33:3	B	Schechter
		35:11 – 36:26		
Or.1102	1	39:15 – 40:8	B	Lewis/Gibson
				1896 CUL 1926
16.314	1	49:12 – 50:22	B	Schechter
16.315	2	50:22 – 51:30	B	Schechter
12.727	2	4:23, 30-31	C	Schechter
		5:4-7, 9-13; 36:19		
		25:8, 13, 17-24		
		26:1-2		
12.867[70]	2	3:14-18, 21-22;	C	Schirmann
		41:16; 4:21; 20:22-23		
		4:22-23		
		26:2-3, 13, 15-17		
		36: 27-31		
AS 213.4	1	25:8, 20-21	C	Yeivin 1974
				Scheiber 1982
AS 213.17	1	31:24 – 33:8	F	Yeivin 1974
				Scheiber 1982

---

[69]   Formerly NS 193.107
[70]   Formerly NS 194.114

Review of Recent Research on the Book of Ben Sira (1980-1996)

By Friedrich Vinzenz Reiterer, Salzburg

How could a person not closely occupied with Ben Sira keep au fait with this book ? For the Ben Sira bibliography being compiled by Professor Nuria Calduch-Benages and me contains more than three thousand single items. So a review of recent Ben Sira research has to be restricted to the material published since 1980, more than 600 titles in total.

There are introductions and referenceworks, containing fundamental information and gathering the results of research.[1] Some of them, such as those of Gilbert (1995; 1996), Kaiser (1994) and Marböck (1992; 1995), are noted because they have appeared recently.[2] Here I take the opportunity of mentioning interesting research and some particular themes. Some old questions about Ben Sira crop up as fresh as ever and merit renewed exploration.

---

[1] Even in this field, there is a considerable number of titles, such that general information seems more popular than specialised research.

[2] M. Gilbert, "Jesus Sirach", RAC fasc. 134 (Stuttgart 1995) 878-906; M. Gilbert, "Siracide", DBS 12 (1996) 1389-1437. O. Kaiser, "Die Weisheit des Jesus Sirach", *Grundriß der Einleitung in die kanonischen und deuterokanonischen Schriften des Alten Testaments 3* (Gütersloh 1994) 97-105. J. Marböck, "Jesus Sirach (Buch)", *Neues Bibel-Lexikon* (Zürich 1992) 338-341; J. Marböck, "Das Buch Jesus Sirach", *Einleitung in das Alte Testament* (ed. E. Zenger-G. Braulik-H. Niehr et al.) (KStTh 1,1; Stuttgart - Berlin - Köln 1995) 285-292.

1. Author's name

Within the Hebrew, Greek and Syriac traditions there are striking differences, further complicated by the different assignations by the Early
Fathers and by Jewish tradition[3], for example

H	B	50,27	Simeon	Ben Jeschua	Ben Eleazar	Ben Sira
		51,30	Simeon	Ben Jeschua	Ben Eleazar	Ben Sira
G		50,27	Jesus	Son of Sirach	Eleazar	the Jerusalemite
G		Prol 7	Jesus			
Syr		51,30	Jeschua	Son of Simeon	Bar Sira	
V			Ecclesiasticus[4]			

Whereas Marböck only indicates the variants, and Gilbert sees "a
problem", Kaiser (1994) suggests a short explanation: He says that the
author's name in H II has been transmitted to Syr, which had an effect
on the G tradition. Thus "Sira" is one of the ancestors. As there is no
complete solution, there is no objection to the generally adopted term
"Ben Sira/ Sirach", which agrees with the rabbinical tradition too.[5]

2. Canonicity

Though written in Hebrew and appreciated among Jews, the Book of
Ben Sira is not in the Hebrew canon. The question of canonicity includes two aspects: (1) How and when was Sira taken into the canon?[6]
(2) To what "canon" did Sira testify?

---

3   Cf. Gilbert, 1995, 879-880.
4   'Imitation of Ecclesiastes' (Marböck).
5   bHagigah 13a; cf.: "Bar Sira" yHagigah 2,1, 77c; Midrash Tanhuma hqt 1.
6   See esp. H.P. Rüger, "Le Siracide: Un livre à la frontière du canon", *Le canon
     de l'Ancien Testament. Sa formation et son histoire* (ed. J.-D. Kaestli-
     O.Wermelinger) (MoBi; Genf 1984) 47-69; H.P. Rüger, "Der Umfang des alt-
     testamentlichen Kanons in den verschiedenen kirchlichen Traditionen", *Die
     Apokryphenfrage im ökumenischen Horizont. Die Stellung der Spätschriften
     des Alten Testaments im biblischen Schrifttum und ihre Bedeutung in den
     kirchlichen Traditionen des Ostens und Westens* (ed. S. Meurer) (Bibel im
     Gespräch 3; Stuttgart 2̲1993 [1989]) 137-144.

(1) Though Gradl maintains that a precise answer why Sira was not included in the Hebrew canon is in the realm of speculation, the book might have been read only in Greek translation.[7] However if so, the question remains, why Sira was appreciated even in rabbinical tradition, although Sira belongs to the books that do not pollute one's hands (Tos. Yadain 2, 13, cf. Seder Olam Rabbah 30).[8] Gilbert agrees with Barthélemy, that the Jewish leaders perhaps wanted to prevent Jews from reading books that are sacred to Christians.[9] This argument can be supported by the observation that Jewish use of Sira increased in the time when normative Judaism was stable and the influence of the sects was being kept under control.[10] The discussion based on the method of 'canonical approach' raised the question of the 'canonical frame'.[11] Recent scholarship suggests that such 'normativity' has to be seen as a process of development.[12]

---

7   F. Gradl, "Das Buch Jesus Sirach (Sir)", *Israel und sein Gott. Einleitung in das Alte Testament* (ed. F. Gradl-F.J. Stendebach) (BiBaB 4; Stuttgart 1992) 193-197, especially 196.

8   Rüger, 1984, 51.

9   D. Barthélemy, "L'état de la Bible juive depuis le début de notre ère jusqu'a la deuxième révolte contre Rome (131-135)", *Le canon de l'Ancien Testament. Sa formation et son histoire* (ed. J.-D. Kaestli-O. Wermelinger) (MoBi; Genf 1984) 9-45, especially 34.

10   Cf. S.Z. Leiman, "Status of the Book of Ben Sira", *The Canonization of Hebrew Scripture: The Talmudic and Midrashic Evidence* (ed. S.Z. Leiman) (Hamden, Connecticut 1976) 92-102.

11   Cf. H.P. Rüger, "Das Werden des christlichen Alten Testamentes", *Zum Problem des biblischen Kanons* (JBTh 3; Neukirchen-Vluyn 1988) 175-189, especially 176; H. Hübner, "Vetus Testamentum und Vetus Testamentum in Novo receptum. Die Frage nach dem Kanon des Alten Testaments aus neutestamentlicher Sicht", *Zum Problem des biblischen Kanons* (JBTh 3; Neukirchen-Vluyn 1988) 147-174.

12   Cf. M. Hengel-R. Deines, "Die Septuaginta als 'christliche Schriftensammlung' und das Problem ihres Kanons", *Verbindliches Zeugnis. I. Kanon - Schrift - Tradition* (ed. W. Pannenberg-Th. Schneider) (DiKi 7, Freiburg-Göttingen 1992) 34-127; M. Hengel, "'Schriftauslegung' und 'Schriftwerdung' in der Zeit des Zweiten Tempels", *Schriftauslegung im antiken Judentum und im Urchristentum* (ed. M. Hengel-H. Löhr) (WUNT 73; Tübingen 1994) 1-71.

(2) An old and often discussed question was which books of the Bible were attested as 'canonical'[13] according to Ben Sira's witness.
Nowadays this question is seldom at the centre of enquiry.

3. Transmission of the Text

Despite the inexplicability[14] of its textual development, analyses show
that there have been two Hebrew versions, a *shorter* and a *longer* one.[15]
According to Rüger and others, H I (between 200-175 B.C.) is the basis
for G I.[16] H II, which was developed between the middle of the 1st
century B.C. and completed before 150 A.D., is the basis for G II, being itself the basis for the Vetus Latina and Vulgate in the 2nd century
A.D. Gilbert (1995, 882) supposes a combination of H I and H II for
the present Peshitta.[17] This is supported by the Arabic version (Kaiser
[1994], Rüger) derived from Syriac, where the variants of H II seem to
have no influence; however one should compare Samaan's[18] remarks

---

13   Cf. A. Eberharter, *Der Kanon des Alten Testaments zur Zeit des Ben Sira. Auf
     Grund der Beziehungen des Sirabuches zu den Schriften des Alten Testaments
     dargestellt* (ATAbh III, 3; Münster 1911); R.D. Wilson, "Ecclesiasticus", PRR
     11 (1900) 480-506.
14   "unklärbar": Gilbert, 1995, 880.
15   Cf. C. Kearns, "Ecclesiasticus, or the Wisdom of Jesus the Son of Sirach", *A
     New Catholic Commentary on Holy Scripture* (ed. R.C. Fuller-L. Johnston-C.
     Kearns) (London 1969) 541-562, especially 547-550.
16   H.P. Rüger, *Text und Textform im hebräischen Sirach. Untersuchungen zur
     Textgeschichte und Textkritik der hebräischen Sirachfragmente aus der Kai-
     roer Geniza* (BZAW 112; Berlin 1970). See also Gilbert (1995), Marböck
     (1992; 1995).
17   M.M. Winter, "The Origins of Ben Sira in Syriac (Part I) (Part II)", *VT* 27
     (1977) 237-253; 494-507; R.J. Owens, "The Early Syriac Text of Ben Sira in
     the Demonstrations of Aphrahat", *JSS* 34 (1989) 39-75.
18   Cf. K.W. Samaan, *Sept traductions arabes de Ben Sira* (EHS XXIII/492;
     Frankfurt a.M. 1994); see the valuable listing of the manuscripts (pp. 444-
     445). The work is a comprehensive collection, which examines the different
     Arabic translations on the basis of their origin; many observations have text-
     critical value, while the details need elucidating in their own context.
     Samaan's findings do not agree with M. Gilbert, "L'Ecclésiastique: Quel texte?
     Quelle autorité", *RB* 49 (1987) 233-250. Instead (even for traditions within
     Arabic), he suggests that Sira was translated largely from the Peshitta (pp. 20.

about G II. The relationship of manuscripts within H and the position of G (I and II) and Syr are always an interesting topic.

After the publication of the Hebrew manuscripts 100 years ago, numerous text-critical studies were all looking for the 'Urtext'. During recent decades, the relationship between the extant Hebrew MSS has been investigated.[19] When research in this field started, there was some hope of reconstructing the 'Urtext', or at least a text near it.[20] As there are so many problems showing that in each version one must assume revisions, the relationships among these versions and with the protocanonical O.T. must be investigated. Therefore recent surveys try to describe relationships between the versions (within H itself and the relationships between H and G or else Syr), and the associations with the protocanonical O.T. It seems that even the 'oldest' text is already an interpretation, so that every scholar is in fact interpreting interpretations. But if the inherent criteria of the kind of interpretation can be found, one can describe what is specific to each, and the comparison may suggest the common base. Interesting work has been done in this field.

---

402). The relationship to G I and G II is indicated; e.g. to 1,10-11, where the influence of G II is discovered (p. 192). The choice of 1,1-12; 24,1-22 and 51,13-30 as the material investigated makes it impossible to study consistently the relationship of the Hebrew manuscripts on the basis of the Arabic translation.

19   Especially the recent investigations on MS F: A. Scheiber, "A Leaf of the Fourth Manuscript of the Ben Sira from the Geniza [25,11 ... -24; Belonging to Paris Manuscript 31,24 ... -33,8]", *Magyar Könyvszemle* 98 (1982) 179-185. A.A. Di Lella, "The Newly Discovered Sixth Manuscript of Ben Sira from the Cairo Geniza", *Bib* 69 (1988) 226-238. P.C. Beentjes, "A Closer Look at the Newly Discovered Sixth Hebrew Manuscript (Ms. F) of Ben Sira", *EstBíb* 51 (1993) 171-186.

20   Cf. Rüger, 1970; similarly A.A. Di Lella, *A Text-Critical and Historical Study of the Hebrew Manuscripts of Sirach* (Ann Arbor 1962). Whereas Rüger in his publication does not consider Ma (see Y. Yadin, *The Ben Sira Scroll from Masada, with Introduction, Emendations and Commentary* [Jerusalem 1965]), although the study was ready in 1965, this text was thoroughly worked over in a critical discussion by L. Schrader (*Leiden und Gerechtigkeit. Studien zu Theologie und Textgeschichte des Sirachbuches* [BET 27; Frankfurt a.M. 1994]).

Schrader's study tries to find new results without discussing prevailing scholarly opinions.[21] As he does not includes Fuß's study, which deals with literary criticism and is scarcely reliable either[22], he again asks for originality and homogeneity. He concludes that there was a first recension parallel with Middle Hebrew which is best attested in Ma and in A[23], whereas B is of poorer quality. Here and in C, a more recent revision has amended the text with rather archaic language (13-53). In the context ofthe Greek translation he speaks of the "Ungenauigkeit und Willkür der griechischen Übersetzung"; 54). As evidence for compilation of the book from single independent collections of student's texts, he suggests, for instance, the decisive "wörtliche Dublette 42,14-15; 20,30-31".[24] Schrader should have kept in mind that there might be matters so important to an author that he forms phrases of his own, and that he can introduce *only* G as an obligatory witness, although he had considered before G as doubtful (20, 30.31 ≠ H, not even the preferred MSS Ma or A; 41,14b.c. 15 ≠ Syr).

The text runs as follows:

[41,14a Παιδείαν ἐν εἰρήνῃ συντηρήσατε τέκνα] 20,30; 41,14b.c σοφία κεκρυμμένη καὶ θησαυρὸς ἀφανής τίς ὠφέλεια ἐν ἀμφοτέροις 30,31; 41,15 κρείσσων ἄνθρωπος ἀποκρύπτων τὴν μωρίαν αὐτοῦ ἤ ἄνθρωπος ἀποκρύπτων τὴν σοφίαν αὐτου 41,16 Τοιγαροῦν ἐντράπητε ἐπὶ τῳ κρίματι[25] μου οὐ γάρ ἐστιν πᾶσαν αἰσχύνην διαφυλάξαι καλόν καὶ οὐ πάντα πᾶσιν ἐν πίστει εὐδοκιμεῖται.

---

21 Schrader, 1994; he does not mention F.V. Reiterer, *"Urtext" und Übersetzungen. Sprachstudie über Sir 44,16-45,26 als Beitrag zur Siraforschung* (ATSAT 12; St. Ottilien 1980), nor P.C. Beentjes, *Jesus Sirach en Tenach: een onderzoek naar en een classificatie van parallellen, met bijzondere aandacht voor hun functie in Sirach 45:6-26* (Nieuwegein 1981), nor B.G. Wright, *No Small Difference. Sirach's Relationship to Its Hebrew Parent Text* (Atlanta 1989).

22 W. Fuß, *Tradition und Komposition im Buche Jesus Sirach* (Tübingen 1962 [Diss.]); his findings seem rather far-fetched.

23 According to N. Calduch-Benages ("Ben Sira e el cànon de les Escriptures", *Butletti de l'Associàció Bíblica de Catalunya* 54 (1996) 51-62), A belongs to HII, whereas B as well as Ma are witnesses of HI-tradition;

24 Schrader, *Leiden und Gerechtigkeit* 59; of course he means 42,14b.c.

25 A. Rahlfs (ed.), *Septuaginta. Id est Vetus Testamentum graece iuxta LXX interpretes II* (Stuttgart 91979): ῥηματί.

20,30 ܣܒܪܬܐ ܓܠܝܬܐ: ܡܣܬܪܬܐ ܕܚܟܡܬܐ: ܐܝܢܐ ܗܢܝܢܐ ܐܝܬ ܒܬܪ̈ܝܗܘܢ

20,31 ܛܒ ܓܒܪܐ [26] ܕܛܫܐ ܣܟܠܘܬܗ: ܡܢ ܓܒܪܐ ܕܢܛܪ ܚܟܡܬܗ

	Siglum	Hebrew
41,14	Ma$^{b.a}$	מה תעלה ב[ש]תיהם [ח]כמה טמונה ושימה מסתרת
	B$^{b.a}$	מה תועלה^{II} בשתיהם חכמה טמונה ואוצר מוסתר^{I}
	Bm	תעלה^{II} מסותרת וסימה^{I}
41,15	Ma$^{b.a}$	מאיש מצפן חכמתו טוב איש מטמ[ן] אולתו
	B$^{b.a}$	מאיש^{I} מצפין^{II} חכמתו טוב איש מצפין אולתו
	Bm	מאדון^{I} יטמין^{II}
41,14a	B$^{d.c}$	מוסר בשת (שמ)^{27} בש . (מוסר)
41,16	Ma$^{b.a}$	[והכ] למו על משפטי מוסר בשת שמעו בנים
= G	B$^{b.a}$	והכלמו על משפטי^{I} מוסר בשת שמעו בנים
14a.16a	Bm	משפטו^{I}

At first sight, one could mention that G and Syr differ in 20,30-31; H (partly) and G complement one another in 41,14.15, but there are so many open questions in H (Ma and B)[28] and G[29], that this passage can be used as evidence only after a detailed analysis. Nevertheless this example impressively shows that the versions must be examined on their own merit if one is investigating both their coincidences with the proto-canonical biblical text, their parallel passages and their differences.

The questions associated with Schrader's approach allow me to indicate relevant research. Reiterer ("Urtext") offers a framework of ques-

---

26   Or ܗܘ ܛܒ

27   Example of difficulties in reading: צ is to be read here according to P.C. Beentjes, "The Reliability of Text-Editions in Ben Sira 41,14-16. A Case Study in Repercussions on Structure and Interpretation", *BTFT* 49 (1988) 188-194, especially 188; ש by P.C. Beentjes, *The Book of Ben Sira in Hebrew* (VTS 68; Leiden 1997).

28   See Beentjes, "Reliability", 188-194, who first requires the inclusion of the textual context and secondly stresses that similar passages relating to "wisdom" function as an introduction for the following section. Such findings presume a deliberate plan for the whole work and, without explicitly investigating the matter, preclude any "accidental" collection of the master's text reworked by pupils.

29   Above all Sir 41,15 and the change of position to be presumed of H (v. 16) and G (v. 14).

tions in order to grasp the relationship of parts of the Hebrew to one another and to comparable passages of the protocanonical O.T. at a text-*describing level*. Such an approach allows also examination of parallel translations in G and Syr, and of trying to describe the Versions. There is no need to interpret or classify the basic text.[30] Only the situation need be noted and the facts to be referred in order to find clues for further deliberations. In particular, Sir 44,16-45,26 is suited for research on parallel protocanonical passages. Though Ma is damaged in small parts, it supports B as an early version; and B in turn, shows G to be a valuable translation. The handling of the Hebrew protocanonical text (if it appears in today's shape) as well as the G translation are independent in their own right, a fact that cannot be said of Syr in relation to H nor of the rest of the Peshitta.[31]

Wright takes up the question of translation technique too and looks at "translation technique" and "the extent to which the grandson's translation reflects dependence on Greek translations of the Hebrew scriptures" (Difference, 10). He goes much further on extent. By doing so, he limits the framework of questions, because of the material that otherwise cannot be dealt with in any other way. He examines comparable texts and allusions from the Pentateuch, from the Deuteronomistic History and from the Prophets. He shows that knowledge of the Hebrew Bible is required, as a pattern for G hardly comes into question. This could even be correct, when there is a correspondence in terminology. It can often be seen that the words are "used independently" by the grandson (225). Although Wright gives examples from Schechter & Taylor, and Eberharter[32], and Reiterer for references to Psalms, Job[33],

---

30 Beentjes, who expressed himself repeatedly as being critical of this deficiency, seeks in vain for an answer.

31 As a consequence, one cannot support the observation that the early books of the Bible in Syr are connected more strongly with the Targumic traditions (as is suggested by Brock), while the late writings are to be considered as more independant. No notable difference could be observed.

32 Eberharter, 1911; cf. J.G. Snaith, "Biblical Quotations in the Hebrew of Ecclesiasticus", *JThS* 18 (1967) 1-12.

33 From a purely terminological viewpoint, see F.V. Reiterer, "Das Verhältnis Ijobs und Ben Siras", *The Book of Job* (ed. W.A.M. Beuken) (BETL 114; Louvain 1994) 405-429; from a thematic viewpoint R. Egger-Wenzel, "Der Gebrauch von חמס bei Ijob und Ben Sira. Ein Vergleich zweier Weisheitsbücher",

and Proverbs (according to Di Lella, Qohelet[34] should be added), all these stand only for knowledge of the Hebrew text of the O.T. However the differences between the vocabulary of Ben Sira and of the LXX cannot be explained. The author says that the differences between the vocabulary of Ben Sira and the LXX can be explained most easily in such a way "that he did not have certain translations to use" (228).[35]

Beentjes, almost simultaneously with Reiterer, inquired into the way Sira used the text of the O.T. During his investigation he treats those examples which are parallel to O.T. texts but whose congruence is the result of later revision (1981, 42-59). He accepts real parallel passages, only if longer passages are concerned or the contexts are similar. He takes ten passages as explicit quotations (21-41). This question occupied him further.[36] In the meantime, he concentrated upon intensive investigation of the manuscripts, because he will publish them as faithfully as possible to the original pattern. I see in this development a natural interest to ensure the textual base.

In 1995, Minissale published a monograph, which offers textual criticism together with a reconstruction of the text from various manuscripts even with emendations.[37] Aiming at evaluation of the Greek text, he proceeds from a reconstructed Hebrew text. He deals with ten

---

Freundschaft im Buch Ben Sira (ed. F.V. Reiterer) (BZAW 244; Berlin - New York 1996), 203-238.

34 Sira's source literature is "especially the Wisdom literature, Proverbs, Job, and Qoheleth"; according to P.W. Skehan-A.A. Di Lella, *The Wisdom of Ben Sira* (AB 39; New York 1987) 40. On the basis of many passages, F.J. Backhaus, "Qohelet und Sirach", *BN* 69 (1993) 32-55, aimed to prove that there were no literary relationships between the two authors, although many themes run in parallel.

35 Here he supports G.B. Caird ("Ben Sira and the Dating of the Septuagint", *Studia Evangelica VII. Papers Presented to the Fifth International Congress on Biblical Studies Held at Oxford* [ed. E.A. Livingstone] [TU 126; Berlin 1982] 95-100), according to which the LXX was not complete in the grandson's time.

36 P.C. Beentjes, "Inverted Quotations in the Bible. A Neglected Stylistic Pattern", *Bib* 63 (1982) 506-523.

37 Compare 33[36],2b: ומחמוטט כמסערה אזנו (MS E, MS F) with ומחמוטט כמסערה אוני and 33[36],3b: ק פת מט ותורתו (MS B) with ותורתו כאורים נאמנה; A. Minissale, *La versione greca del Siracide. Confronto con il testo ebraico alla luce dell'attività midrascica e del metodo targumico* (AnBib 133; Rom 1995) 79. The emendations are basically a scholarly aid, but a criterion would be advantageous.

pericopes[38] that are tested by the following criteria: Where is the Greek text spoiled? What is the value of different textual readings? Where are thematic discrepancies? How can the method of translation be described? Where are additions or elisions in G? The way the Greek translator has rendered the text is rightly understood as an interpretation. The translation is supposed to be influenced by the methods of the Targum. In the tabular part of his monograph, Minissale mostly reproduces only hemistichs (not texts with context!) based usually on poetic viewpoints, and, for instance, on law, wisdom, history, Israel, priesthood, and eschatology, sometimes noting analogy to the Targum (204 n. 66). The approach is ingenious, but many passages of textual criticism are more like asserted than argued, often just describing content.

From his examples, one may take 41,14-16,[39] on his way of only dealing with the text. Minissale offers the text according to Ma, but he eliminates B because of its being near to Aramaic (here one could question whether in such examples [B], the same interests could have been at work as in the Targum?), but he deals briefly with the textual situation, although he sees 41,14a.16 as parallelism (in the position of 16) and uses the Greek verse numbering, which gives rise to problems.

In the "note testuali e filologiche" (102), he does not note מוסר בש שם מוסר בשת that is omitted. Among "lettura diversa" he should have thougt about a special motive for changing the Greek order (perhaps the G sequence is even original), but he takes over the explanation of Levi,[40] which explains ἐν εἰρήνη as a mistake and an addition by B. He does not reckon that the passage full of problems might be written in 14a (= 14a.16a) according to G numeration. If the unit begins thus, the problem of the imperative being in the middle of the text (v. 16) could be solved and imperatives would not then be unexpected within the unit. But if the poem begins with 14b.c.15, then the function of the short saying at the beginning of the poem (didactic example?) should

---

38 The author deals with 4,20-6,4; 6,18-37; 10,19-11,6; 31,25-32,13 (= Smend; Ziegler 34,25-35,13); 32,14-33,6 (= Smend; Ziegler 35,14-36,6); 37,16-31; 41,14-42,8; 42,15-25; 44,1-15; 51,13-30.

39 Treated in the framework of 41,14-42,6 from p. 99 onwards; these verses (41,14-16), as an opening passage, are rather independent.

40 I. Lévi, L'Ecclésiastique ou la sagesse de Jésus, fils de Sira. Texte original hébreu, édité traduit et commenté. Premiére partie (ch. XXXIX,15, à XLIX,11) (BEHE.R 10,1; Paris 1898) XLVII.

be made clear. Minissale's analysis is much impeded by the inconse-
quence of the numeration[41] in the second section of his investigation,
which brings such a lot of material and single arguments (words,
phrases lines, verses, but without any recognizable attention to literary
units).

Because of its significance, the Syriac translation must be mentioned. Winter doubts whether one can find its roots at all. Brock[42]
collects the facts about the Peshitta: time of origin (1st or 2nd Century
A.D.), its name (from 9th Century onwards in contrast with other
Syriac translations) and its relation to the Biblical traditions of that
time. The Pentateuch resembles that of the Targumim; the other books,
in particular the Deuterocanonical books resemble the LXX, except for
Sira, which traces back to H.

Nelson's investigation[43] outlines the history of the discovery of the
Hebrew texts and the development of the G I and G II tradition. He describes Syriac textual editions, and offers a numerical synopsis for
39,27-44,17; he also provides a translation and examines aphorisms for
the Syriac and the other versions. After a hardly connotated listing of
the facts, he offers a few results (in extracts): Syr goes with Ma and B
(27[28] times; plus once without Ma), Syr and G (12 times) without
Ma; Syr, G and Ma correspond 7 times against B; Syr and Ma against B
(4 times), Syr and G against B (4 times). On the whole, the B text in
this part is similar to Syr but there is no simple scheme for a history of
origin. Syr uses an H text, more recent than Ma, but older than the MSS
of Cairo. It came into being for Jewish readers speaking Syriac (from

---

41 One assumes that Minissale numerates according to either Ziegler or Rahlfs,
    even if he does not say so. To illustrate the difficulty of determining the nu-
    meration, one may take the following examples: 31,4 (p. 156) = Smend
    (Ziegler 34,4); 36,7a (p. 157) = Ziegler 33,7 (v 7b does not exist; Smend
    36,5b; Vulg. 36,7 [Smend 36,5a = Ziegler 33,6]); 32,17a = Smend (Ziegler
    35,17a); 36,23a = Ziegler (Smend 36,18); 37,17a (p. 159) = Smend 37,17a
    (according to Ziegler there is no v 17b); 37,18a (S. 159) = Ziegler 18a (Smend
    17b); 37,18b (p. 159) = Ziegler 18b (Smend 18a); 37,18c (p. 159) = Ziegler
    18c (Smend 18b); there are many other examples. A concordance of verse
    numbers would at least offer a chance of overcoming such confusion.

42 S.P. Brock, "Bibelübersetzungen I, 4 Peschitta", TRE 6 (1980) 182-185; 188-
    189.

43 M.D. Nelson, *The Syriac Version of the Wisdom of Ben Sira Compared to the
    Greek and Hebrew Materials* (SBLDS 107; Atlanta, Georgia 1988).

40 A.D. onwards known in Edessa) in the 2nd Century A.D. Up to the middle of the 5th Century, it was being revised by Christians. The translation is also valuable for linguistic studies on the Syriac language. This is attested through various additions to Payne Smith by Margoliouth.[44]

4. Numeration

The problem of numeration is often pointed out because all Greek manuscripts show signs that the order of leaves has been switched. But the information about the verses concerned is rare and divergent: 33,16-36,13 is suggested to belong after 30,25, therefore the counting begins after 36,13 with 30,26.[45] Kaiser (1994) says that the passages 33,13b-36,13a should be placed between 30,26/27; Marböck (1992;1995) concludes most correctly that 30,25-33,13a was switched with 33,13b-36,16. Since the sequence has been lost, a standard versification must be set so that everybody can find a cited text.

The text editions (and the translations into modern languages) are essential to the propagation of the numeration and to the availability of the scholarly research. The edition of Rahlfs, often used up to the present time (compare Minissale's mixture), offers a correction in numeration. Since Ziegler's edition, there has been a normative text,[46] which has been adopted by the H edition of 1973.[47] In common practice, many exegetes go from one way of numeration to another, so there is much confusion. One can only escape with the help of a numerical synopsis, as for example is offered by Nelson (37-42). As the numeration

44 J.P. Margoliouth, *Supplement to the Thesaurus Syriacus of Robert Payne Smith* (Hildesheim-New York 1981).

45 Gradl, 194; similarly, but somewhat more precisely A. Lefèvre, "Ecclesiasticus (Sirazide)", *Einleitung in die Heilige Schrift I* (ed. A. Robert - A. Feuillet) (Wien-Freiburg-Basel 1963) 756-762 and 763.

46 J. Ziegler, *Sapientia Iesu Filii Sirach* (Septuaginta. Vetus Testamentum Graecum auctoritate Societatis Litterarum Gottingensis editum XII,2; Göttingen 1965 [²1980]).

47 ספר בן סירא: המקור קונקורדנציה וניתוח אוצר המלים (*The Historical Dictionary of the Hebrew Language*) (Jerusalem 1973); cf. also P. Boccaccio-G. Berardi, *Ecclesiasticus. Textus hebraeus secundum fragmenta reperta* (Rom 1986).

by Rahlfs and Ziegler differs also in other sections of the Greek text, one must be careful. For the chapters in disorder one should follow Ziegler's order of lines: 30,24a.b; 33;13b.c (30,25a.b)[48]; 34,1a.b (31,1a.b) ... 33,13a (36,10a), 33,16b (36,10b) etc.[49] Syr and Vulgate have not made this change, but they have their own system of numeration.[50]

5. Information concerning Ben Sira's person

Most exegetes are careful when they deal with the person of Ben Sira. They emphasize that the name is known, but concerning his profession and social position they disagree. Since Smend,[51] it has been presumed that Sira must have been a member of the Jewish upper class; he belonged to the scribes, who were the natural teachers because of their specific knowledge of the Torah and acted as judges. Kaiser (1994) presumes that they knew about the customs of foreign peoples and that they were the competent teachers of their contemporaries because of their own experience of life (100). He thinks Sira was probably a priest.[52] Kieweler assumes that he was a public official and perhaps a

---

48   References in parenthesis are the verse numbers of Rahlfs.
49   My colleagues and I have produced a verse-by-verse synopsis of the editions of Ziegler, Rahlfs, Syr (Mosul) and Vulgata, which is to appear in the framework of the Sira bibliography (also ready for press).
50   I am using a self-produced edition that presents every Version and its verse number stichometrically. This work is to serve as the basis for a study edition of Sira that presents both H and Syr unvocalized, and G according to Ziegler (noting significant text-critical variants). In addition, a concordance of the three major Versions is to appear in one volume, offering vocalized texts. Furthermore, a grammatical analysis is planned, so that even those less experienced can work with this text.
51   R. Smend, *Die Weisheit des Jesus Sirach erklärt* (Berlin 1906) 345-346. Cf. R. Gordis, "The Social Background of Wisdom Literature", *HUCA* 18 (1943/ 1944) 77-118 (= R. Gordis, *Poets, Prophets and Sages. Essays in Biblical Interpretation* [Bloomington-London 1971] 160-197).
52   So also H. Stadelmann, *Ben Sira als Schriftgelehrter. Eine Untersuchung zum Berufsbild des vormakkabäischen Sofer unter Berücksichtigung seines Verhältnisses zu Priester-, Propheten- und Weisheitslehrertum* (WUNT 2,6;

member of the gerousia.[53] Kaiser assumes that Sira was either of Levite or priestly origin, but Marböck would not agree[54] and has restated his position (1992, 339). Sira's avowed sympathy for liturgical matters and the priesthood could arise from the danger that these institutions faced. There had already been conflicts long before Sira's time because of the (strong) influence of the priests, even in politics.[55]

An original suggestion comes from Wischmeyer, with the question whether Sira perhaps was a physician.[56] I go along with Tcherikover's opinion that Sira came from the poorer class. Living in poor circumstances, he gained wisdom and then rose into the upper class, so that he had access to the powerful of his time.[57] This opinion adds meaning to the passages in the Book of Ben Sira describing poverty and viewing the danger of falling into poverty as a bitter humiliation.

Sira may have been a man of advanced years,[58] but the hints are few that he had been a member of the gerousia. Especially where people get the advice of listening to the old, there are only hints concerning contact between these two groups in a private and spontaneous way within daily life. The parallelism between Duauf and the picture of the sage or

---

Tübingen 1980) 271ff; J.F.A. Sawyer, "Was Jeshua Ben Sira a Priest?" (PWCJS 8 Division A; Jerusalem 1982) 65-71.

53 H.W. Kieweler, *Ben Sira zwischen Judentum und Hellenismus. Eine kritische Auseinandersetzung mit Th. Middendorp* (BEAT 30; Wien 1992) 55.

54 J. Marböck, "Sir 38,24-39,11: Der schriftgelehrte Weise. Ein Beitrag zur Gestalt und Lehre Ben Siras", *La sagesse de l'Ancien Testament. Nouvelle édition mise à jour* (ed. M. Gilbert) (BETL 51; Louvain ²1990) 293-316; 421-423, especially 306 (¹1979; = J. Marböck, *Gottes Weisheit unter uns. Zur Theologie des Buches Sirach* [ed. I. Fischer] [HBS 6; Freiburg-Basel-Wien et al. 1995] 25-51); K.W. Burton, *Sirach and the Judaic Doctrine of Creation* ([Diss.] Glasgow 1987) 63.

55 These conflicts were the forerunners of the quarrels between Onias III and Jason (175/174 B.C.). The conflict escalated under Antiochus IV Epiphanes in Jerusalem. Around 200 B.C., the Jewish moneyed nobility (the Tobiad Joseph and his sons) resided partly in Jerusalem (Josephus, Ant. 12, 4.9). See especially Kieweler, 31-68.

56 O. Wischmeyer, *Die Kultur des Buches Jesus Sirach* (BZNW 77; Berlin-New York 1995) 47 note 55.

57 V. Tcherikover, "Jerusalem on the Eve of the Hellenistic Reform", *Hellenistic Civilization and the Jews* (ed. V. Tcherikover) (Philadelphia 1961 [New York ⁶1982]) 117-151, especially 148.

58 According to D.S. Williams, "The Date of Ecclesiasticus", *VT* 44 (1994), 565, Sira was about 60 years old.

the ideal scribe (and the working class) has been examined[59], but nothing is said there about how Sira dealt with the literature of his environment.

6. Date of Ben Sira

The opinion that Sira was active towards the end of the 3rd Century B.C. has given way to the opinion of his working at the beginning of the 2nd Century. Whereas Gilbert says that "agreement seems to have been reached" that "Ben Sira wrote ... 190 B.C.E.",[60] Crenshaw sets a later date: Sira "can be dated with confidence to the decade between 190 and 180 B.C.E.".[61] Kaiser's battery of evidence shows that Jochanan/ Onias was already dead according to Sir 50,1-21, whereas the troubles around 175 had not yet occurred.[62]

The grandson, who went to Egypt about 132 B.C. (date of translation according to Marböck 1993;1995), translated the book into Greek at the time of Ptolemey VIII, who ruled 170-164 and 145-116 B.C.[63] under the byname Euergetes.[64]

7. Composition of the Book

There are different positions on the criteria of composition of the book and on ways of finding them out. Sections that can be delineated are

---

59 R.J. Williams, "The Sages of Ancient Egypt in the Light of Recent Scholarship", *JAOS* 101 (1981) 10; J.Th. Sanders, "On Ben Sira 24 and Wisdom's Mother Isis" (PWCJS 8 Division A; Jerusalem 1982) 62-63.

60 M. Gilbert, "Wisdom Literature", *Jewish Writings of the Second Temple Period. Apocrypha, Pseudepigrapha, Qumran Sectarian Writings, Philo, Josephus* (ed. M.E. Stone) (CRINT 2/II; Assen-Philadelphia 1984) 282-324, especially 291.

61 J.L. Crenshaw, "Proverbs, Book of", ABD 5 (New York-London-Toronto 1992) 514.

62 Cf. Flavius Jos. Ant. Jud. XII,224; Williams, 563-565.

63 Prol. 28 suggests the ruler's death, that is, 116 B.C. (Gilbert, 1995, 880).

64 Like Ptolemaios III (246-221 B.C.)

suggested in Smend (23 subsections),[65] Peters (10 subsections)[66] and Segal (8 subsections).[67] But according to Lefèvre the book is "a collection of proverbs without internal order and about the most diverse circumstances".[68] If that view be accepted, it determines exegesis, "because exegesis depends on whether the separate proverbs are taken as parts of a larger whole or as originally independent elements" (Schrader, 64). For this reason, this question and that of the unity of disputed passages[69] become even more evident.

For many scholars, the Book of Ben Sira could be divided into three major parts: 1-23; 24-43; 44-50/51 (e.g. Kaiser 1994), or 1-23; 24-42,14[70]; 42,15-51,30 (e.g. Marböck 1993; 1995)[71] and the appendix 51,[72] where the parts dealing with wisdom[73] and those dealing with

---

65   R. Smend, *Die Weisheit des Jesus Sirach erklärt* (Berlin 1906) xx-xxxiv
66   N. Peters, *Das Buch Jesus Sirach oder Ecclesiasticus* (EHAT 25; Münster 1913) xli-xlii.
67   M.Z. Segal, ספר בן סירא השלם (Jerusalem ³1972) 15-16 (Hebrew).
68   A. Lefèvre, "Ecclesiasticus (Sirazide)", *Einleitung in die Heilige Schrift I* (ed. A. Robert & A. Feuillet) (Wien-Freiburg-Basel 1963) 756-762. F. Gradl, 194: "ein durchgehend logischer Aufbau des Buches ist nicht erkennbar".
69   P.C. Beentjes, "'Full Wisdom is Fear of the Lord'. Ben Sira 19,20-20,31: Context, Composition and Concept", *EstB* 47 (1989) 27-45.
70   Wischmeyer, 153, follows the division (1-24) of J. Marböck, *Weisheit im Wandel. Untersuchungen zur Weisheitstheologie bei Ben Sira* (BBB 37; Bonn 1971) 47-49, who has evidently changed his mind about the first part of the book ending here.
71   Th.R. Lee, *Studies in the Form of Sirach [Ecclesiasticus] 44-50* (SBLDS 75; Atlanta, Georgia 1986) 229-234, considers Sir 49,14-16, according to Greek prototypes, to be an encomiastic conclusion, serving as a transition to the praise of Simeon; see N. Peters, "Das Buch der Weisheit Jesus des Sohnes Sirach oder Ecclesiasticus", *Die Weisheitsbücher des Alten Testamentes* (ed. N. Peters) (Münster 1914) 422; similarly Wischmeyer, 153, although she is apparently not acquainted with Lee.
72   Gradl, 194, speaks of the redacted final form, since he regards the theme of wisdom in Chaps. 1; 24; 51 as editorial framework; Marböck, 1995, 289, explicitly mentions that, for 51,13-29 (as for a few other passages, namely 36,1-17 and 51,12a-o), authenticity is questionable. More restricted is the finding of Schrader, 69-95 in relation to Th. Middendorp, *Die Stellung Jesu Ben Siras zwischen Judentum und Hellenismus* (Leiden 1973) 125-136, since he attempts to demonstrate later insertions (e.g. 8,1-2; 42,8) suggesting a redaction in the Maccabean period.
73   According to Marböck, 1992, 39, the corresponding units are: 1,1-10; 4,11-19; 6,18-37; 14,20-15,10; 24; 32,14-33,6; 38,24-39,11; 51,13-30. On these see O.

God's activity (Kaiser, 101-102) prove to have a particular structuring function. Thus Kaiser finds ten parts, marked by new beginnings (1,1; 4,11; 6,18; 14,20; 24,1; 32,14; 39,12; 44,1; 50,25; 51,1).[74] In the detailed arrangement he relies on Skehan & Di Lella (4-6), who offer a thematically oriented differentiated arrangement in a sensible way. Marböck sees further structuring hints in groups of texts that he views as expressing major themes, such as 'fear of God' (1,11-2,18; 10,19-24; 25,6-11; 40,18-27) [75], 'true and false shame' (4,20-30; 41,16-42,8) [76], and 'order in creation' (15,11-18,14; 33,7-15; 39,12-35; and 42,15-43,33), [77] so that he can trace a network full of meaning which has much in its favour but is far from simplifying the picture.

The presentation of an internal structure requires an internal homogeneity which Rickenbacher (1973) takes as a starting point. In his view, the order of the literary units within the book of Ben Sira produces evidence for its structure.[78] Jüngling suggests that biographical notes are the framework of composition.[79] Schrader, however, sees only a mechanistic collection of originally independent elements.[80]

Rickenbacher, *Weisheitsperikopen bei Ben Sira* (OBO 1; Freiburg-Göttingen 1973) passim. With the finding "of different levels of structure," J.D. Harvey, "Toward a Degree of Order in Ben Sira's Book", *ZAW* 105 (1993) 52-62, is more basic.

74 Four in the first, four in the second, and two in the third part of the book.

75 In his judgement, Marböck is evidently influenced by J. Haspecker, *Gottesfurcht bei Jesus Sirach. Ihre religiöse Struktur und ihre literarische und doktrinäre Bedeutung* (AnBib 30; Rom 1967).

76 I. Krammer, "Scham im Zusammenhang mit Freundschaft", *Freundschaft im Buch Ben Sira* (ed. F.V. Reiterer) (BZAW 244; Berlin-New York 1996) 171-201.

77 Compare the study of G.L. Prato, *Il problema della teodicea in Ben Sira. Composizioni dei contrari e richiamo alle origine* (AnBib 65; Rom 1975), who treats further texts on the themes.

78 Also Haspecker, 93.118; Middendorp, 33-34, sees a school textbook, which is based on a Greek model, and in which nationalism encounters the world-citizenship of the Stoic philosophers.

79 Cf. H.-W. Jüngling, "Der Bauplan des Buches Jesus Sirach", *Den Armen eine frohe Botschaft*; (Fs Bischof F. Kamphaus; [Hrsg. J. Hainz - H.W. Jüngling - R. Sebott] Frankfurt 1997) 87-105.

80 According to Schrader, fundamental theological tensions originate here within the texts, since Sira deals with a collection of originally independent elements that do not originate from Jesus Sirach himself (300); in contrast to other statements in the study, this thesis is consistently maintained from start to fin-

8. Central themes: external and internal cultural influence

(a) According to Marböck, certain themes in the Book of Ben Sira are more strongly stressed than in the other literature of O.T. (even than the related book of Proverbs) or are exaggerated because of dangers arising from the Hellenistic way of life. Examples are the warning against rulers and rich people (8,10-19; 11,29-34; 12,8-18; 13,1-13), taking the part of the helpless and poor (34,21-27; 35,15-20; Marböck 1995); warning against standing surety (29,14-20), advice about keeping company with women (9,1-9), attitude towards matrimony (25-26), behaviour at home (29,21-28; 36,31), educational problems (30,1-13; 42,9-14) and above all friendship (6,5-17; 22,19-26; 27,16-21; 37,1-6). Acquaintance with Greek literature (Theognis) and demotic wisdom (Phibis in Papyrus Insinger) arise from this scope.[81]

In 7,18; 9,10; 11,29-34; 12,8-9; and 33,6, Kaiser sees a major topic because friendship reflects the "increasing isolation of the individual in such times of change".[82] The positive side of these new developments through Hellenistic influences includes esteem for travel (34,9-13; 39,4), the position of the physician (38,1-15) and advice about a banquet (32,13).[83] There must be added the role of the sage, by analogy to the philosophers (38,24-39,11), when Sira expressly wants to call him back to Biblical tradition. Marböck emphasizes Sira's acquaintance

---

ish. However in the study, one does not discover what really is genuinely from Sirach; by contrast, see K.W. Burton, 222: "The whole of Sirach's text is a well planned symphony, every note, every movement is part of the whole. There are subtleties and allusions throughout which must be seen as notes which give fullness and harmony to his message".

81   Gilbert (1995, 884-885) is cautious on looking at Hellenistic influence.
82   "zunehmende Isolation des Einzelnen ..., wie sie in derartigen Wendezeiten auftreten"; O. Kaiser, "Gottesgewißheit und Weltbewußtsein in der frühhellenis-tischen jüdischen Weisheit", Der Mensch unter dem Schicksal. Studien zur Geschichte, Theologie und Gegenwartsbedeutung der Weisheit (ed. O. Kaiser) (BZAW 161; Berlin - New York 1985) 122-134 (= in: Glaube und Toleranz. Das theologische Erbe der Aufklärung [ed. T. Rendtorff] [Gütersloh 1982] 76-88, especially 128-130). The theme of friendship was the subject of a symposium on Sira (June 1995), published in F.V. Reiterer (ed.), Freundschaft im Buch Ben Sira (BZAW 244; Berlin-New York 1996).
83   Kaiser, 1982; Kaiser 1995, 102.

with the Stoa[84] in the topics of liberty (15,11-17)[85] and self-control (22,27-23,6; 38,16-23). Besides, Sira provides evidence of the internal cultural situation in his days (Marböck 1994).

(b) Sanders shows Sira's relation to pagan literature; he finds various allusions,[86] indicating that Sira knew Greek literature, but not in a relevant way. Sira depends more on wisdom from Egypt, especially Papyrus Insinger.[87] Sanders and others think of a date before or after the early Ptolemaic time.[88] Sanders examines the texts which Humbert, Morenz, Fuß, and Couroyer suggest to be parallels.[89] He himself deals in detail with the passages on shame. The parallelism "allows us to observe Ben Sira's process of selection and utilization at work" (94) in which Sira had on Phibis in an expressive and more comprehensive way than on Theognis (98) so that one could even speak of borrowing (101-103) according to Sanders. The intensive discussion about Sira's contacts with non-Biblical literature has been emphasized with regard of the excessive text of Sir 24 and the question of the influence of the Isis aretalogy. This influence is treated by Ringgren[90] and above all by

---

84   Marböck 1995; this point is emphatically advocated by R. Pautrel, "Ben Sira et le Stoicïsme", *RSR* 51 (1963) 535-549, but subsequently subjected to criticism.

85   Kaiser, 1995, 103; particularly the similarity to Post-Deuteronomistic ideas of decision-making.

86   J.Th. Sanders, *Ben Sira and Demotic Wisdom* (SBLMS 28; Chico, California 1983) mentions, for instance, the Iliad. After examination of the parallel passages adduced by Middendorp, he considers only one as convincing (39-40) In his judgment, a relation with passages quoted from the Odyssey are not convincing (40-41).

87   In the context of the Satire on the Trades, Sira has taken over from Insinger "both the content and the point of view ..., and this borrowing is more obvious and his reliance on foreign tradition more pronounced than was the case with any of the Hellenic gnomic materials" (Sanders, 1983, 69).

88   A.Volten, *Das demotische Weisheitsbuch* (Copenhagen 1941) 70.

89   Sanders, 69-80 on P. Humbert, "Le livre de l'Ecclésiastique de Jésus-Sirach", *Recherches sur les sources égyptiennes de la littérature sapientiale d'Israël* (ed. P. Humbert) (Neuchâtel 1929) 125-144. Sanders, 68-69, on S. Morenz, "Eine weitere Spur der Weisheit Amenopes in der Bibel", *Religion und Geschichte des alten Ägypten* (ed. S. Morenz) (Weimar 1975) 412-416. Sanders, 80-91, on Fuß. Sanders, 91-92, on B. Couroyer, "Un égyptianisme dans Ben Sira 4,11", *RB* 82 (1975) 206-217.

90   H. Ringgren, *Word and Wisdom; Studies in the Hypostatization of Divine Qualities and Functions in the Ancient Near East* (Uppsala 1947) 146.

Conzelmann.[91] But Gilbert,[92] following Skehan,[93] does not agree. They suggest greater influence from Proverbs on Sira and so they think this Isis connection to be improbable, whereas Sanders[94] refuses such an influence. However, others in our time think of it as a probability again (e.g. Kieweler).

(c) Since Middendorp's and Hengel's[95] treatises, the question of Hellenistic influence on Judaism has attracted more interest. In a careful way, Kieweler (16-63) works on the main political, administrative and cultural influences on Judaean Palestine.[96] He shows how external circumstances marked life by the imposed balance between adaptation and withdrawal during the long literary history of Israel, especially in the Post-Exilic Period. Under this assumption, Sira takes pains to preserve the heritage of his people and deals intensively with the trends of his time. With ideas from Hellenistic education (37-47), though withdrawing from it, Sira gathered disciples at the synagogue, mentioned for the first time, to teach them the Law of Moses (64-65). He studies Greek philosophers (Ionian natural philosophy, Bias, Xenophanes, Heraklitus, Demokritus, Epicurus, Zeno), older and more recent poets (Homer,[97] Hesiod,[98] Homeric hymns, fables of Aesop, Alcaios, Theognis, Pindar, Herodotus), the tragedians Aeschylus, Sophocles and Euripides, the comedians Aristophanes and Menander,[99] as well as the

---

91 H. Conzelmann, "Die Mutter der Weisheit", *BEvTh* 65 (1974) 167-176 (= in: *Zeit und Geschichte* [FS R. Bultmann [ed. E. Dinkler] Tübingen 1964], 225-234 [= "The Mother of Wisdom", *The Future of Our Religious Past* [ed. J.M. Robinson] [New York 1971] 230-243]).

92 M. Gilbert, "L'éloge de la Sagesse (Siracide 24)", *RTL* 5 (1974) 326-348.

93 P.W. Skehan, "Structures in Poems on Wisdom: Proverbs 8 and Sirach 24", *CBQ* 41 (1979) 365-379.

94 Sanders, 1983, 45-50; Sanders, 1982.

95 M. Hengel, *Judentum und Hellenismus. Studien zu ihrer Begegnung unter besonderer Berücksichtigung Palästinas bis zur Mitte des 2. Jh.s. v.Chr.* (WUNT 10; Tübingen ²1973).

96 On the role of the high-priest at that time see K.D. Schunk, "Hoherpriester und Politiker? Die Stellung der Hohenpriester von Jaddua bis Jonatan zur jüdischen Gemeinde und zum hellenistischen Staat", *VT* 44 (1994) 498-512.

97 In contrast to Hesiod, Homer moves in an aristocratic world.

98 Hesiod's Epos "Theognis" is the first ancient attempt at a systematic theology; Kieweler, 107.

99 C. Wildberg, *Ursprung, Funktion und Inhalt der Weisheit bei Jesus Sirach und in den Sentenzen des Menander* (Marburg 1985) [Dipl.].

historian and philosopher Xenophon. Although Kieweler works independently, the presentation is one-sided because of his debate with Middendorp so that he does not allow other authors to have their say. He shows that Middendorp hardly noticed any historical factor that might have influenced Sira's position. Ben Sira is not intermediate "between Judaism and Hellenism" (268), but he is an Israelite under Hellenistic influence marked by international contacts. He does not live in a vacuum but at the end of a long line of evolution. "The opposition to the Hellenistic system of authority took root, as almost always, in the spiritual and religious environment, which led to a reconsideration of the Patriarchal heritage" (267). On the other hand, he is, for instance, influenced by Homer, Pindar, and especially Theognis (91-105. 201-206; 137-195), and, in the *Praise of the Fathers* by the Isis aretalogy. On the other hand, the compactness of the work, which is based on a new conception of wisdom, shows the originality of the author. "This wordly wisdom relates Ben Sira to observation and maintenance of the Law" (269). Although these generalizing statements are persuasive, neither Kieweler nor Middendorp consider differences in the textual material (various H manuscripts, G I and Syr) by which one might perhaps detect trends and pecularities of tradition within the Hebrew or at least the Greek and Syriac material.[100]

(d) As one can see, the contacts with Greek culture are noted again and again, especially in that late Egyptian form that occurred in Alexandria. At the same time, Sira was firmly rooted in Biblical tradition. Kieweler hints that Sira's obvious attitude of mind is typical of Judaism before the Destruction of the Second Temple (272). So Sira is a witness of the Judaism of his time and perhaps even one of the creators of that culture.

This theme is taken up by Wischmeyer, whose refreshing work indicates that Sira's age was far from narrowing culture in the direction of arts and literature, as in our modern era. She tries to define "Kultur" more precisely. This concept includes the broad area of society and politics, and "the broad area of material and immaterial products of culture, art, music, literature and education" (20). She distinguishes the following groups of themes: family, work and profession, society, poli-

---

[100] The same additional question could also have been considered by Wischmeyer, 53 (though she makes an exception in her discussion of the upper echelons of society); her result proves the efficacy of such comparisons.

tics and state, law,[101] material culture, manners and customs, arts and music, language and literature, education and learning, helpful mental guidance (Seelenführung) and the relation between religion and culture. As to family, Sira's ideas presuppose life in town.[102] He is not really interested in large-scale politics or affairs of the state[103] He takes over its traditional appreciation. Wischmeyer describes Sira as a fatherly friend, who is seen as 'pater familias' but who views the members of the family as his equals. "In general, Jesus Sirach does not speak simply in Old Testament and Patriarchal manner of many children as a great benefit. Rather he stresses the idea of responsibility for correct bringing up of children and for their prosperity" (29). The remarks about women show that a good wife can behave like a sage (the ultimate achievement in the development of mankind). Sira holds monogamy in high esteem and, as Wischmeyer suggests, his noble and decent way of life is not ascetic.

The task of parents is the education of the children. Though there are no rules about relations between brothers and sisters, Sira deals with slaves according to the legal status of his time, but he exceeds it in reference to the affection from him. In Sira's opinion, a friend (passim 27-41) belongs as a private partner to the family. However, as often been emphazed by Kaiser, the author does not adequately consider the role of a reliable friend or a group of friends in times of politically radical change.[104]

Wischmeyer sees the profession of farmer, which was very important in those days, only in a metaphorical way or mentioned by chance; Sira had no ideal of country life. So in his sage education, there is no fresh impetus on the subject of work (43).[105] Sira is cautious about

---

101 Even if Sira touches on judges and law-courts only incidentally, the Torah still remains the foundation of legal thought and action, and the source of ethical and juristic norms (ibid., 73-82).

102 Wischmeyer considers Sira as a town-dwelling landowner (ibid., 43 note 32; 70-74).

103 Since Sira does not develop a theory or approach to the distribution of power or the essence of government, a gap remains into which other groups forced their way.

104 J. Corley, *Ben Sira's Teaching on Friendship* ([Diss.] Washington 1996), to be published in BJSt.

105 This statement would be qualified by consideration of already available studies, e.g. F.V. Reiterer, "Die Stellung Ben Siras zur Arbeit". Notizen zu einem

commerce, where one has to act in a prudent, cool and conscientious way. He is more positive about professions such as physician or artist (45-48).

Society is traditionally organized and the influence of the upper class, scarcely the representatives of culture, depends on their financial power. Wischmeyer thinks that these people are to be found among the high priest's remote relatives. But Sira points out that wealth, which he views positively (55-56), and social prestige are not automatically inter-related. The sages[106] as well as the rich are people risen to a higher so-cial level, who "would drastically change the tradional structure of the Judaean society" (61). They stand on the side of the conservative land-owners, confronting the progressive and rich merchants. For Sira there is no "natural" environment, but there is only creation. Within this framework, he deals, for instance, with hills, rocks, deserts, water, brooks, many kinds of animals (often mentioned metaphorically), plants, household utensils and food or its consumption (83-101). On manners and customs, Ben Sira touches upon gestures, social conduct, visits, table-manners, hospitality, presents, games and amusement, en-tertainment, child care, planning of life, wedding, death[107] and funeral (102-119). Apart from the reference to essential trades, the author holds the artistic aim to be decisive (38,28.29). Music is to be found every-where in the O.T. Sira speaks of it in the religious domain as well as in the profane (from the drinking song to the funeral march), at which "it is the task of the creator of proverbs to examine these songs for their

kaum berücksichtigten Thema sirazidischer Lehre", *Ein Gott - eine Offen-barung* (FS N. Füglister [ed. F.V. Reiterer] Würzburg 1991) 257-289, with bibliographical references.

106 "The sage dominates and instructs in all areas of public and private life at home and abroad. So he instructs on politics, juridical and domestic matters. He is a teacher of religion and customs; he instructs on public and private ethics. Since he recieves his teaching direct from Divine wisdom, he is an incontest-able authority and an essential support of rulers and Jews alike" (Wischmeyer, 63; translation JCR).

107 Here the author ignores discussions such as that of F.V. Reiterer, "Deutung und Wertung des Todes durch Ben Sira", *Die alttestamentliche Botschaft als Wegweisung* (FS H. Reinelt [ed. J. Zmijewski] Stuttgart 1990) 203-236, with bibliographical references; also to be noted the recent work of Schrader, 237-252 (incidentally also lacking any review of the literature on the topic).

metre" (134.120-135).[108] "Ben Sira often mentions the role of speech as an instrument of human culture in Classical diction" (140) and he teaches a high ethical obligation in speech (143-145),[109] in which he does not allow aesthetic dimensions to be neglected (145-146). On education and learning, Wischmeyer doubts whether proof could be given of any system of public schools in the O.T.; she concieves of instruction given by elders, who teach wisdom in private. On law, however, there is the tradition of transmission by priests. In contrast to the sage, there is the fool, who does not, however, form a vocational group. The fool is characterized by lack of religion and self-control (e.g. in drinking, sexual intercourse and possessions) and especially by unsuitable speech (176-182). "Sira's personal and oral understanding of wisdom aims at a culture of wisdom poetry" (185).

Ben Sira summarises theological instruction in three areas: What is God's creation? What is mankind? What is God's history with mankind? (187-198) All doctrines focus on the idea that true justice is the fear of God (198). In agreement with Hengel (1973, 252-254),[110] Wischmeyer understands identification of wisdom with knowledge of law as a strategy to combat Hellenism. Creation, mankind, and human life are interwoven with God's law, so that wisdom in a new way becomes instruction for conduct of life (199-200).

Wischmeyer's chapter on mental guidance (Seelenführung) is ingenious and sensible. She draws a remarkable picture of the sage as a leader in internal problems and as a man having insight into the mind. But the question is not how religious attitude and experience can be explained psychologically; the question "is the psyche itself and its

---

108 He does not exploit the discussion by J. Marböck, "קו - eine Bezeichnung für das hebräische Metrum?", VT 20 (1970) 236-239 (= J. Marböck, *Gottes Weisheit unter uns. Zur Theologie des Buches Sirach*, [HBS 6 [ed. I. Fischer] Freiburg-Basel-Wien 1995] 144-146).

109 Recently: J. Okoye, *Speech in Ben Sira with Special Reference to 5,9-6,1* (EHS XXIII/535; Frankfurt a.M. 1995); A.A. Di Lella, "Use and Abuse of the Tongue: Ben Sira 5,9-6,1", *'Jedes Ding hat seine Zeit ...'. Studien zur israelitischen und altorientalischen Weisheit* (FS D. Michel; ed. A.A. Diesel et al.) (BZAW 241; Berlin-New York 1996) 33-48.

110 Especially J. Marböck, "Gesetz und Weisheit. Zum Verständnis des Gesetzes bei Jesus Ben Sira", BZ 20 (1976) 1-21 (= J. Marböck, *Gottes Weisheit unter uns. Zur Theologie des Buches Sirach*, [HBS 6 [ed. I. Fischer] Freiburg-Basel-Wien et al. 1995] 52-72).

cultural outline, which in Sira's time and country was always religious" (206). Internal powers in instruction are the mind and wisdom themselves. Camp sees the role of feminine wisdom as the guardian of morals and tradition in analogy by woman.[111] In Post-Exilic times, the family, individualism and private piety became more important (272-274). As a consequence, the social position of the woman improved. In addition, wisdom took on more of the role of mediator between God and mankind or Israel, respectively (235-237). In line with the statements of Camp, Wischmeyer uses erotic comments on wisdom. "In the eyes of Ben Sira, the erotic allusions are not a Topos, but this Topos is filled with new meaning by his instruction. For he approaches the feelings of his pupils, the youth of Jerusalem, with his Topos. The mental culture is not only an intellectual or formal educative process, but a process of stretching in which the inner strength of the pupils is drawn out and modeled by Wisdom, their teacher, in the same way as this happens in love for a woman" (235). Although marked by inner freedom, sovereignty, and optimism, the intellectual elite were trained by trust in the good God, in which awareness of mortality and sin teaches modesty for everybody (247).[112]

Sira's religious interpretation and his relationship with culture are the summary of everything said above, where the author works out the synthesis and indicates the paradigmatics with rare clarity. This concise study, offering many interesting aspects, is excellent. Wischmeyer is often rather apodictic and hardly enters into discussion. But the result offers a convincing picture of Sira and his cultured effect.

---

111 C. Camp, *Wisdom and the Feminine in the Book of Proverbs* (Sheffield 1985) 146-147.

112 A contrasting judgment is offered by Schrader, who (influenced by his conception of Sira as a resigned and pessimistic old man) sees a false veneer of optimism, particularly about suffering and death. There is no evidence of God's goodness, but only of punitive and probationary suffering. Earlier he notes in amazement that one may encounter in individual statements a remarkably profound understanding of suffering (304), which points to its mysterious character (ibid., 307).

9. Wisdom, Law and Creation

In line with Marböck (1976, 1-21; 1971, 93-96) and other scholars,[113] Schnabel equates wisdom and law. He chooses the relation between wisdom and creation as his theme and concludes that creation is a way of revealing wisdom.[114] In a section about wisdom and the history of salvation, he includes the origin of wisdom from God, its assigment to Israel, its relationship to worship and its association with the fear of God. "Ben Sira the scribe and priest incorporated the priestly, the prophetic, and the sapiential traditions of Israel and presented wisdom as being active and essential in all realms of reality: in nature and in history, in the world and in the life of God's people" (28).

By analogy, Schnabel investigates the law's relation to creation. He considers it unthinkable to put law on a par with the order of creation, only because both of them appear in one text dealing with creation (17,11-12).[115] He considers certain terms with other usage applications in themselves (e.g. תורה as a destiny of death imposed by God [in 41,1], as well as חק and ייי דבר), showing that God has given an inner order to his creation. In 24,23, the law seems to be identified with wisdom as mentioned before, and seems to paraphrase a universal cosmic law different from the Sinaitic revelation. Law plays a part in the history of salvation and its relation to the fear of God belongs to the "fundamental admonition".[116] The function of the law is in its normative role for morals and social conduct. It is a measure of piety, it regu-

---

113 Cf. G.T. Sheppard, "Wisdom and Torah: The Interpretation of Deuteronomy Underlying Sirach 24,23", *Biblical and Near Eastern Studies* (FS W.S. LaSor [ed. G.A. Tuttle] Grand Rapids 1978) 166-176; G.T. Sheppard, *Wisdom as a Hermeneutical Construct. A Study of the Sapientializing of the Old Testament* (BZAW 151; Berlin - New York 1980) 18-83; D.J. Harrington, "The Wisdom of the Scribe According to Ben Sira", *Ideal Figures in Ancient Judaism. Profiles and Paradigms* (ed. J.J. Collins - G.W.E. Nickelsburg) (SBL 12; Ann Arbor, Michigan 1980) 181-188; G.W.E. Nickelsburg, *Jewish Literature between the Bible and the Mishnah. A Historical and Literary Introduction* (Philadelphia 1982) 59.

114 E.J. Schnabel, *Law and Wisdom from Ben Sira to Paul; A Tradition-Historical Enquiry into the Relation of Law, Wisdom, and Ethics* (WUNT 2/16; Tübingen 1985) 16-19; also earlier Segal, on 1,6; Rickenbacher, 41.

115 In this, he rightly expresses himself against making such a parallelisation; see Marböck, 1971, 87-88; Marböck, 1976, 5-6 [1995, 57-58].

116 Thus Haspecker, 287-289.

lates worship and jurisdiction, and it is the basis of doctrine (29-55). Although Schnabel generally pays adequate attention to literal biblical references within every relevant unit, alluding to Haspecker, he concludes that though "the law is never the subject of a longer pericope, it is nevertheless of fundamental importance to Ben Sira" (62), a conclusion which I had drawn independently. Sira's poetic strength can hardly be doubted and he supports his intentions in a striking way through the arrangement, so that the position of the whole poem, too, is especially relevant.[117] My own inquiries show that there are inclusions that embrace poems with wisdom.[118] Besides these envelopes over the whole book or within single passages, one can see that wisdom can often be found in the introductions of units and marks the whole text.[119] At the end of units, wisdom is used in the function of conclusion.[120] In contrast to wisdom, there is never an inclusion with law. Sometimes we find νόμος in the introductory verse of a unit.[121] As in 19,20 and 21,11, νόμος may refer to wisdom. Several times, law is to be found in the closing verse of a unit.[122] This observation shows the different emphases on wisdom and law, although there is clear evidence that they are equated. Besides, it is improbable that Sira is thinking here mostly of the Torah of Moses, as Schnabel believes (62). Moreover he examines passages showing identification of wisdom and law, which have been suggested by historical events (87) and their theological (philosophical) background. "The fact that this identification is referred to in 19 passages altogether and often occurs at key positions in the different pericopes, shows how important this theologoumenon is for Ben Sira" (89). However he did not think of the fact that the law often submits to

---

117 According to an unpublished manuscript by F.V. Reiterer, *Weisheit und Gesetz im Buch Ben Sira*, a paper given at the SBL International Meeting in Budapest (1995).

118 Namely 6,18-37 (18b; 37d); 14,20-15,10 (14,20a; 15,10a); 38,24-39,11 (38, 24a; 39,10a [10-11]; 41,14-15 (41,14b; 41,15b).

119 As in 4,11a (4,11-20); 6,18b (6,18-37); 19,20a (19,20-30; σοφία and νόμος); 21,11b (21,11-22,2; νόμος and σοφία); 24,1a (24,1-22); 50,27d (50,27-29); 51,13b (51,13-30).

120 Namely 1,10c (1,1-10); 1,20a (1,11-20); 11,15a (11,10-15); 20,31b (20,27-31); 25,10a (25,1-10); 43,33b (42,15-43,33); 44,15a (44,1-15); 45,26a (45,23-26).

121 Namely 19,20a (19,20-30; σοφία and νόμος); 21,11b (21,11-22,2; νόμος and σοφία); 24,23 (24,23-34).

122 Namely 19,17 (18,30-19,17); 45,5 (45,1-5).

wisdom and does not stand on the same level.[123] As a consequence, he sees that law and wisdom (apparently with equal status) are the basis and requirement, the contents and the range, the gain and result of practical and personal piety (89).

Jolley also deals with "the function of Torah in Sirach" in an interesting investigation, which, however, does not consider significant relevant literature. He works on the semantic field of the Torah - also in comparison to other comparable terms such as ברית[124] especially in Sira; he rejects restriction to the Deuteronomic law[125], but sees it (as the whole Bible) as God's gift to Moses. However one must always remember that this Mosaic law goes back to the beginning of the creation (16-55). In a wider step, Jolley deals with the historical background and its intellectual history (Sira's opponents, death and immortality, free will and fate, punishment and retribution, the political and religious situation). Moreover he examines 1,11-30; 14,20-15,10; and 24,1-34 as single texts. Summing up, he declares that "torah is to be used in study and worship as the guide to how one should live. Left by itself, the Torah ... has no autonomy and is of no educational value. It must be studied, and this is what Ben Sira encourages his readers to do. ... Wisdom has come to Israel to give Torah life ... Torah and Wisdom are inseparably linked together in Sirach in a synergistic relationship ..." (147-148). Someone gains wisdom in obedience to God's will, which is to be found in the Torah, the Five Books of Moses (150). Sira does not see the crisis of his time without doing anything, but stresses obedience to the Torah as a response to the Hellenistic challenge (154).

---

[123] It is becoming ever clearer that studies in their analysis of the meaning of a literary unit must consider the poetic framework more closely than hitherto has been done.

[124] On this word M.A. Jolley, *The Function of Torah in Sirach (Wisdom Literature)* (Southern Baptist Theological Seminary 1993) [Diss.], states that it occurs 8 times in the Praise of the Fathers (46-48). He does not see "sieben Bundesschlüsse", as Marböck indicates for its structural function in the Praise of the Fathers; J. Marböck, "Die 'Geschichte Israels' als 'Bundesgeschichte' nach dem Sirachbuch", *Der neue Bund im Alten. Studien zur Bundestheologie der beiden Testamente* (ed. E. Zenger) (QD 146; Freiburg-Basel-Wien 1993), 177-197 (= in: J. Marböck, *Gottes Weisheit unter uns. Zur Theologie des Buches Sirach*, [HBS 6 [ed. I. Fischer] Freiburg-Basel-Wien et al. 1995] 103-123).

[125] Sheppard, 1978, 166-176.

In retrospect, it seems that both studies confer a precedence on the Torah, the Mosaic revelation (of the Pentateuch). In each study, wisdom is the practical result. According to Jolley, wisdom is obedience to law; according to Schnabel, it is the basis of practical and personal piety.

10. Creation and Intertestamental literature

In a similar way to the concept 'fear of God', creation plays a central part in Sira.[126] Often creation is referred to incidentally and, in some texts, it is dealt with more comprehensively. In one section, Schnabel investigated the relations to wisdom and law. Burton made a special study on this theme, which concluded that Sira was scarcely influenced by wisdom literature, but especially by Psalms, as someone "familiar with cult and the temple" might do, and by the stories of creation in Gen 1 and Gen 2-3. In particular, however, Sira used Deutero-Isaiah,[127] where eschatological features are to be found, as well as the beginning of apocalyptic literature (9-99). He stresses the parallelism between Deutero-Isaiah and Sira within the theme "Creator of all", which he sees in Isa 44,24; 45,22; and 45,7, and in Sir 11,14; 18,1; and 43,33; here he picks up a thread leading to P, where the theme is implicitly present (36-38).[128] God's title of ὁ κτίστης ἁπάντων (Sir 24,6) is not to be found anywhere in the Old Testament, but occurs three times in Jubilees (11,17; 22,27; 45,5). The search for the resting place of wisdom and "the heavenly journeys in search of secret knowledge" (97) is similar to 2 Enoch, so that the parallels cannot be overlooked. In a detailed investigation, Burton deals with personified wisdom in creation (1,1-10), mankind's free will (15,14-20), mankind's position in creation (16,24-17,14), God and mankind (18,1-14), wisdom as a gift, the para-

---

126 Of the book, 30 chapters include at least 100 terminological references; as listed in the manuscript of Reiterer SBL Annual Meeting at Mainz (1993), as yet unpublished.

127 P.C.Beentjes, "Relations between Ben Sira and the Book of Isaiah", *The Book of Isaiah* (ed. J. Vermeylen) (BETL 81; Louvain 1989) 155-159.

128 On this, see the note about the different use of הכל in the two books (Burton, 78-79).

dise of wisdom (24), inequality in creation (33,7-19),[129] divine order and control, and the hymn on God's achievements (42,15-43,33). To sum up: in Sira's work, creation is more than a subordinate theme. On the contrary, it is the central structure for Sira's entire way of thinking, being an essential part of his teaching, which is rooted in tradition, beginning with J up to the book of Jubilees. The work shows itself to be entirely independent; this can be seen especially in Chapter 24. Torah, temple, worship, the people, the individual and his decisions: they were all important only in the praise of God, the creator of everything (219-222). Sira's statements about creation form an advent to apocalyptic literature and the New Testament (Rom 11,33-36; 225).

Without any knowledge of Burton, Argall examined revelation, creation and judgment by comparing the apocalyptic book of 1 Enoch and Sira, two books partly of the same era,[130] in which he assesses literary features, significant grammatical forms, and words (4). His study arose from the two references to Enoch in Sira, showing that "Sira had at least *some* appreciation for Enoch as a revealer figure, however heated his polemic against some purveyors of esoteric tradition" (11; 13).[131] Argall points to the prophetic authority in Chap. 24, by which Sira saw himself as a revealer. Here wisdom is a mystically revealed dimension. As in a love story (57), wisdom turns towards the admirer,

---

129 Burton uses only the edition of Rahlfs: 33,10-15 (= Ziegler 36,10-15). In this case the textual base has implications in terms of content, since in v. 13b (treated by Burton on p. 161), instead of πᾶσαι αἱ ὁδοὶ αὐτου (Rahlfs), Ziegler gives πλάσαι αὐτο as original.

130 1Enoch is a composite work, probably dating from between the fourth and first centuries B.C.; R.A. Argall, *1 Enoch and Sirach: A Comparative Literary and Conceptual Analysis of the Themes of Revelation, Creation and Judgement* (SBL 08; Atlanta, Georgia 1995) 6.

131 He presupposes that the two passages belong to the original textual stock. Whereas P.C. Beentjes, "The 'Praise of the Famous' and Its Prologue. Some Observations on Ben Sira 44:1-15 and the Question on Enoch in 44:16", *BTFT* 45 (1984) 374-383, and Skehan - Di Lella, 499, consider 44,16 as secondary, is this verse classified as original by Middendorp, 53-54.109.112.134 and J. Marböck, "Henoch-Adam-der Thronwagen. Zu frühjüdischen pseudepigraphischen Traditionen bei Ben Sira", *BZ* NF 25 (1981) 103-111 (= in: J. Marböck, *Gottes Weisheit unter uns. Zur Theologie des Buches Sirach*, [HBS 6 [ed. I. Fischer] Freiburg-Basel-Wien et al. 1995] 133-143); see also Wright, 155. Yadin, 38 suspects a secondary transposition (49,14a; 44,16b; 44,16a; 49,14b).

who desires it and in marriage is revealed its secrets; here by mutual references to 51,17.26 a connection to school is given. The sage thinks of the Torah, handles it properly and can teach it and impart its concealed contents[132] to his pupils.[133] In 1 Enoch and Sira, wisdom is of heavenly origin, has a life-giving function, takes the role of a person as revealer (esp. 1 Enoch 32 and Sir 24) and leads to a written book (92-98). Within creation too, Argall sees an observable and a hidden aspect. He sees the sizable facts of creation (e.g. mankind, sun and moon, storm, wind, abyss and sea) as achievements of God (135-155),[134] but with a double thrust: they can be useful or can do damage. Even when they are destructive, they fulfil a positive function, being able to serve God's judgment. The hidden aspects of creation show "the inability of humankind to comprehend the great expanse of creation" (155).[135] Although the origin of wisdom has been revealed to Ben Sira and to Israel, they do not now have complete insight through creation, but can understand the results of the phenomena. The author sees a parallel between Sira and 1 Enoch in the way that creation can be viewed from heaven and from earth, and in that both "teach the importance of obedience" (164). Dividing the text into genres (divine warrior hymn,[136] disputation speech,[137] and woe oracle[138]) he compares the theme of judgment in both books and concludes that there are "fundamentally different views of eschatology in *1 Enoch* and Sirach" (240). From Deutero-Isaiah and Trito-Isaiah, Sira takes over the contest with the Gentiles, not only to recompense them for their evil deeds against Israel, but also to save and gather the dispersed. On the other hand, Sira omits themes like the descending of the warrior, the role of fire and storm, as well as the renewal of creation. Hence a new interpretation in Sira's meaning of the doctrine of contrasts is achieved. In the words of

---

132 Argall, 53-73; he illustrates the theme with 24; 4,1-19; 6,18-37; 14,20-15,10; 51,13-30.

133 Argall, 73-91 makes a fitting reference to the teaching situation: "Ben Sira himself is an enlightened teacher of revealed wisdom" (91).

134 Represented in 16,24-17,14; 33/36,7-15; 39,12-35; 42,15-43,33.

135 Represented in the similarly constructed sections: 1,1-10 and 24,3-7.

136 Sir 35/32,22b-26; 36,1-22 in Argall's view, which corresponds to Rahlfs' chapter divisions, but differs from Ziegler's verse divisions (= 33,1-13a; 36,16b-22 Greek).

137 Cf. 5,1-8; 11,14-28; 15,11-16,23; 23,16-21.

138 Cf. 2,12-14; 41,8-9.

the disputation speech, wrong behaviour is spoken of, as well as the
false assumption that one could escape God and hide from him in creation (220-235). In the woe oracles, Sira addresses sinners, especially
those who leave the way of wisdom and forget the Torah. He is thinking of Jews who have turned to other systems of wisdom (239). 1
Enoch and Sira agree about the divine warrior as a motif of eschatological judgement.[139]

Levison joins this field of research, depicting Adam in the early
Jewish literature: Sira and the book of Wisdom, Philo, the Book of
Jubilees, Josephus Flavius, 4 Ezra, 2 Baruch, the Apocalypse of Moses
and Vita Adae et Evae.[140] The praise of Adam he sees founded in Sira
not making any comparable statement about Israel, so he puts Adam,
the first human, as the first Israelite in the Adam tradition. So he introduces Adam into the venerable line of ancestors of Israel. In all the passages examined, he sees allusions to Gen 1-3; Sira, however, does not
follow the original Biblical context, but subordinates the thematic elements to his conception of theodicy. To show God's sovereignty over a
world in which good as well as evil can be found, Sira builds up arguments on the order of creation. He shows mankind, originating from the
earth (Sir 36/33), as mortal and earthly, and as returning to earth (Sir
40). Sira further interprets Gen 1-3 in such a way that he omits all pejo-
rative connotations. He uses יצר as "neutral ...; the tree of knowledge is
the capacity to distinguish between good and evil; death is a part of
God's original order for the cosmos. Even mortality ... is the basis for
God's mercy" (48). With this positive interpretation Sira stands alone in
early Jewish literature (148.150).

---

139 The author fails to provide a definition of "eschatological". For Sira he seems
to assume that the occurence of misfortune, or at least of death without the
prospect of an afterlife, belongs to this domain.

140 J.R. Levison, *Portraits of Adam in Early Judaism. From Sirach to 2 Baruch*
(JSPE.S 1; Sheffield 1988) 33-48, deals with 15,9-16,4; 16,17-17,24; 17,25-
18,14; 24,28; 33,7-13 according to Rahlfs, unmentioned in the bibliography (=
Ziegler 36,10); 40,1-11.27; 49,16.

11. The Praise of the Fathers

The *Praise of the Fathers*, being the oldest Midrash, is really fascinating. So, nearly every scholar dealing with Sira gives shorter or longer notes on it, or picks out certain themes from it. Besides many recent articles, some books go beyond a meditative treatment, for instance Maertens.[141] Lee questions the scholarly tradition about the literary context and extent of the hymn. He sees that 42,15-43,33 and 44-49; 50 correspond in the same way as Psalm 104 and Psalm 105. He investigates both Biblical[142] and Intertestamental texts[143] (in which he includes Deuterocanonical texts), and New Testament texts[144] as interrelated. After a glance at Pre-Rabbinical midrash, he turns to Hellenistic biography and finds a few points of contact. As he does not find any basis for further investigation, he deals with hymnic texts of the time. He finds a poetic aim in the area of eulogy, panegyric hymn or encomium. As he notices an "enthusiastic delineation of the high priest Simon son of Onias"[145] as the aim of the poem, he esteems the single examples as a subordinate genre (82). After detailed and wide-ranging investigation of the encomium (82-206) in Greek literature, he finds all the corresponding elements in Sir 44-50 (206-239).

Mack takes another line. Less fully than Lee, whose investigation was known to him, he deals with Sira's original texts and their problems, but, so to speak, he reports the gist of Sira. He feels as though Sira is speaking to him as a scholarly colleague,[146] working in another field, and he regrets that so "little effort has been devoted to solving the

---

141 Th. Maertens, *L'Éloge des Pères (Sir 44-50)* (Brüssel 1956); Th. Maertens, "L'Éloge des Pères", *CLV*(B) 26 (1955) 1-6; 27 (1956) 1-11; 28 (1956) 1-5; 30 (1956) 1-10; (B) 31 (1956) 1-11; 32 (1957) 1-11; 33 (1957) 1-10; 35 (1957) 1-11; 36 (1957) 1-8; 37 (1958) 1-11; 38 (1958) 1-8.

142 Ps 78; 105; 106; 135; 136; Ez 20; Neh 9 ; Lee, 23-29.

143 1 Macc 2,51-60; 3 Macc 6,4-8; 4 Macc 16,15-32; 18,9-19; Jdt 16,1-7; Wis 10; Cant 2,17-3,2; Lee, 29-48.

144 Hebr 11; Acts 7.

145 As does I. Lévi, "Sirach, the Wisdom of Jesus the Son of", JE 11 (London - New York 1905) 388-397 (quotation 389).

146 B.L. Mack, *Wisdom and the Hebrew Epic. Ben Sira's Hymn in Praise of the Fathers* (Chicago 1985) xii.

problems of the hymn".[147] His literary analysis stimulated by 44,1-2, combines far-tanging poetic approaches.[148] As general pattern of characterization, he finds designation of office, mention of election, reference to covenant,[149] mention of the person's piety, an account of their deeds, reference to the historical situation and mention of reward (18-36). On the basis of the structure he observed in Sir 44-49 with a king and a prophet facing each other, he deals with relevant themes such as succession and the concept of a sacred story. "Ben Sira understood the contemporary form of Second Temple Judaism as an appropriate climax to Israel's covenantal history" (56), of which Sira sees himself as a learned interpreter.[150] In the history of tradition the hymn stands near to the Pentateuchal redaction. It is especially distinguished from the chronistic line and Ezra-Nehemiah by the "exclusivist notion of Jewish identity" (119) which is recorded there. Ben Sira "is familiar with Hellenistic historiography, biography, and the encomium, but each provides models only for certain aspects" (120-137). Moreover the author deals with wisdom and the Hellenistic paideia (140-171). Both aims - the manifestation of divine intention (wisdom) and the social order - have been reached by Sira in a very autonomous way.

Because both studies were oriented by the history of ideas, they could not fulfil the wish for a comprehensive investigation of the *Praise of the Fathers*. Petraglio tried to do this in his extensive and monumental work. He holds Sira to be a master of the Hebrew language and his work to be pure rehashing of the history and books of his people. In the introduction, he deals with the extent of rehashing. He sees 42,15-43,11 and 44-50 as equivalent: God's activity in nature and

---

[147] As is evident from the previous statements and a look at the contemporary literature, he could find only one book and three articles (ibid., 3).

[148] He considers Sir 44,16; 48,9-11 and 49,14-16 to be later additions and does not deal further with (ibid., 17).

[149] In this context, he considers the structuring with seven covenants, proposed by Haspecker, 85 note 94 (subsequently also Marböck, 1993, 177-197) to be significant in terms of form (although partial in terms of content), since this element plays a role for all the people; Mack, 20,39.

[150] Hence also the praise of the "scholar-sage as a scholar-sage" (Mack, 91-104), who is in any case subordinate to the "Mosaic office" (ibid., 106).

in history.[151] Besides, he also goes through the text section by section and offers a translation, in parts a paraphrase, on the basis of the Greek text. Then Hebrew variants are added, though without noting the manuscripts. The subsequent detailed interpretation uses Biblical texts as references in an extensive way, together with secondary literature. Petraglio even uses Intertestament literature (39-40) such as Enoch. He partly gives spiritual emphasis and works up thematic references. Each unit ends with a summary. An ingenious device in some parts is to use the form of a letter (e.g. 35-37,79-81,135-138), in which he addresses some of the named Biblical figures in Sira's name. He even ends the whole investigation in this form. This voluminous study can be put to good use in any further inquiry into the *Praise of the Fathers*. But his treatment of textual criticism, literary study, poetic form and literary influence of the environment needs revision.

12. Ben Sira's attitude towards woman

Though Marböck suggests that in today's opinion Sira's attitude to woman is indecent,[152] he himself (1992), Kaiser (1994) and Gilbert (1995) do not allude to this theme, which one could think to be of no interest in Sira research. As an example of most recent time, Schrader deals with the theme not without emotions. Although he does not think of this book as a biographical source, he sees "certain personal traits of the author" that "lay in a disturbed relation to the female sex" (97, 100). In late O.T. times, there was a prevailing opinion that sin had come into the world through the fall of the angels (1 Enoch 6-16; 7,1-6;

---

151   Chap. 24 is an example of it; R. Petraglio, *Il libro che contamina le mani. Ben Sirac rilegge il libro e la storia d'Israele* (Theologia 4; Palermo 1993), 11-20, especially 17.

152   Marböck (1994, 292). Similarly Skehan - Di Lella, 91: "Moreover, Ben Sira wrote his book only for the instruction and enlightenment of young men in a male-centered and male-dominated society; hence his vocabulary and grammar are masculine-oriented. It was not his intention to instruct women. When we take these factors into account, we can understand why Ben Sira speaks about women in the way he does, even though today we may disagree with much of what he says and how he says it"; but Sira himself is in no way prejudiced against women.

15,2-16, 1; Jub 5,1-6; 10,1.5-9.11).[153] Sirach amended this opinion. He
mentions that woman is the cause of all evil.[154] Moreover, he sees
precedents in Judaism, even before his time, e.g. Qoh 7,26.[155] A hundred years later, there were consequences in Vita Adae et Evae and in
the Greek version of the Apocalypsis Mosis (§ 22). From here, Judaism
(Mishnah, Abot I,5; II,7) and Early Christianity (1Tim 2,14)[156] were
strongly marked; he frankly recognizes comparable statements from Israel's environment.

Schrader had a predecessor in Trenchard, who believed that he was
the first to fill the gap in the research on Sira's statements about
women.[157] He considers Sira a misogynist who is full of prejudice
against women, not only in his doctrine but also personally. Whereas
one can find some positive signs within his treatment of the text, the
summaries are full of negative statements. His investigation is made up
of five sections: woman as good wife; as mother and widow; as evil
woman; as adulteress and prostitute; and as daughter. Even in the first
section, a good woman is good only in so far as she is seen beside her
husband, but "the fact that she is a woman is for him a negative status"
(38). Positive aspects are wiped out, and he presumes at least unsaid
negative aspects, even about a woman as mother (56), because sin

---

153 B. Malina, "Some Observations on the Origin of Sin in Judaism and St. Paul",
     CBQ 31 (1969) 18-34, especially 24.
154 In no way does Schrader seek to bring his thesis into theological agreement
     with Sir 11,15 (חטא ודרכים ישרים מיי הוא); this is all the more astonishing, since
     he considers A as a valuable textual witness.
155 Here also he dismisses the suggestion that מָר in the phrase מָר מִמָּוֶת (Qoh 7,26)
     should be interpreted as "strong" on the basis of the semantic field of מרר in
     Ugaritic, Aramaic, and Arabic (N. Lohfink, "War Kohelet ein Frauenfeind?",
     La sagesse de l'Ancien Testament. Nouvelle édition mise à jour [ed. M. Gil-
     bert] [BETL 51; Louvain ²1990] 259-287, especially 281-282); L. Schwien-
     horst-Schönberger, *"Nicht im Menschen gründet das Glück" (Koh 2,24). Kohe-
     let im Spannungsfeld jüdischer Weisheit und hellenistischer Philosophie* (HBS
     2; Freiburg-Basel-Wien et al. 1994), sees it exclusively as a warning against
     the evil unchaste quarrelsome woman (175-180). Th. Krüger, "'Frau Weisheit'
     in Koh 7,26?", *Bib* 73 (1992) 394-403, explains the passage by reference to
     Lady Wisdom in Ben Sira, in which it ceases to provide a covenant on women.
156 Oddly enough he places 1Cor 14,34-36 there.
157 W.C. Trenchard, *Ben Sira's View of Women, a Literary Analysis* (BJSt 38;
     Chicago 1982) 167.

comes from woman anyway (81-82).[158] In comparison between sons and daughters, Trenchard views texts that are critical of sons as irrelevant and disregards them, and concludes that "sons may bring joy and fulfillment. Daughters bring trouble and anxiety" (164), indicating Sira's "incredibly negative statement about women" (163).

According to Trenchard, Sira "makes remarks about women that are among the most obscene and negative in ancient literature" (172). Moderate,[159] neutral, or positive theological[160] interpretations are ignored or rejeted by the author. One cannot ignore Trenchard's error of approach in failing to compare attitudes[161] in texts from Sira's environment.[162] Here exegesis benefits from scholarly studies by women on texts concerned. Camp, Archer and Wischmeyer[163] do not regard him as a misogynist; they clearly see problems in a historical background in which an increase in the negative side of patriarchy is not concealed.

---

158 F.R. Tennant, "The Teaching of Ecclesiasticus and Wisdom on the Introduction of Sin and Death", *JThS* 2 (1901) 207-223.

159 G. von Rad, *Weisheit in Israel* (Neukirchen-Vluyn 1970 [²1982]), 335.

160 J.W. Gaspar, *Social Ideas in the Wisdom Literature of the Old Testament* (Catholic University of America Studies in Sacred Theology 2,8; Washington D.C. 1947); K.E. Bailey, "Women in Ben Sirach and in the New Testament", *For Me to Live* (FS J.L. Kelso, ed. R.A. Coughenour) (Cleveland 1972) 56-73; H. McKeating, "Jesus Ben Sira's Attitude to Women", *ExpTim* 85 (1973/1974) 85-87; M. Gilbert, "Ben Sira et la femme", *RTL* 7 (1976) 426-442; G. Maier, *Mensch und freier Wille. Nach den jüdischen Religionsparteien zwischen Ben Sira und Paulus* (WUNT 12; Tübingen 1971) 96; B. Vawter, *The Book of Sirach. Part 1 with a Commentary* (PBS 40; New York 1962) 7.

161 Skehan - Di Lella, 90-92.

162 Cf. M.R. Lefkowitz - M.B. Fant, *Women in Greece and Rome. A Source Book in Translation* (London [1977] ²1992); S.B. Pomeroy, *Women in Hellenistic Egypt. From Alexander to Cleopatra* (Detroit 1990); R. Hawley-D. Levick (ed.), *Women in Antiquity. New Assessments* (London-New York 1995).

163 C.V. Camp, "The Female Sage in Ancient Israel and in the Biblical Wisdom Literature", *The Sage in Israel and the Ancient Near East* (ed. J.G. Gammie - L.G. Perdue) (Winona Lake 1990) 185-203; C.V. Camp, "Understanding a Patriarchy: Women in Second Century Jerusalem through the Eyes of Ben Sira", *"Women Like This". New Perspectives on Jewish Women in the Greco-Roman World* (ed. A.-J. Levine) (SBL 1, Atlanta 1991) 1-39, with bibliographical references. L.J. Archer, *Her Price Is beyond Rubies. The Jewish Woman in Graeco-Roman Palestine* (JSOT.S 60; Sheffield 1990), with bibliographical references. Wischmeyer, 29-31.

13. Concluding notice

Every theme and every approach to Sira tend to sweep aside all other problems. For everybody dealing long with the book of Sira, it is obvious, that the variety of ways of arguments and the comprehensive differentiation of the particular themes (seen in the whole book) do not allow us to speak of one leading theme in Sira's work.

This review cannot be exhaustive, because of the large number of works on Sira. Much must still be done in examining the inner structure of single literary units, where poetic analysis can clarify the content. The work of Calduch-Benages about Sira 2 shows how anthropology, religion and theology can be emphasized.[164] "Whoever touches pitch gets dirty", Sira says (13,1a), but whoever deals with Sira's poetry gets caught up in his ideas, in spite of a written witness that raises many problems.

---

164 Cf. N. Calduch-Benages, *En el Crisol de la Prueba. Estudio Exegético de Sir 2* (Rome 1994) (Diss., Pontificio Instituto Biblico).

Structure and Redaction History of the Book of Ben Sira
Review and Prospects*

By Johannes Marböck, Graz

The questions of structure and development of the Wisdom of Ben Sira represent two extensive and much discussed topics of research. However daring or audacious an approach may be, a reminder of some approaches so far can perhaps serve as a guideline or orientation for further research, or at least as an impulse for a dialogue. Although the two questions can hardly be separated, it seems appropriate to start with a general survey of the form of the book and to continue with observations on the structure in order to enquire into a possible and plausible idea of the development of the Wisdom of Ben Sira.

1. Structure of the book

In his dissertation, Jolley has recently pointed at the lack of research into form and structure of the Book of Ben Sira.[1] So after a critical survey of models for the structure of Ben Sira suggested during the last two hundred years, some observations on attempts of structuring will be presented, with examples, and their consequences will be discussed.

---

* For the English translation of the paper, I would like to express thanks to Mrs Gertrud Madl, Graz
[1] M.A. Jolley, *The Function of Torah in Sirach* (UMI Diss 9406300; Ann Arbor 1995) 160-161.

1.1 Models and tendencies in the history of research

The difficulty of finding a structure of the extensive and, in content, pluriform Book of Ben Sira can be illustrated on the one hand by the statement in the commentary of Skehan & Di Lella: "Except for chaps. 44-50 ... the book manifests no particular order of subject matter or obvious coherence";[2] on the other hand, Roth[3] and Harvey[4] try to demonstrate an inner logic for the structure of the book. Needless to say, the text problem exacerbates the uncertainty behind all the suggestions made. Beforehand and now, there were and are opponents and proponents of a coherent structure of the book. Moreover, the question of thematic structures of larger units beyond formal divisions, and of the book seems to be gaining emphasis. As introduction, let us remember traditions of ancient exegesis, in particular two scholars who read the book systematically and structured it. Thus Nicolaus of Lyra distinguished two large parts: Chapters 1-43 as a rational and argumentative instruction of the love of wisdom, and Chapter 44 onwards with examples.[5] Cornelius a Lapide[6] divided the book into three units: Chapters 1-23 (praise of wisdom with commandments and teachings about various virtues); Chapters 24-42,14 (praise of wisdom and presentation of its ethics); and Chapters 42,15-51,30 (examples of these virtues in the praising of God and his creation as well as in the *Praise of the Fathers*).

---

2   P.W. Skehan - A.A. Di Lella, *The Wisdom of Ben Sira* (AB 39; New York 1987) 4. On the inclusio between 1,11-30 and the acrostic poem in 51,13-30, however, the commentary says "that the book was planned in the form in which we have it by a single compiler, namely, Ben Sira himself" (74). Likewise. W.O.E. Oesterley, *Introduction to the Books of the Apocrypha* (London 1958) 229: "here and there ... signs of some attempt to coordinate the subject-matter are discernible; but the attempts are desultory, and generally speaking the material is mixed up in disorderly fashion."

3   W. Roth, "On the Gnomic-Discursive Wisdom of Jesus Ben Sirach", *Semeia* 17 (1980) 59-79.

4   J.D. Harvey, "Toward a Degree of Order in Ben Sira's Book", *ZAW* 105 (1993) 52-62.

5   Nikolaus de Lyra, *Postilla super totam Bibliam* Vol. 3 (Strassburg 1492 [Nachdruck Hildesheim 1971]) in Ecclesiasticum 1,1. See H.G. Reventlow, *Epochen der Bibelauslegung.* Vol. 2: Von der Spätantike bis zum ausgehenden Mittelalter (München 1994) 259-271.

6   Cornelius a Lapide, *Commentarius in Ecclesiasticum* (ed. secunda ab Auctore aucta et correcta, Antwerpen 1643) 25.

The principle of arrangement could be in line with the Decalogue. Most ancient scholars accepted the principle of a double or triple division of the Book of Sirach which recurs in numerous variations.

Even Eichhorn, the founder of modern introduction to the Old Testament, reckoned with a composition consisting of three collections: Chapters 1-23; 24-42,14; and 42,15-50,24 (with colophon), and pointed at the use of the theme of wisdom.[7] Bretschneider rejected the development of the book out of three larger coherent collections by references to both the Classical gnomic and the textual interchanges from Chapter 30 onward. He rejected a thematic arrangement: "Cum haec sit libri condicio, errant qui certum quendam in eo quaerant ordinem, quod quibusdam visum est".[8] To Fritzsche, however, the book is "ein Ganzes, das im Einzelnen nach Inhalt und Form tüchtig verarbeitet wurde" (a whole that was carefully worked in content and form).[9] He divided it into seven large units: 1,1-16,21; 16,22-23,27; 24,1-30,24/33,12-36,16a /30,25-27; 30,28-33,11/36,16b-22; 36,23-39,11; 39,12-42,14; 42,15-50,26, excluding Chapter 50,27-29 and Chapter 51. Zöckler accepted this arrangement and acknowledged that Sirach was more than a collector or dumb compiler; nevertheless "kann an eine streng einheitliche Konzeption des Ganzen durch Einen Verfasser nicht gedacht werden" (one cannot concieve a strictly unified idea of the whole by one author).[10] Inspired by the five books of the Pentateuch and by the division of the Book of Psalms into five sections, Edersheim distinguishes between five parts (1-23; 24-32; 33-43; 44-50,21; 50,22-51,30), which he considers a coherent and consequent work despite all its diversities.[11] To Spicq, a division into five parts is also likely (1,1-16,23;

---

7   J.G. Eichhorn, *Einleitung in die apokryphischen Schriften des Alten Testaments* (Leipzig 1795) 51. L. Alonso-Schökel, *Proverbios y Eclesiastico* (LiSa VIII,1; Madrid 1968) 144, 227, 299, was the first in recent times to describe this broad structure. He is followed by V. Morla Asensio, *Eclesiastico. Texto y Comentario*, Salamanem/Madrid / Estella 1992.

8   C.G. Bretschneider, *Liber Jesu Siracidae Graece* ad fidem codicum et versionum emendatus et perpetua annotatione illustratus (Ratisbonae 1806) 17-18.

9   O.F. Fritzsche, *Die Weisheit Jesus-Sirach's* (KEH zu den Apokryphen des Alten Testaments 5; Leipzig 1859) xxvii; on the structure, xxxii-xxxiii.

10   O. Zöckler, *Die Apokryphen des Alten Testaments* nebst einem Anhang über die Pseudepigraphenliteratur (KK; München 1891) 256.

11   A. Edersheim, "Ecclesiasticus. Introduction and Commentary", *Apocrypha* II (ed. H. Wace) (London 1888) 18-20.

16,24-23,27; 24,1-32,13; 32,14-42,14; 42,15-50,29). The book, as it has
developed, has a homogeneous background and was given its form by
the author, though; but it has no clear order, or rather structure.[12] Although the general characterization of the five parts is not expressive,
and, as for Fritzsche, the division of the theodicy section of 15,11-18,14
at 16,24 is a problem, his reference to an increasingly narrow focus of
the book from universal wisdom (1,1-10) to Israel (24; 44-50) is noteworthy.

The great impulse for a structure came from the commentary of
Smend; thus the paragraphs with the Praise of Wisdom and the Exhortation to Teach Wisdom are "in sich abgeschlossene Ganze zugleich als
Einleitung zu den folgenden Abschnitten" (a self-contained whole as
well as an introduction to the following sections).[13] Not only is there
"fast überall ein gewisser Zusammenhang" (almost everywhere a certain coherence) but this is true also for the whole arrangement, particularly from 38,24 onward. However it is questionable whether all statements on wisdom should be taken as of the same weight without regard
to form and function (e.g. Sir 8,8.9; 10,30-11,1; 16,24-25; 18,28-29;
27,4-7 ...).[14]

As a consequence, two major commentaries attempted to show that
there was a reduction of wisdom sections essential for the structure and
that the Book of Ben Sira had a symmetrical overall structure. Peters
divided the work into two large sections (A, B), each of five parts each
(A: 1,1-4,10; 4,11-6,17; 6,18-14,19; 14,20-20,26; 20,27-23,27; B: 24,1-
32,13; 32,14-38,23; 38,24-41,13; 41,14-42,14; 42,15-50,29. Appendix:
51,1-30) for which "die in die Sprüche des Siraziden eingebetteten allgemeinen Ausführungen über die Weisheit als Fingerzeige für die
schriftstellerische Scheidung der Teile betrachtet werden dürfen" (the
general statements about wisdom that are embedded in the sayings of
the Siracid can be seen as markers for the author's division of the

---

12   C. Spicq, *L'Ecclésiastique* (SB[PC]; Paris 1951) 553-554. A. van den Born,
     Wijsheid van Jesus Sirach (BOT; Roermond 1968) 7, 19, 133, 168, 194, 213,
     divides the book into two or preferably five larger sections: 1,1-23,27; 24,1-
     32,13; 32,14-39,11; 39,12-42,14; 42,15-50,29.
13   R. Smend, *Die Weisheit des Jesus Sirach* (Berlin 1906) xxxiv-xxxvii.
14   Cf. L. Schrader, *Leiden und Gerechtigkeit*. Studien zu Theologie und Text-
     geschichte des Sirachbuches (BET 27; Frankfurt 1994) 62.

parts).[15] The model of Peters echoes in the explanation of Sirach by Hamp,[16] as well as in Eberharter's commentary.[17] The structure suggested by Segal met with an even livelier response; he distinguished between two parts consisting of four units each (1,1-4,10; 4,11-6,17; 6,18-14,19; 14,20-23,27 and 24,1-32[35],13; 32[35],14-38,23; 38,24-43,33; 44,1-50,29) and Chapter 51 as appendix.[18] Segal viewed the work composed as model led on the Book of Proverbs and "from a literary viewpoint well constructed".[19] This demarcation of units by Segal, with a disputable separation of God's Wisdom in Creation (42,15-43,33) from the Praise of the Fathers, is accepted with minor differences,[20] though, by Skehan-Di Lella, Harvey and Schrader.[21] Pfeiffer also favours a composition of two parts: Chapters 1-23 and 24-50. He could not detect a clear demarcation within each part, except for 42,15-50,26.[22]

In summary of the views presented so far, wisdom sections function in different ways as markers of new units. Any literary-thematic structuring is either refused or remains very (too) general and is therefore neither helpful nor convincing. The monograph by Haspecker[23] on the Fear of God and by Prato[24] on the theodicy sections showed that theo-

---

15 N. Peters, *Das Buch Jesus Sirach oder Ecclesiasticus* (EHAT 25; Münster 1913) xli (xxxix-xlii).

16 V. Hamp, *Sirach* (EB; Würzburg 1954).

17 A. Eberharter, *Das Buch Jesus Sirach oder Ecclesiasticus* (HSAT VI/5; Bonn 1925) 8-9, divides in 2,1-42,14, and 42,15-50,29, but for the subdivisions he follows Peters. Chapter 1 is introduction and Chapter 51 appendix. O. Schilling, *Das Buch Jesus Sirach* (HBK VII/2; Freiburg 1956), repeats the 10 sections from Peters.

18 M.Z. Segal, *Seper ben-Sira haššalem* (Jerusalem 21958) vi-viii (table of contents), 16.

19 M.H. Segal (ed.), "Ben Sira, Wisdom of ( )", *EncJud* 4, 552 (550-553).

20 For Skehan - Di Lella, *Ben Sira*, Section VI opens in 33,19 (Segal: 32[35],14).

21 Schrader, *Leiden und Gerechtigkeit*, 65: "So könnte es gewesen sein; als Arbeitshypothese ist diese Aufteilung brauchbar."

22 R.H. Pfeiffer, *History of New Testament Times*. With an Introduction to the Apocrypha (Westport 1973 [New-York 1949]) 353-354 (332-408); similarly J. Vella, *Eclesiastico* (BAC 312; Madrid 1970) 5: Sir 1-23; 24-42,14; 42,15-43,33 and 44-50.51.

23 J. Haspecker, *Gottesfurcht bei Jesus Sirach. Ihre religiöse Struktur und ihre literarische und doktrinäre Bedeutung* (AnBib 30; Rom 1967).

24 G.L. Prato, *Il problema della teodicea in Ben Sira. Composizione dei contrari e richiamo alle origini* (AnBib 65; Rom 1975).

logical themes also determine the literary structure of the book, or rather of later units, stronger than it seemed at first sight. These monographs may have led to the attempt by Roth to show an inner factual-thematic logic for both the overall structure of the book and for larger units.[25] The general structure of Ben Sira reflects the curriculum of a student of wisdom. It begins with commandments and prohibitions, continues with closer argument and reflexion, and ends with long textual units. In the 'first edition' of Ben Sira's book (Chapters 1-23; 51) Roth distinguishes four units opened by wisdom texts (1,1-4,10; 4,11-6,17; 6,18-14,19; 14,20-23,27) along the lines of Proverbs. The themes are in alphabetical order (3,1ff: אב; 4,20ff: בשת; 7,1ff: גאוה; 15,11ff: דעה) The following units begin with wisdom sections and end with autobiographical notes (24,1-32,13; 32,14-38,23; 38,24-50,29). There is an increasing emphasis on the person of the author towards the end of the book. Roth has numerous, constructive observations , such as the alphabetic arrangement of themes from 6,18ff, especially from 14,20ff, and the variety of different forms and themes within 38,24-50,29. But do they favour a quadruple division of the book? However his attempt to correlate criteria of literary structure and subject-matter is remarkable, for instance in his remarks on the handling of traditional sayings to build literary units (e.g. 8,8f; 21,15; 39,1-3), in the theme of 6,18-14,19 (socially oriented) contrary to 14,20-23,27 (theologically, individually oriented), and finally in 32,14-38,23 (polarity and discernment in ethical matters). Harvey took over the symmetrical structure of Segal, and tried to elaborate the structure even more than Roth though less plausible.[26]

1.2 Elements of a structure

Let me gather recurring elements of structure from the oulined history of research. Firstly the wisdom sections as markers for the opening of larger units have been mentioned since Eichhorn and particularly since Smend. The texts that recur are 1,1-10; 4,11-19; 6,18-37; 14,20-15,10; ch 24; 32(35),14-33(36),6; 38,24-39,11; 51,13-30. From Chapter 24,

---

25 Roth, "Gnomic-Discursive Wisdom", 59-79.
26 Harvey, "*Degree of Order*", 52-62.

there are also autobiographical notes (24,30-34; 33,16-19; 39,12.32; also 50,27; 51,13ff).

Peters was the first to point at the large literary frame of Ben Sira in line with the Book of Proverbs.[27] The presentation of wisdom in Sir 1 and the acrostic on the quest for wisdom in 51,13-30 parallel the introduction in Prov 1-9 and the acrostic text of Prov 31,10-31. Gilbert would include Chapters 2 and 51,1-12 in this structure too: the exhortation to be ready for trials in the service of the Lord (2,1-18) and the concluding thanksgiving prayer for the gift of allowing such trials (51,1-12). This would introduce a double inclusio.[28] However less certain is the suggestion of Di Lella that 1,11-30 is an alphabetical poem of 22 lines[29] and that 51,13-30 is a frame text, like those mentioned above.[30]

The Praise of Wisdom in Chapter 24 is undoubtedly central in the book. It functions as a new introduction and reminds of the origin of wisdom in God and its relation to creation, paralleling 1,1-10. It seems, however, that Chapter 24 is a blockade for the connection between 22,27-23,27 and 25,1-11. Sir 23,16.22-23 and 25,1.2.7 include numerical sayings; a common theme is φόβος κυρίου (23,19.27; 25,6.11), and further catchwords are: εἴδη (23,16; 25,2), μοιχός (23,23c; 25,2d), βουλή (23,1b; 25,4b.5b), γλῶσσα (22,27d; 25,7b.8b), διανόημα (23,2a; 25,5b). Certainly, these are hints about the development of the book as it now stands.[31] But it is not conceivable to derive a large two-part division (1-23; 24-50) from the centrality of Sir 24.[32] There are good rea-

---

27 Peters, *Jesus Sirach*, XL.
28 M. Gilbert, "L'action de grâce de Ben Sira (Sir 51,1-12)", *Ce Dieu qui vient* (FS. B. Renaud; [ed. R. Kuntzmann]) (LD 159; Paris 1995) 231-242. For Spicq, *L'Ecclésiastique*, 554, the mention of Adam in 49,16 forms a kind of responsio to Sir 1,10 (universality of wisdom). As a further observation, the increasing emphasis on praise as an activity of the wise should be mentioned: Sir 15,9-10; 17,6-10; 18,1-7; 32(35),16b-17; 39,5-6; 39,12-15.32-35; 42,15-43,33; 44-49.50; 51.
29 See A.A. Di Lella, 'Fear of the Lord as Wisdom: Ben Sira 1,11-30' as included in this volume.
30 Skehan - Di Lella, *Ben Sira*, 74, 576.
31 J. Marböck, *Weisheit im Wandel*. Untersuchungen zur Weisheitstheologie bei Ben Sira (BBB 37; Bonn 1971) 41-43.
32 Note especially the positions of Peters, Segal, and Pfeiffer in the foregoing review of divisions.

sons to consider Sir 42,15-43,33; 44-49.50 a final great diptych about God's wisdom and sovereignty in creation and history, a unit highly independent in form and content. Evidence for this view is a series of formal and textual connections, as at the beginning (42,15; 44), at the end (43,30; 45,25; 50,22), in the transition (43,33-44,1; cf. 1,9), and finally, by the motif of glory (כבוד: 43,12; 44,2.13.19 ...).[33] Thus a general three-part division of the book can be suggested, as did Cornelius a Lapide, Eichhorn, Morla Asensio and Alonso-Schökel.

Thus there are the following structural elements:
- a frame enclosing the book (Chapters 1-2 and 51);
- wisdom paragraphs as markers of new sections of different weight;
- a tendency towards larger more compact units at the end of the book (from 38,24 on);
- emphasis on the history of Israel in the middle and at the end of the book (24; 36; 44-50), and on the Praise of Wisdom and the Praise of God;
- themes throughout the book (wisdom, fear of God, theodicy, praise) that fit into particular larger units in different ways.

1.3 Structure of particular sections

Even if there is actually no direct progressive structure or line of thought through the whole book, yet some single, larger sections seem to have been structured more carefully in form and content than many critics since Bretschneider would admit. So let me take some examples of how the studies of Haspecker and Prato on the one hand and those of

---

33   J. Marböck, "Die 'Geschichte Israels' als 'Bundesgeschichte' nach dem Sirachbuch", *Der Neue Bund im Alten*. Zur Bundestheologie der beiden Testamente (ed. E. Zenger) (QD 146; Freiburg 1993) 181 (177-197); P.C. Beentjes, "The 'Praise of the Famous' and its Prologue. Some observations on Ben Sira 44:1-15 and the question of Enoch in 44:16", *BTFT*. 45 (1984) 374-383; B.L. Mack, *Wisdom and Hebrew Epic*. Ben Sira's Hymn in Praise of the Fathers (Chicago - London 1985) 189-193. Scholars who consider 42,15-50,29 as an independent unit are Eichhorn, Fritzsche, Zöckler, Peters, Spicq, Pfeiffer, and Schilling. For Eberharter, Van den Born and A. Minissale, *Siracide* (Ecclesiastico) (Rome 1980), Sir 42,15-50,29 represents Part 2 of the Wisdom of Sirach.

Roth and Harvey on the other hand can perhaps clarify the structure of the book. I take Sir 1,1-4,10; 4,11-6,17, and 19,20-23,27.

1.3.1 Sir 1,1-4,10

The text represents the first major composition of the book with manifold literary and thematic cross-references, which can be explained more fully by a cursory glance at the structure and themes of the subsections. Four sub-sections form the thematic introduction to the book: fundamental statements about wisdom and fear of God (1,1-2,18); the parental commandment (3,1-16); the attitude of humility and goodness (3,17-31); helpful demeanour towards the poor (4,1-10).

Sir 1,1-2,18 is a compact treatise, despite its manifold literary techniques,[34] starting with a thematic presentation (1,1-27): wisdom as God's gift to those who fear him (1,1-10); the fear of God as source of all good (1,11-13); wisdom and fear of God (1,14-20: beginning - crown - root); fear of God and sin (1,21-25); with 1,26-27 as a reminder which ends with a direct personal address.

The second sub-section (1,28-2,18) as an admonition aims at a religious decision to be made. There is a switch from warnings against hypocrisy (1,28-30: μη ...) to positive admonition for steadfastness in trials (2,1-6), and to trust in God's mercy (2,7-11) and to lamentations (2,12-14) with statements about the fear of God and fulfilment of God's will (2,15-16). The last paragraph (2,17-18) is again a reminder (in line with 2,1.4) and self-exhortation (1st person pl.).

The section on the parental commandment (3,1-16) is one of the most carefully prepared and independent compositions in the Book of Ben Sira[35]. It can be divided into opening (3,1-2) with exhortation to hear and statement of theme; statements (3,3-7) with promises on atonement for sin (v.3 and. v.14), and fear of God (v.7); the first parenesis (3,8-11), positive-negative and כבוד (vv.8.10.11); the second parenesis (3,12-15) with support for an ageing father (v.14) with a

---

34 Haspecker, *Gottesfurcht*, 94-100.
35 Haspecker, *Gottesfurcht*, 126:"eine der sorgfältigsten und wohl auch eigenständigsten Kompositionen im Buch Sirach".

promise of atonement (as vv.3-4); final theological condemnation (3,16, as 3,2).[36]

The next sub-section (3,17-31) about humility and goodness includes a parenesis about gentleness (πραΰτης/ענוה) and humility (ταπεινόω) with justifications (3,17-20); warnings against a presumptuous mind (3,21-24) with justifications; examples of hautiness of heart and wisdom of heart (3,25-29): כבד לב 3,26-27; חכם לב 3,29); a concluding reference to the reward of good deeds and goodness (3,30-31, echoing 3,1.14-16: atonement of sin, thought for the future).[37]

The last sub-section (4,1-10) about readiness to help the poor includes warnings against a poor attitude towards the poor with justification (4,1-5.6b); positive admonitions (4,7-10); a final promise (4,10cd): father to the orphan as a son of God as climax.

All four units have the same structural elements: the changing of thematic statements (3rd person) with direct address in the parenesis (positive - negative), and final emphasis and restatement (1,26-27; 2,17-18; 3,16.30-31; 4,10).

The deliberate arrangement of 3,1-16.17-31; 4,1-10 is indicated by the catchword *father* at beginning and end (3,1 and 4,10).[38] God calls the father of the poor his son; honour of father and mother by a son in 3,1-16 is reciprocated in 4,10 by God himself acting as father and mother.[39] That means that God's care does not extend only to father and mother, fatherless poor (orphans) but also to people who so act as father or mother. The emphasis on the atoning power of beneficence (צדקה/ἐλεημοσύνη) as an inclusio in 3,3.14 and in 3,30-31 adds to the impression of a larger composition; 3,30 at the same time announces the theme of the following paragraph. In the Greek text, this line could be traced by ἐλεημοσύνη as far back as mercy (ἔλεος) of the merciful (ἐλεήμων) God in 2,11.18. Moreover, these three sections are woven together in manifold ways by a wider network of catchwords and mo-

---

36 R. Bohlen, *Die Ehrung der Eltern bei Ben Sira*. Studien zur Motivation und Interpretation eines familienethischen Grundwertes in frühhellenistischer Zeit (TThSt 51; Trier 1991) 64-74.

37 Haspecker, *Gottesfurcht*, 186-187.

38 Skehan - Di Lella, *Ben Sira*, prefer for 4,10d G: "and he will be more tender to you than a mother" instead of Ms A: "and he will be kindly to you and will deliver you from the pit".

39 W.H. Irwin, "Fear of God, the Analogy of Friendship and Ben Sira's Theodicy", *Bib* 76 (1995) 554-555 (551-559).

tifs, which cannot be completely unravelled here. May a few examples suffice.

For instance the motifs of the hearing of the prayer or a plea (3,5b; 4,6b); the cursing of a mother or of the embittered poor (3,9; 4,5b.6a)[40]; παροπγίζω (3,16b; 4,2b.3a)[41] and λυπεῖν towards a father or the hungry (3,12 G; MS A: עזב ; 4,2 MS A: אל תפוח) appear in G in 3,1-16 and 4,1-10 in a beautiful concentric structure. Key motifs connect 3,17-20 and 4,7-10, the beginning and the end of the two units, namely, ענוה/ πραΰτης in 3,17 (as also 19b) and 4,8b; also ταπεινόω in 3,18a and 4,7b; *finding grace* in 3,18b (G, MS C) and 4,10d (MS A).

Statements about instruction in wisdom and fear of God in 1,1-2,18 are implemented and particularized in the three instructional subsections about honour to parents, about humility and modesty, and about dealing with the poor. The same apllies also to the motif of mercy and beneficience in the fear of God, which appears centrally in the subsection on parents in 3,7, and especially to the statements on ענוה/ πραΰτης - πραΰς as humility before God and modesty and friendliness towards man, in particular the socially inferior and poor.[42] The πραΰτης of 1,27 reappears in 3,17.19 and 4,8; in the same list ταπεινόω / ταπείνωσις of 2,4.17 reappears in 3,18 and 4,7. In Sir 3,19, God reveals his mysteries to the humble, but in 1,30c he reveals the secrets of the proud in judgment. The statements on the fruits of wisdom and the fear of God in 1,11-13; 1,14-20 are echoed plentifully by the promises about honouring parents in the same order: the experience of joy (εὐφραίνω / εὐφροσύνη 1,11.12; 2,9; 3,5); a long life (μακροημέρευσις 1,12.20; 3,6); blessing (εὐλογία 1,13; 3,8); God's saving or remembering in the moment or day of plight (θλῖψις 2,11; 3,15); the motif of humiliation and shame (ἀτιμία 1,30b; 3,10), for those boasting before God or parents.

This collection of observations taken from many studies allows the conclusion that Sir 1,1-4,10 can be viewed as an intended literary composition with a clear conceptual structure: Sir 3,1-16; 3,17-31 and 4,1-10 are examples of the practice of the fear of God in daily life with concluding promises and affirmations made by God. The position of the explanation about humility in 3,17-31 between 3,1-16 (parents) and

---

40   Cf. 3,16b G: "Accursed by God is he who provokes his mother".

41   MS A 2b: תחעלם; 3a: מעי דך - καρδίαν παρωργισμένην.

42   Haspecker, *Gottesfurcht*, 186-187.

4,1-10 (the poor) enhances the weight of a religious and social basic attitude. A short survey on what follows in 4,11-6,17 may enhance the conclusions.

1.3.2 Sir 4,11-6,17

The following remarks illustrate the diversity of the structure of 4,11-6,17 and its integrity in the book as a whole. The boundary given by the wisdom sections 4,11-19 and 6,18ff is asserted interestingly by the inclusio with the motif of examination, and testing of the loyalty and love of the student of wisdom by Wisdom itself at the beginning of 4,17 (MS A: בחר נסיון; G: πειράζειν)[43] and the winning of a loyal friend by testing (πειρασμός - ניסין) in the final section 6,7 (MS A: 6,6). A broad formal structure is built up with a list of vetitives with אל in 4,20-6,4 (as also 7,1-20.34-35; Chap. 8-9,12) and the positive illustration following in the concluding section on friendship 6,5-17 (MS A 6,4-18).

It is difficult to delimit smaller units precisely in form and theme, except for 4,11-19 and 6,5-17, since the themes overlap. The major catchwords *speech/tongue* (λόγος, γλῶσσα 4,23-24.25.29; 5,9-15; 6,1) already appear in the statements about bashfulness/dishonour (בשת - αἰσχύνη 4,20-26; also 5,14; 6,1b G)[44] and sin/sinner (4,21.26; 5,4-8.9; 6,1c G [MS A 5,16]). Framed by the catchword *wealth* (χρήμασιν: 5,1.8; MS A 5,1: חילך; 5,8: נכסי שקר), 5,1-8 forms a subsection with a warning against wrong trust in money and power, the theological dispute 5,3.4-8 about pity and God's judgment being the core of it. Sir 6,2(1)-4(3) takes up 5,2 (G: ἐπιθυμίαι καρδίας - נפשך תאות) warning against destructive greed (נפש - βουλὴ ψυχῆς). The conclusion about good/bad speech in 6,1 G (5,15b MS A) as well as 6,4(3) about greed twice anticipates the theme of 6,5-17 (שונא/אוהב - φίλος/ἐχθρός). In addition to this connection by catchwords, there is Prato's observation of the double aspect of reality,[45] not only in a series of warnings and positive illustrations between 4,20-6,4 and 6,5-17 but also in the actual themes of true and false shame (4,20f), especially on the question of

---

43   For a discussion of the text see Skehan - Di Lella, *Ben Sira*, 170, 172.
44   Roth, "Gnomic-Discursive Wisdom", 74, sees in 4,20-28 the body of Section *beth* (בשת) in an alphabetic-climactic arrangement in Sir 1,1-23,27.
45   Prato, *Il problema della teodicea*, 366-369.

theodicy, of pity, and judgement of God towards the sinner in 5,(3)4-8 and in the statements about speech (5,10.13 and the warnings against the δίγλωσσος 5,9.14; 6,1).

Several interesting hints at the wider coherence of the Book of Ben Sira can be found in the strongly wovened themes of 4,11-6,17. Thus the revelation (גלה - ἀποκαλύπτειν) of hidden things (מסתרי - κρυπτά) of Wisdom to the faithful student in 4,18 reminds of God's promises of the revelation of His mysteries (סוד - μυστήρια) to the humble in 3,19. It is only in these two places that revelation of secrets means something positive; in 1,30c on the contrary, God reveals the secret of the sinner. The warning in 5,5 against adding sin to sin out of light-minded trust in atonement repeats exactly the characterization of a hardened heart of 3,27, the opposite of the humble of 3,17-20, in a different context. The motif of testing in the hinge texts 4,17 and 6,7(6) finally connects the whole paragraph with the parenesis on the fear of God (2,1-18), in which it is said in 2,1 that the pious must be prepared for examination and testing. Human friendship is not only to be seen in the context of examination and fear of God but the testing of the pious is also in the service of the friendship with God;[46] Sir 44,20d mentions Abraham as a model since he was found faithful under testing.[47]

The promises of Wisdom in 4,11-19 refer back to the blessings of wisdom and fear of God in 1,11-12 too, e.g. *joy* 4,12, as in 1,11.12; *blessing* 4,13b, as in 1,13b; *glory* 4,13, as in 1,11. The major theme of good upright speech within 4,23-6,1 is remarkably the only concrete example of the practice of the fear of God, which is mentioned already in 1,29 at the beginning of the parenesis (1,28-2,18). The presence and efficacy of wisdom in Jerusalem according to 24,10 seems to be anticipated in the motif that the service of wisdom is service in the Temple (4,14). These few observations suggest accepting a certain structure for 4,11-6,17[48] as well as its purposeful integration into the larger context.

Prato has presented further reflections on 9,17-11,28 within the important section 6,18-14,19.[49] Besides the fear of God (6,37; 7,29; 9,16;

---

[46] Irwin, "Fear of God", 551-559.

[47] See the contribution by N. Calduch-Benages to this volume.

[48] Harvey, "Degree of Order", 55, summarizes: Applying Wisdom Personally; see I.J. Okoye, *Speech in Ben Sira* with special reference to 5,9-6,1 (EHS 535; Frankfurt 1995) 12-18.

[49] Prato, *Il problema della teodicea*, 369-378.

10,19-24),[50] the themes of transience and death (7,17.36; 10,9-11; 11,25-26; 14,11-19) in relation to pride and arrogance might be of significance for the whole structure.[51]

1.3.3 Sir 19,20-23,27

As a last example, let me repeat a few observations made by Beentjes on Sir 19,20-20,31 and on the prayer in 22,27-23,6,[52] texts which - with the exception of the theodicy section (15,11-18,14)[53] - have found little attention so by those scholars who regard 14,20-23,27 as a large section.

With its themes of wisdom-law and fear of God, Sir 19,20-24 represents a small sub-section, which is reminiscent of the opening of the book (1,1-10.25-27). Framing elements (טוב-sayings in 19,24 and 20,31; *wisdom* in 19,20 and 20,31; κωλύειν ἁμαρτάνειν in 19,28 and 20,21) as well as sayings with ἐστιν, which appear frequently only within 19,20-20,31, relate to a larger sub-section of 19,20-20,31; in addition, there are numerous networks of catchwords. The concern is the illustration of true wisdom in opposites, especially in behaviour in speech: silence and speech at the right/wrong time (20,1-8); the wise and the foolish person in speech and presents (20,9-17); the speech of the foolish person (20,18-26); the wise person in speech and manner (20,27-31). After basic statements on sin, the sequel (21,1-22,26) illustrates fear of God and law (21,1-10.11), wisdom and foolishness, and concludes (as in 6,5-17 and 19,13-17) with a section about friendship (22,19-26). The next sub-section (22,27-23,27) consists of the prayer in 22,27-23,6 with a completely analogous bipartite structure (22,27-23,1, decency of the mouth; and 23,2-6, decency of desire). This structure is

---

50 Haspecker, *Gottesfurcht*, 130-140.
51 Roth, "Gnomic-Discursive Wisdom", 74-75: "hortative ethical and society-oriented in character" with גאוה (7,17; 10,5-18) in central position; Harvey, "Degree of Order", 55-56: Applying Wisdom Socially, distinguishes 7,1-36; 8,1-9,18; 10,1-11,9; 11,10-28; 11,29-12,18; 13,1-23; 13,24-14,19 with summaries in 7,36; 9,14-18; 11,7-9; 12,16-18; 13,21-23; 14,18-19.
52 P.C. Beentjes, "'Full Wisdom is Fear of the Lord'. Ben Sira 19,20-20,31: Context, Composition and Concept", *EstBib* 47 (1989) 27-45; id., "Sirach 22:27-23:6 in zijn Context", *BTFT* 39 (1978) 144-151.
53 Cf. Prato, *Il problema della teodicea*, 208-299.

made concrete in two ways: in 23,7-15 by *mouth/lips* (see 22,27ff) and in 23,16-27 by *desire*. The concluding verse (23,27) is not only a summary for 22,27-23,27: "Thus all who dwell on the earth shall know, and all who remain in the world shall understand, that nothing is better than the fear of the Lord, nothing sweeter than obeying his commandments." This saying with κρείσσων forms a nice inclusio to 19,24 (as also 20,31) and leaves 19,20-23,27 to be understood as a larger section.[54] Thus one may ask whether this text could not be seen as a separate section beside 14,20-19,17, or at least within 14,20-23,27. The issue of the development of the book is raised by the question whether 23,27 concludes the first big part of the book,.

1.3.4 Some general ideas about structure

Before sketching our ideas of the literary development, let me summarize a few preliminary consequences of the structure.

Various earlier studies and observations suggest a more complex literary and thematic structure of larger sections, in parts valid even of the entire book, than widely supposed.

Exact, literary and thematic analysis of larger sections of the Greek text or in the Hebrew manuscripts is still needed.

Literary and thematic structures are more plausible if more points of view are considered (text criticism, stylistics, poetics, vocabulary, thematic connections ...).

A great variety of possible shapes for particular sections apply very different instructional strategies beyond the literary and thematic structure. That means that Ben Sira's great themes and concerns such as wisdom, fear of God testing and praise can affect particular sections and topics in different ways, as Roth tried to show and as needs further study.[55]

---

54 Cf. Peters, *Jesus Sirach*, xii and 168.
55 Cf. J. Marböck, "Das Buch Jesus Sirach", *Einleitung in das Alte Testament* (Hrsg. E. Zenger u.a.) (KStTh 1,1; Stuttgart 1995) 285-292.

2. *Problems regarding the Redaction history of the Book of Ben Sira*

The redaction history of this large and diverse book of wisdom has engaged scholars for more than 200 years. Eichhorn (1795) believed that the book consisted of three collections, "schriftlichen Aufsätzen des jüdischen Weisen" (written essays of the Jewish sage), which the author had compiled at different times,[56] a model heavily criticized by Bretschneider.[57] Ewald[58] believed that the history of Hebrew proverbial poetry in Ben Sira's book had been focused after a complex process. He supposed that Chapters 1-16,21 and 16,22-36,22 were two older books of proverbs dating from the 4th or 3rd Century B.C.E., the original arrangement of which Ewald tried to reconstruct; only 36,23-51,30 (without 39,12-35) were attributed to Jesus Sirach. Fritzsche too believed that the author had organized "was er im Laufe der Zeit stückweis niedergeschrieben hatte" (what he had written down piece by piece in the course of time)[59]. Subsequent processes include systems of structuring and the extent of the thematic and logical arrangement of the material. I take problems with Chapters 24 and 51 as examples after collecting the most main evidence for a gradual development of the book. The present discussion is devoted to the stages of redaction by Ben Sira himself as well as to a possibly early relecture.

2.1. Evidence for gradual composition

The formal and thematic compactness of a series of texts suggests an oral or written version originally independent of a larger literary context, e.g. the two large units about creation (42,15-43,33) and history (44-49.50), selfpraise of Wisdom (Chapter 24), the image of the scribe (38,24-39,11), the sections about theodicy (15,11-18,14; 39,12-35), and prayer and its practice (22,27-23,27). A purposeful literary redactional work is testified by the many autobiographical notes, as observed by many scholars, which announce that the work be continued after the

---

56   Eichhorn, *Einleitung in die apokryphischen Schriften*, 51-52.
57   Bretschneider, *Liber Jesu Siracidae Graece*, 17-24.
58   G.H.A. Ewald, *Geschichte des Volkes Israel* IV (Göttingen [3]1864) 342-347.
59   Fritzsche, *Weisheit Jesus Sirach's*, xxxii.

sections on wisdom with 24,30-34; 33(30),16(25)-19(28); 39,12.32.[60]
The breaking-up of a series (of vetitives) by inserting thematically
closed units also suggests a progressive shaping, as in the texts about
friendship (6,5-17) and quest for wisdom (6,18-37) within the warnings
(4,20-6,1; 7,1-20.34-35; Chs. 8-9.11. In addition, the recurrence of
themes is made plausible by redactional compilation of extant instructional texts.[61]

2.2. Sir 24 and 51

Roth takes Chapter 24 as the start of the first expansion (24,1-32,13) of
the original version of the book (1,1-23,27 and 51,1-30).[62] However the
question of the function of Sir 24 in the development of the composition seems to be more complex. The break in the coherent text mentioned above between 22,27-23,27 and 25,1-11 by 24,1-29 could well
be understood as a first conclusion, that is in a double sense: as inclusio
for 1,1-10.11-27 about origin and blessing of wisdom and fear of God
as well as a positive counterpart to the adulterous woman in 23,25-26,
who is denied all the blessings and fruits of wisdom of 24,12.16.20
(taking root, spreading of twigs, sweet memory) in the same arrangement; in addition, the theme of inheritance (for Jacob) appearing in Sir
24,8.23 can be found in a negative meaning in 23,12.[63] The praise of
wisdom originally meant for a solemn conclusion now received the si-
multaneous function of opening a new part of the book by means of the
epilogue in the 1st person, hinting at the author's plans for 24,30-34.

---

60 Especially Roth, "Gnomic-Discursive Wisdom", 60-61, 65. Earlier Peters, *Jesus Sirach*, xl.

61 Fritzsche, *Weisheit Jesus Sirach's*, xxxii. Schrader, *Leiden und Gerechtigkeit*,
59.

62 Roth, "Gnomic-Discursive Wisdom", 60, 74. The other sections that were
added are 32,14-38,23; 38,24-50,29.

63 Marböck, *Weisheit im Wandel*, 42-43; A. Lefèvre, *Introduction critique à
l'Ancien Testament* (éd. H. Cazelles) (Paris 1973) 729; recently Beentjes, "Full
Wisdom is Fear of the Lord"; id., "Sirach 22:27-23:6", 150; also M. Gilbert,
Introduction au Livre de Ben Sira ou Siracide ou Ecclésiastique (Rome 1988)
54-55; O. Wischmeyer, *Die Kultur des Buches Jesus Sirach* (BZNW 77; Berlin
1995) 153, 82.

Chapter 51 seems to be a similar crux not only in the structure but also in the redaction history of Ben Sira. At the beginning of literary-historical research on the book, it was briefly dismissed as an appendix or supplement to the colophon in 50,27-29[64] of disputed authenticity. It now receives a new place in the studies on the redaction history of the book. In Roth's opinion, 51,1-30 represents the end of the original Book of Ben Sira (1,1-23,27).[65] As early as 1913, Peters understood the chapter as a review and conclusion of the entire book, as intended by the author: Sir 51,1-12 as a thanksgiving psalm and 51,13-30 as a poem about the quest for wisdom modelled on the acrostic poem of the wise housewife at the end of the Book of Proverbs (Prov 31,10-31).[66] Gilbert elucidated this suggestion and considers Chapter 51 as the last stage of redaction by Sirach himself.[67] There is hardly any compelling ground in the present discussion on literary criticism to doubt the authenticity of 51,1-12 and 51,13-30. [68]

The question of the number of larger redactions and editions must be left open, as rather hypothetical, especially from 32,14ff onward, if one accepts that the work was probably composed in several stages by Ben Sira himself. To regard however Sir 38,24-50,29 as the last and only big redaction, as is Roth's conviction, seems to be unlikely and difficult. A break after 42,14 (38,24-42,14) could well be recommended formally and in content.

2.3. New questions: early additions and revisions of Ben Sira's book?

Apart from critical opinions about the thanksgiving litany (Sir 51,12a-o)[69] which probably originated in Qumran circles and an occasional verse (e.g. 44,16), Middendorp followed Ewald in questioning the authenticity of several other texts of Sirach on the basis of literary and

64	Fritzsche, *Weisheit Jesus Sirach's*, 307-308; Zöckler, *Die Apokryphen des Alten Testaments*, 256.
65	Roth, "Gnomic-Discursive Wisdom", 60, 74.
66	Peters, *Jesus Sirach*, xl, 437.
67	Gilbert, "L'action de grâce", 240-242.
68	So recently Skehan - Di Lella, *Ben Sira*, 74, 563, 576-577; Schrader, *Leiden und Gerechtigkeit*, 71-74, 75-82; Gilbert, "L'action de grâce", 241.
69	Skehan - Di Lella, *Ben Sira*, 569-570.

thematic discrepancies in the context of the book, namely the prayer for the salvation of Zion (36,1-17), the statements on Elijah (48,10-11), Enoch, Joseph, Shem, Shet and Adam (49,14-16) and 51,30. He reckoned with an eschatologically oriented revision in the Maccabean era.[70] The problem has been taken up anew by Schrader, who has presented the most elaborate attempt at the redaction history of the book beyond Sirach.[71]

According to Schrader, Ben Sira's original book was a collection of the disorderly posthumous works by a disciple, to whom also 50,27-29 is attributed. The structure of the entire book with its blocklike, mechanically associative assembled single pieces is thoroughly planned.[72] Schrader, in discussion with Middendorp about non-Siracid additions and revisions, does not see any reason why the thanksgiving psalm (51,1-12) or 51,1-30 as a whole should be of post-Siracid origin. Revision in Maccabean time would be 48,10 only (against Middendorp without 48,11)[73] and the petition for judgment against the heathen in 35(32),18(22)-20(26) and the deliverance of Zion (36,1-22)[74] dating between 167 and 164 B.C.E.[75] Questions to be put to Schrader are why the extensive arrangement of the book could not be attributed to the Siracid himself, and whether the literary and thematic shape of separate sections, or rather their connections, is not even more intensive than expected (as in 1,11-2,18). For an eschatological revision in Maccabean time, one needs to examine how far sapiential and eschatologic-apocalyptical traditions in particular texts can safely be separated in late wisdom literature.

---

70 Th. Middendorp, *Die Stellung Jesu Ben Siras zwischen Judentum und Hellenismus* (Leiden 1973) 113-136.
71 Schrader, *Leiden und Gerechtigkeit*, 58-95: Die Entstehung des Sirachbuches.
72 Schrader, *Leiden und Gerechtigkeit*, 58-68.
73 Schrader, *Leiden und Gerechtigkeit*, 82-87.
74 G: 33,1-13a; 36,16b-22.
75 Schrader, *Leiden und Gerechtigkeit*, 87-93.

Ben Sira Manuscripts from Qumran and Masada *

By Corrado Martone, Torino

The Qumran sect has been defined as an "Israel in miniature".[1] In the large library of this Israel in miniature, remains of all the books of the Hebrew Bible have been found.[2] Among the 220 Biblical manuscripts which, in the course of time, have been found in the Qumran caves, there are also fragments of the Hebrew text of Ben Sira, whose importance cannot be underestimated. Another major testimony of the Hebrew text of our book was found during the Masada excavations by Y.Yadin and his team. The Ben Sira manuscripts from Qumran and Masada are the focus of the present paper.

1. Ben Sira Manuscripts from Qumran

In the second volume of the series *Discoveries in the Judaean Desert*, devoted to the texts stamming from the so-called "Petites Grottes" (that is Cave 2 and 3, Cave 6-10), M. Baillet published two fragments containing a small portion of the Hebrew text of Ben Sira.[3] Unfortunately the two

---

*   I would like to thank the organizational committee for granting me the privilege of participating in the Ben Sira Conference.

1   M.A. Knibb, *The Qumran Community* (Cambridge 1987) 130.

2   The only exception is the Book of Esther. Nevertheless, fragments of a narrative work that could be a source of this book have been found in Qumran Cave 4. See J.T. Milik, "Les modèles araméens du livre d'Esther dans la grotte 4 de Qumrân", *Mémorial Jean Starcky. Vol. II* (eds. E. Puech & F. García Martínez) (Paris 1992) 321-406.

3   M. Baillet, *Discoveries in the Judaean Desert of Jordan* III (Oxford, UK) 1962, 75-77.

fragments are in such a bad state that it is not simple to draw conclusions from them: nevertheless, some comments are in order.

The two fragments are part of the same manuscript, which was found in the 2nd Qumran cave; to this manuscript was assigned the series number 18 (2Q18 or 2QSir). The manuscript has been dated by its script to the transitional phase between the Hasmonean and the Herodian period, he middle ist Century B.C.E., on the basis of palaeographic criteria established by F.M. Cross in a seminal study.[4] The first fragment of the manuscript is in very bad state and it has been identified as a part of Ben Sira, just because this identification, as we shall see, is probable for the second fragment of the same manuscript. In Fragment 1, we can see two lines where just five letters are readable, namely one letter in the first line and four letters in the second line. However the reading of three of the four letters of the second line is far from certain. These difficulties notwithstanding, and on the basis of two hypotheses about the letters of the second line, Baillet reconstructs two passages of our book: in the first line, just a *taw* is readable and, if we read in the 2nd line a *he*, an *aleph*, a *yod* and a final *nun*, it is possible to reconstruct Sir 6,14-15:

1 [אוהב אמונה אוהב] ת[קוף ומוצאו מצא הון]
2 [לאהוב אמונ]ה אין [מחיר ואין משקל לטובתו]

This reconstruction is based on a reading of the 3rd letter of the 2nd line as a *yod*: this reading is not impossible but it presupposes, to use F.M Cross' terminology, an "idiosyncratic" shape of the letter because of its abnormal length. However if one reads in the 2nd line a *he*, an *aleph*, a *resh* and a final *kaph*, one can reconstruct Sir 1,19-20, a passage which is not to be found in the mediaeval manuscripts of our book:

1 [שכל ודעת תביע וכבוד] ת[ומכיה תרים]
2 [שרש חכמה יראת יהוה וענפי] ארך [ימים]

Palaeographically, this reconstruction is, in my opinion, much more likely. On the basis of this reconstruction, furthermore, one can see an arrangement by hemistichs, which is the most striking characteristic of the second fragment of our manuscript.

Although not well preserved, the second fragment allows a far more certain reconstruction than the first one. It contains 13 lines and preserves

---

4   F.M. Cross, "The Development of the Jewish Scripts", *The Bible and the Ancient Near East. Essays in Honor of William Foxwell Albright* (ed. G.E. Wright) (Garden City, NY 1961) 170-264.

just the last letter or letters of lines 1, 3, 7 to 12. Baillet identified this fragment as a passage of the Hebrew text of Ben Sira, namely Sir 6,20-31.

1 ב[ל רסח הנלכלכי אל ולו ליואל איה הבוקע]
2 [הכילשהל רחאי אלו וילע היהת אשמ ןבאכ]
3 חכ]נ איה םיברל אלו אוה ןכ רסומה יכ]
[...] 4
[...] 5
6 [היתלובחתב ץקת לאו האשו הכמכש טה]
7 ה[יכרד רמש ךדאמ לכבו הילא ברק הכשפנ לכב]
8 הפ[רת לאו התקזחתהו אצמו שקב רקחו שרד]
9 גנע[תל ךל ךפהנו התחונמ אצמת רוחאל יכ]
10 םתכ ידגב [התלבחו זע ןוכמ התשר ךל היהתו]
11 תל[כת ליתפ היתרסומו הלוע בהז ילע]
12 הנרטעת תראפת ת[רטעו הנשבלת דובכ ידגב]
[...] 13

This fragment is important for what concerns the textual history of our book. On the basis of the preserved letters, we can see a Hebrew text of Ben Sira dating *at least* to the middle 1st Century B.C.E. which is not only very similar to the Geniza text but also that, if Baillet's reconstruction is correct, seems also to present the arrangement by hemistics that we find in the Geniza text.

For the relationship between the Qumran and the Geniza texts, the perfect correspondence should be noted between the two readable words of line 12 and Sir 6,31 as witnessed by the Geniza text. Furthermore, the arrangement by hemistics to be found in both manuscripts would seem to confirm the old hypothesis that Paul Kahle put forward before the publication of the Ben Sira Manuscript from Qumran Cave 2.[5] According to his hypothesis, the Cairo text of Ben Sira was copied from Qumran manuscripts. The Syriac letter of Patriarch Timotheus tells us that shortly before 800 C.E. many Hebrew manuscripts were discovered in a cave near Jericho. So Kahle assumes that "it is very likely that the Hebrew text of Ecclesiasticus, of which great parts were discovered in the Cairo Geniza also came from the Cave".[6] If so, Timotheus' letter is ancient testimony to the Qumran Corpus.

---

5   P. Kahle, "The Age of the Scrolls", *VT* 1 (1951) 38-48.
6   P. Kahle, "Age", 46.

Unfortunately it is not possible to ascertain whether Baillet's reconstruction is correct. However careful measurement of the available room for letters to be reconstructed supports such a reconstruction and therefore Kahle's hypothesis.

Another major testimony of a portion of our book was published in 1965 by James Sanders in the 4th volume of the series *Discoveries in the Judaean Desert.*[7] The scroll containing the portion of Ben Sira text comes from Qumran Cave 11 and was given the series number 11Q5 and the title 11QPs(alms)[a]. This scroll contains some Psalms arranged in a sequence different from the Masoretic Text, as well as other pseudepigraphical compositions. Column XXI, lines 10 to 17 reproduces the Hebrew text of Sir 51,13 ff. This text exhibits a Herodian script dating from the first half of the first century C.E. and is much better preserved than the Cave 2 fragment. In the sequence of the scroll, the Ben Sira text follows the text of Ps 138,1-8 and precedes a pseudepigraphical composition entitled by Sanders "Apostrophe to Zion". The Hebrew text runs as follows:

11 אני נער בטרם תעיתי ובקשתיה באה לי בתרה ועד

12 סופה אדורשנה גם גרע נץ בבשול ענבים ישמחו לב

13 דרכה רגלי במישור כי מנעורי ידעתיה הטיתי כמהט

14 אוזני והרבה מצאתי לקח ועלה היתה לי למלמדי אתן

15 הודי זמותי אשחקה קנאתי בטוב ולוא אושב חריתי

16 נפשי בה ופני לוא השיבותי טרתי נפשי בה וברומיה לוא

17 אשלה ידי פרש [...] מערמיה אתבונן כפי הברותי אל

18 [...] ל [...]

I quote J.A. Sanders' translation:

> I was a young man before I had erred when I looked for her.
> She came to me in her beauty when finally I sought her out.
> Even (as) a blossom drops in the ripening of grapes, making glad the heart,
> (so) my foot trod in uprightness; for from my young manhood have I known her.
> I inclined my ear but a little and great was the persuasion I found.
> And she became for me a nurse; to my teacher I give my ardour.
> I purposed to make sport: I was zealous for pleasure, without pause.
> I kindled my desire for her without distraction.
> I bestirred my desire for her, and on her heights I do not waver.
> I opened my hands ... and perceive her unseen parts.
> I cleansed my hands.

---

7   J.A. Sanders, *The Psalms Scroll of Qumran Cave 11 (11QPs[a])* (Discoveries of the Judaean Desert of Jordan IV) (Oxford, GB 1965) 79-85.

This portion of the Hebrew text of Ben Sira is preserved also in the manuscript from the Genizah and offers therefore, because of its antiquity, an invaluable device for what concerns the study of the textual development of our book. I would like to focus on two major characteristics of this text. The first one is the acrostic form of the hymn preserved in the Qumran text. G. Bickell[8], on the basis of his retro-version from the Syriac of this text, put forward the hypothesis that the original form of the hymn was based on an acrostic structure. It is worth noting that Bickell's hypothesis was formulated in 1882, that is to say 14 years before the discovery of the Genizah fragments of Ben Sira. Furthermore, the Geniza text does not preserve the original acrostic form of the hymn since it presents many difficulties as for the alphabetic sequence from *aleph* to *mem*.

The text from Cave 11, on the other hand, presents a perfect acrostic sequence from *aleph* to *kaph*. But from *mem* on, where the Cairo text is better preserved, our scroll presents just two words at the beginning of Col. XXII, which, after a *vacat*, are followed, as we have seen, by the so-called "Apostrophe to Zion". The Qumran text of Sirach from Cave 11 presents us with a form of the hymn from before a process of textual transmission, in which it underwent several corruptions with almost complete loss of the acrostic structure. The scroll represents a form very close to the original.[9]

As for the relationship between the Qumran text and the Greek text, the synopsis prepared by Sanders shows that, although there are many differences that cannot be overlooked, the closeness of the two texts is undeniable. The analysis of such differences allows us to highlight another major characteristic of the Cave 11 text of Sirach. The RSV translation of the Greek text runs as follows.

> While I was still young, before I went on my travels,
> I sought wisdom openly in my prayer.
> Before the temple I asked for her,
> and I will search for her to the last.
> From blossom to ripening grape

---

8   See *ZKT* 6 (1882) 326-30.
9   On this acrostic hymn, see also I. Rabinowitz, "The Qumran Hebrew Original of Ben Sira's Concluding Acrostic on Wisdom", *HUCA* 42 (1971) 173-84; P.W. Skehan, "The Acrostic Poem in Sirach 51:13-20", *HTR* 64 (1971) 387-400.

> my heart delighted in her;
> my foot entered upon the straight path;
> and I found for myself much instruction.
> I made progress therein;
> to him who gives wisdom I will give glory.
> and I was zealous for the good;
> and I shall never be put to shame.
> My soul grappled with wisdom,
> and in my conduct I was strict;
> and lamented my ignorance of her.
> I directed my soul to her,
> and through purification I found her.

There can be little doubt that the Greek version tends to modify the original Hebrew text. In order to understand the lines of such modifications we must analyse a particular characteristic of our hymn, namely its passages that leave room for erotic interpretation.

In his edition of the text, J.A. Sanders wrote that the author of the hymn "dedicated his normally developing passions and desires to the pleasures of life with Wisdom and did so unstintingly, without pause, without distraction and without respite";[10] Sanders adds that our hymn is "a Wisdom teacher's song of his experience of intimate knowledge of Wisdom in his youth. The experience is related in mute but distinctly erotic tones".[11] This interpretation has been reassessed by T. Muraoka in 1978.[12] After a detailed linguistic analysis of the hymn, this scholar concludes that the relationship between the author and the personification of Wisdom is described in terms of sexual intercourse. In order to give an example of Muraoka's analysis, I mention his interpretation of the word *yd* ("hand"), which is most probably used euphemistically in our hymn as not only in Biblical but also in Qumran Hebrew (1QS VII,13). This interpretation throws new light on the text of the Geniza which in the line 19 reads "my hand opens her portal". Furthermore, Sanders indicated the term *rgl* ("foot") as a possible euphemism in line 4 of the Qumran text: "my foot trod in uprightness".[13]

---

10   Sanders, *Psalms Scroll*, 84.
11   Sanders, *Psalms Scroll*, 85.
12   T. Muraoka, "Sir. 51,13-30: An Erotic Hymn to Wisdom?", *JSJ* 10 (1979) 166-178.
13   Sanders, *Psalms Scroll*, 81.

On the other hand, we are surely not faced with a secular song, since the poet wants to highlight the analogy between his religious zeal for Wisdom and "a man's intimate association and physical union with his female companion". The description of Wisdom as a bride is not unfamiliar in the Jewish literature, as we see especially in the book of Proverbs (e.g. 8,2). Qumran literature offers an example of the opposite imagery, as we most probably find in the composition entitled *The Wiles of the Wicked Woman* (4Q184), published by John Allegro in 1967[14], in which the Wisdom of the enemies of the sect is depicted as a harlot. I quote some passages from this composition in F. García Martínez's translation:[15]

> (1) She [...] utters futility and in [...] She is always looking for depravities, and whets the words of her mouth (2) and implies insult and is busy leading the community astray with nonsense. Her heart weaves traps, her kidneys [nets]. (3) [Her eyes] have been defiled with evil, her hands go down to the pit, her feet sink to act wickedly and to walk towards crimes. (4) [Her ...] are foundations of darkness and there are sins -plenty in her wings. [Her ...] are night gloom and her clothes [...] (5) Her veils are shadows of the twilight and her adornments diseases of corruption. Her beds are couches of corruption (6) [...] of deep ditches. Her lodgings are couches of darkness and in the heart of the night are her tents. In the foundations of gloom she sets up her dwelling (7) and camps in the tent of silence. In the midst of eternal fire is her inheritance and those who shine do not enter. (8) She is the start of all the ways of wickedness. She is the ruination of all who inherit her, and the calamity of all those who grasp her. (9) For her paths are paths of death, and her roads track to sin. Her trails lead astray towards wickedness (10) and her pathways to the guilt of transgression. Her gates are the gates of death, and in the entrance to her house, Sheol proceeds. (11) All those who go to her will not come back and all those who inherit her will sink to the pit. She hides in ambush, in secret places (12) [...] ... [...] ....She raises her eyebrows impudently... to sidetrack into the paths of the pit and seduce the sons of men with smooth words.

If these interpretations of the Ben Sira Psalm from Qumran Cave 11 are correct, there can be little doubt that we can explain the differences between the Greek and the Qumran text as an attempt on the part of the Greek translator to avoid too explicit terms to be found in the Hebrew text. Furthermore, this text is incorporated in a group of Psalms claiming

---

14   J.M. Allegro, *Discoveries in the Judaean Desert of Jordan V* (Oxford, UK 1968) 82-85.

15   F. García Martínez, *The Dead Sea Scrolls Translated. The Qumran Texts in English* (Leiden - New York - Cologne 1994) 379-380.

Davidic authorship. Therefore the Psalm was not part of the original Book of Ben Sira. Otherwise it would hardly have been included in the Qumran Scroll.[16]

2. The Ben Sira Text from Masada

The most extensive Ben Sira manuscript from the Judaean Desert comes not from Qumran but from the fortress of Masada. The Masada finds include a group of Aramaic and Hebrew ostraca and papyrus fragments in Latin, several biblical texts, a copy of the *Song for the Sabbath Sacrifice*, a composition well attested in Qumran too and many fragments in Hebrew, Aramaic, Greek and Latin.

On 8 April 1964, Y. Yadin and his team discovered in one of the casemates of the eastern wall of Masada's fortress, a scroll containing Chapters 39,27-44,17 of the Hebrew text of Ben Sira.[17] Leaving aside for a moment the major problems that these fragments pose for what concerns the Hebrew original of our book, I shall focus on a few palaeographical observations in order to arrange the manuscript from a chronological point of view. Since the majority of letters present characteristics typical of a very late stage of Hasmonean formal script, which already presents some early Herodian characteristics one can place our manuscript between 4QSam^a and 1QM in the Tables of the aforementioned study of F.M. Cross and to date it, therefore, between 40 B.C.E. and 20 C.E. Besides palaeographical data, archaeology offers a *terminus ante quem* in order to date our scroll, since the Masada fortress was destroyed by Roman troops in 73 C.E.

The arrangement of the text in the manuscript supports Baillet's reconstruction that we have seen in the discussion of the Ben Sira fragments from Qumran Cave 2. Each verse has been written on a separate line and each line is divided into two hemistichs. The same

---

16   Sanders, *Psalms Scroll*, 83.
17   Y. Yadin, *The Ben Sira Scroll from Masada: With Introduction, Emendations and Commentary* (Jerusalem 1965).

arrangement of the text is to be found in some Psalms manuscripts from Masada published by Yadin.[18]

What is the relationship between the text of Ben Sira found at Masada and the other available texts of the book? To answer this question, Yadin's edition provides three tables in which the various agreements and differences are recorded. Table 1 records 52 instances in which the text of the scroll is in agreement with the *marginal reading* of MS B of the Geniza as opposed to the main text of MS B. Table 2 records 39 instances in which the text of the scroll is in agreement with B text and contrasts with B margin. Table 3 records 90 instances in which the text of the scroll differs from both B margin and B text.

A close study of these Tables elicits clues about the textual history of our book. First, the text of the scroll confirms the reading of B margin against that of B text in those instances in which B text presents a more common Hebrew word and B margin a more difficult aramaism. An example is word סימה in B margin, which corresponds to the word אוצר of B text in Sir 41,14. The Masada scroll confirms that the aramaism סימה, which is to be found in the fragments of the *Testament of Levi* from Qumran too, is the original reading of our book, whereas the reading of B text is a clear example of *lectio facilior*.

However Table 2 offers instances in which the Masada scroll agrees with B text against B margin, which represents an explanation of B text. So we read in Sir 44,2: "Great honour did the Most High allot". In this passage, the Hebrew text of the Masada scroll and of B text has simply חלק עליון, whereas B margin specifies חלק עליון להם, referred to the above mentioned "our fathers in their generations".

The most important data on which to evaluate the Greek translation of Ben Sira are those recorded in Table 3, in which, as we have seen, are recorded those instances of differences both from B margin and B text. Many of these instances agree with the Greek. The number of these occurrences, as Y. Yadin points out, could be much larger "since in many instances where the variants are pure synonyms, it is impossible to reconstruct the exact Hebrew text drawn on by the Grandson".[19] At any rate, the analysis of some passages in which the text of the Scroll is in

---

18   Y. Yadin, "The Excavation of Masada - 1963/64: Preliminary Report", *IEJ* 15 (1965) 1-120.
19   Yadin, *Ben Sira Scroll*, 9, note 30.

agreement with the Greek and differs from both B margin and B text
highlights the significance of the Greek text.

In Sir 40,13 the expression χρήματα ἀδίκων corresponds in B text to
the clearly mistaken מחול אל חול ("from the sand to the sand"), most
probably derived from מארץ אל ארץ which we find in verse 11 of the
same chapter. On the other hand, the text of the scroll presents an
expression which can be undoubedtly considered as the *Vorlage* of the
Greek, that is to say חיל מעול ("wealth from iniquity").

Another instance in which the Greek text is confirmed by the Masada
Scroll is Sir 40,30. This verse runs as follows: ἐν στόματι ἀναιδοῦς
γλυκανθήσεται ἐπαίτησις. The Greek phrase ἐν στόματι ἀναιδοῦς
corresponds in the Hebrew text of B to the slightly different phrase לאש
עוז נפש, whereas the Masada Scroll is in perfect agreement with the Greek
with the phrase בפי עז נפש.

Another interesting instance is that to be found in Sir 41,4c where the
Greek reads: εἴτε δέκα εἴτε ἑκατὸν εἴτε χίλια ἔτη. This passage, in
which Ben Sira is speaking of the eternity of death, has a different shape
in the text handed down by the Hebrew text of MS B. The numbers of
the years is reversed, from 1000 to 10. The original sequence reflected in
the Greek text is witnessed by the Masada Scroll that reads לעשר מאה
ואלף שנים. Furthermore, the Masada scroll also reflects the wording of the
Greek in that it has the word "years" at the end of the hemistich, whereas
the Hebrew of MS B puts it right after the numeral "thousands".

In Sir 41,5 the Greek text is again better than the Hebrew text of MS
B: τέκνα βδελυρὰ γίνεται τέκνα ἁμαρτολῶν ("abominable sons are
the sons of sinners"). The Hebrew text of MS B presents some
difficulties, reading נין נימאס דבר רעים, whereas the text of the Masada
scroll seems more reliable: נין נמאס תלדות רעים.

Sir 42,6b provides another instance where the Masada scroll confirms
the faithfulness of the Greek text, in which Ben Sira urges his disciples to
keep evil wives under control: καὶ ὅπυ χεῖρες πολλαὶ κλεῖσον. The text
of MS B presents some difficulties as for the sense of phrase, in that it
reads ומקוק ידים רפות תפתח: "and open the place where there are weak
hands". The Masada scroll, on the other hand, offers a text which is
undoubtedly the Vorlage of the Greek: ומקוק ידים רבות מפתח: "and where
many hands are, a key". It is worth noting, furthermore, that this reading
of the Masada scroll confirms the emendations of I. Lévi to the Hebrew

of MS B in his edition of this manuscript published at the beginning of our century.

Another contribution of the Masada scroll to the evaluation of the Greek text of Ben Sira lies in its containing some verses lacking in MS B and handed down by the Greek translation. One can see for example Sir 42,18: ἔγνω γὰρ ὁ ὕψιστος πᾶσαν εἴδησιν καὶ ἐνέβλεψεν εἰς σημεῖον αἰῶνος. The Hebrew form of this verse is not handed down by MS B from the Geniza but is present in our scroll, which runs as follows: כי יעד עליון דע]ת ו]יביט אתיות עולם ("for the Most High possesseth knowledge and seeth what cometh to eternity").

Another example of this sort is Sir 42,22: ὡς πάντα τὰ ἔργα αὐτοῦ ἐπιθυμητὰ καὶ ὡς σπινθῆρός ἐστιν θεωρῆσαι. This verse, too, has survived in Hebrew only in the Masada scroll: כל מעשיו נחמדים עד ניצוץ מראה ("All His works are lovely even unto a spark and a fleeting vision"). Thanks to the Masada scroll, we can choose the right reading of the Greek manuscript which is not καὶ ὡς, but ἕως (until) as is witnessed by עד of the Hebrew text.

One more verse lacking in MS B is Sir 44,12; the Greek form of this verse runs as: ἐν ταῖς διαθήκαις ἔστε τὸ σπέρμα αὐτῶν καὶ τὰ τέκνα αὐτῶν δι'αὐτούς. We find the Hebrew form of the first hemistic of this verse in the Masada scroll: בבריתם עמד זרעם ("in their covenant their seed abideth"). As for the second hemistic, the first, and only, readable word in the Masada scroll is וצאצאהם ("and their offspring") which perfectly fits the Greek καὶ τὰ τέκνα αὐτῶν.

Some conclusions can be drawn from this brief survey of the relationships between the Hebrew text of Ben Sira handed down by the Masada scroll and the other main known texts. First, as Yadin stated, the text of the Scroll is essentially identical with that of the Geniza manuscripts, despite the many variants. Even if we have analysed mostly variant readings, the majority of the verses agree in all the textual witnesses. *Quo dicto*, another conclusion we can draw from this analysis concerns the relationship between B text and B margin. Contrary to *communis opinio,* the Masada scroll suggests that B text is a popular version with *lectiones faciliores*, and the marginal glosses represent a more reliable manuscript that it hands down more difficult readings.

3. The Book of Ben Sira and Qumran Literature

The last section of this paper deals with the relationship between the Book of Ben Sira and the Qumran literature as a whole. In the first period of the Qumran discoveries when nearly all the main texts were available to scholars, two major articles appeared on this subject. The first was published by Manfred Lehmann,[20] and the second by Jean Carmignac.[21] M. Lehmann stressed the parallels between the Book of Ben Sira and liturgical compositions from Qumran, namely the *Hodayot* (1QH) and the liturgical sections of the *Rule of the War of the Sons of Light against the Sons of Darkness* (1QM) in order to bring out the link between Ben Sira and later Jewish liturgy. Lehmann's work lists parallels between the formula used for Thanksgiving liturgy in Ben Sira 51,1 ff. and many passages of the *Hodayot*.

Carmignac's article is a sort of continuation of Lehmann's, as the author himself points out. To evaluate *Les rapports entre l'Écclesiastique et Qumrân*, Carmignac analyses Biblical quotations to be found in both Ben Sira and Qumran literature, similar terminology and similar themes. The main conclusion Carmignac draws from the analysis is on one hand that the affinities in Biblical quotations and vocabulary may be due to a more general Jewish culture shared by the Book of Ben Sira and the Qumran literature. On the other hand, Carmignac notes that "Les affinités de pensée sont indiscutables et, même en tenant compte du patrimoine commun à tous le Juifs de cette époque, elles suggèrent assez nettement une influence directe (sans doute de l'*Écclesiastique* sur les auteurs qoumrâniens)". Furthermore, the book of Ben Sira leaves much more room for human freedom than Qumran authors do, so that it is hardly conceivable to assume a Qumran origin for our book.

Besides these two articles, both published in the early 1960s, very little has been written about the relationship between Qumran literature and the Book of Ben Sira. Noteworthy is an article by John Priest,[22] which explains the appearance on the part of Ben Sira of David after Phinehas in the Hymn of the Fathers in the light of the doctrine of the two Messiahs, as found in the Qumran literature.

---

20   "Ben Sira and the Qumran Literature", *RevQ* 3 (1961) 103-16.
21   "Les rapports entre l'Écclesiastique et Qumrân", *RevQ* 3 (1961) 209-18.
22   "Ben Sira 45,25 in the light of the Qumran Literature", *RevQ* 5 (1964) 106-118.

In recent years, a spate of new texts have been published, mostly from Qumran Cave 4. Among the newly published fragments at least one presents striking affinities with a major passage of the book of Ben Sira. This text (4Q525) is in a Herodian script and can be dated palaeographically to the end of the 1st Century B.C.E. I would like first of all to quote Fragment 2, Col. II, that is to say the most interesting section of this text for what concerns parallels with Ben Sira.

(1) [Blessed is the one who speaks the truth] with a pure heart and does not slander with his tongue. Blessed are those who adhere to his laws, (2) and do not adhere to perversed paths. Blessed are those who rejoice in her and do not explore insane paths. (3) Blessed are those who search for her with pure hands and do not importune her with treacherous heart. Blessed is the man who attains Wisdom (4) and walks in the Law of the Most High and dedicates his heart to her ways, and is constrained by her discipline and always takes pleasure in her punishments (5) and does not forsake her in the hardship of [his] wrongs, and in the time of anguish does not discard her and does not forget her [in the days of] terror (6) and in the distress of his soul does not loathe her. For he always thinks of her, and in his distress he meditates on [the law] (7) [and throughout] his [whole] life [he thinks] of her, and places her] in front of his eyes, in order not to walk in paths of [evil ...][23]

This text was published by E. Puech in 1992[24] but it had been described by J. Starcky as follows: "Un manuscrit de caractère sapientiel contient une série de macarismes pour ceux qui accomplissent les commandements ('šry ...) et la description des tourments qui attendent les impies".[25] The significance of this text is the clear Jewish link between Sir 14,20-15,1 and Matthew 5,3-10. Furthermore, our text is closer to the Book of Ben Sira than to the Matthean passage. Like Ben Sira, 4Q525 stresses the Wisdom character of the macharisms, whereas the eschatological character that we find in the Matthean text would seem to be lacking. However the allusion in Fragment 15 to the eternal punishments that most probably will be undergone by one who does not follow Wisdom, sets 4Q525 as a perfect watershed between Ben Sira 14,20-15,1 and Matthew 5,3-10.

In summary, the few examples analysed here show that the Qumran literature is an invaluable tool for a better understanding of the Book of

---

23   Adopted from the translation by García Martínez, *Dea Sea Scrolls*, 395.
24   "4Q525 et les péricopes des béatitudes en Ben Sira et Matthieu", *RB* 98 (1991) 80-106.
25   "Le travail d'édition des fragments manuscrits de Qumrân", *RB* 73 (1956) 67.

Ben Sira and that further investigation on this subject will be required, when all the Qumran and the Masada texts have been published.

Reading the Hebrew Ben Sira Manuscripts Synoptically
A New Hypothesis

By Pancratius C. Beentjes, Nieuwegein

During the last five years, I have been working on a Hebrew text edition of the Book of Ben Sira, which should also contain a synopsis.[1] Both the text edition of all extant Hebrew Ben Sira manuscripts, and the synopsis of all parallel texts are presented in a new way, the considerations and pecularities of which are illustrated and elaborated in the first part of this article.

Preparing a particular section of the synopsis, namely the part relating to MS B and the Masada Scroll, I discovered a textual phenomenon that has not to my knowledge been described before. On the basis of twelve couples of verses, I suggest the theory that certain variant readings in Hebrew Ben Sira manuscripts could have been caused by dictation.

1. The need for a new text edition and synopsis

Various text editions were published quite soon after the discovery in 1896 of some Hebrew fragments, identified as parts of the Book of Ben Sira.[2] Some new Hebrew manuscripts and fragments of the Book of

---

1   Pancratius C. Beentjes, *The Book of Ben Sira in Hebrew.* A Text Edition of all Extant Hebrew Manuscripts & a Synopsis of all Parallel Hebrew Ben Sira Texts (VTS 68; Leiden 1997).

2   A.E. Cowley - Ad. Neubauer, *The Original Hebrew of a Portion of Ecclesiasticus*, Oxford 1897; S. Schechter & C. Taylor, *The Wisdom of Ben Sira*, Cambridge 1899 (repr. Amsterdam, 1979); I. Knabenbauer, *Commentarius in Ecclesiasticum* (Cursus Scripturae Sacrae 6) Paris 1902; H.L .Strack, *Die Sprüche*

Ben Sira were discovered between 1931 and 1960.[3] However especially after the discovery of the Ben Sira Scroll from Masada in 1964, a completely new edition was needed, to include all hitherto recovered texts.[4] In 1968, F.Vattioni published a useful polyglot[5] but his Hebrew text was based on Lévi's edition, which contains many imperfections and errors.[6] The most recent text edition was published in 1973 under the direction of Ze'ev Ben-Ḥayyim, as a result of an extended project of 'The Academy of the Hebrew Language and the Shrine of the Book'.[7]

Since the end of the 1970s during intensive preoccupation with the Hebrew text of the Book of Ben Sira, I have become increasingly concerned about instances in which current text editions had given users a false impression of the texts of the recovered Hebrew manuscripts.[8] For instance both Vattioni and Ben-Ḥayyim rendered the Hebrew texts in

---

Jesus', des Sohnes Sirachs, Leipzig 1903; I. Lévi, *The Hebrew Text of the Book of Ecclesiasticus* (SSS 3) Leiden 1904 (3rd ed. 1969); F.Vigouroux, *L'Ecclésiastique* (La Sainte Bible Polyglotte, 5) Paris 1904, 1-239; 885-970; N. Peters, *Liber Jesu Filii Sirach sive Ecclesiasticus hebraice*, Freiburg i.Br., 1905; R. Smend, *Die Weisheit des Jesus Sirach, hebräisch und deutsch*, Berlin 1906.

3   J: Marcus, *The Newly Discovered Original Hebrew of Ben Sira (Ecclesiasticus xxxii,16-xxxiv,1)*, Philadelphia 1931; J. Schirmann, 'Dap hadaš mittôk seper ben-Sîra ha-'ibrî', *Tarbiz* 27(1957-1958) 440-443; J. Schirmann, 'Dappîm nôsepîm mittôk seper ben-Sîra'', *Tarbiz* 29(1959-1960) 125-134; M. Baillet, J.T. Milik, R. de Vaux, *Discoveries in the Judean Desert* III: *Les 'Petites Grottes' de Qumran*, Oxford 1962; J.A. Sanders, *Discoveries in the Judean Desert* IV: *The Psalms Scroll of Qumran Cave 11 (11 QPsa)*, Oxford 1965; Y. Yadin, *The Ben Sira Scroll from Masada*, Jerusalem 1965.

4   The edition of M.H. Segal, *Seper ben-Sîra' haššalem* (Jerusalem 1933; 2nd ed. 1958) provided only MSS A-B-C-D-E. Moreover the passages of Ben Sira that had not then been discovered were *retranslated* by Segal from Greek and Syriac into Hebrew. For these two reasons this text edition is unreliable.

5   F. Vattioni, *Ecclesiastico*. Testo ebraico con apparato critico e versioni greca, latina e siriaca (Testi 1) Napoli 1968.

6   In the edition of P. Boccaccio - G. Berardi, *Ecclesiasticus*, Roma 1976 ('Ad usum scholarum'), only the discoveries before 1931 were incorporated.

7   *The Book of Ben Sira*. Text, Concordance and an Analysis of the Vocabulary (The Historical Dictionary of the Hebrew Language), Jerusalem 1973.

8   The way in which such inaccuracy can lead to exegetical misconstructions has been aired in : P.C. Beentjes, 'The Reliability of Text-Editions in Ben Sira 41,14-16', *BTFT* 49 (1988) 188-194.

the order of the *Greek* verses, i.e. not in the sequence of the recovered *Hebrew* manuscripts.[9]

Meantime, A. Scheiber published a sixth Hebrew manuscript (F) of the Book of Ben Sira, and two minor fragments of MS C in 1982. Unfortunately he published those texts in a little known Hungarian periodical[10] and it took another six years before his article was noticed by A.A. Di Lella, who provided a more accurate text-critical edition of MS F.[11]

With this in mind at the end of the 1980s, I came up with the idea of publishing a new text edition of the Hebrew Book of Ben Sira. Such an edition should contain only the actual texts of the recovered Hebrew Ben Sira manuscripts, e.g. verses in the order found in the manuscripts and without reconstructions for illegible consonants or for larger gaps in the manuscripts. A second major reason for preparing a new text edition of the Hebrew Book of Ben Sira was to present a *synopsis* of all the extant Hebrew Ben Sira material.

1.1 Method and approach

Once the decision was taken to prepare a Ben Sira synopsis, I was faced with some delicate questions of method and approach. At the outset, the text edition was intended merely as a running synopsis. However this option was abandoned for several reasons.

(1) In MSS B, E, F, and the Masada Scroll, the Hebrew text is arranged *stichometrically*: each (half of a) verse is written in two distinct columns, which are clearly marked off by a rather wide blank space. By contrast, MSS A, C, D and 11QPsᵃSir present a *continuous* Hebrew text and the space of every line has been completely utilized. Not only is there no blank between the first and the second half of a colon, but neither is there a blank between one line and the next. An editor want-

---

9   See, for instance, in both editions Sir 3,25; 7,15; 11,32-12,1; 31,21-22; 31,27-28; 36,18 ff.; 37,24-25; 41,14-16; 42,9; 44,15; 46,16-20; 48,7-8; 51,19-20. See also Sir 36,1-11a. 11b-17 [Ben-Ḥayyim] and Sir 49,15-50,1 [Vattioni].

10 A. Scheiber, 'A New Leaf of the Fourth Manuscript of the Ben Sira from the Geniza', *Magyar Könyvszemle* 98 (1982) 179-185.

11 A.A. Di Lella, 'The Newly Discovered Sixth Manuscript of Ben Sira from the Cairo Geniza', *Bib* 69 (1988) 226-238.

ing to put together these two types of manuscripts is faced with a serious problem. Which of the two principles should he favour in order to present the material synoptically ? The only effective way would be to opt for the *stichometric* rendering, also on grounds of frequency. The manuscripts written stichometrically preserve in total about 1000 verses, whereas the non-stichometric manuscripts preserve about 550 verses. However if these latter manuscripts be edited stichometrically, their essential feature would be completely lost.

(2) Special problems arose also for MS C, which is an *anthology* from the Book of Ben Sira.[12] To the editor who wants to 'synopticize' this manuscript with the parallel texts of MSS A, B, and D, the 'chaotic' sequence of the verses of MS C (e.g. Sir 3,14-18.21-22; 41,16; 4,21; 20,22-23; 4,22-23) poses a serious problem. To present MS C synoptically, one has to rearrange the anthological verses into an assumed 'original' order, but then all characteristics of the anthological MS C disappear at once.

(3) A third problem of approach is *'erratic verses'*, which are to be found in MSS A and B. For instance in MS A, the Hebrew text of Sir 27,5-6 has been transmitted between Sir 6,22 and 6,23. In MS B, this feature occurs several times. For example, the text of Sir 7,21 occurs between Sir 10,24 and 10,25, and Sir 27,16 between Sir 31,2 and 31,3.

How should one reproduce such 'erratic verses'? By lifting them out of their original context, the editor is *creating a new text* that has never existed. The same could be said about rearranging continuous texts stichometrically and about the complete destruction of MS C's characteristics.

Considering these facts, I had no other choice but to render all the extant material in a *twofold* way. In *Part I* of the text edition, each Hebrew Ben Sira text is included according to the factual presentation of the manuscripts themselves. In this part, the reader will therefore find the verses arranged exactly as they were in the recovered Hebrew manuscripts. In the 'non-colometric' texts (MSS A, C, D and 11QPs^a), a slash (/) indicates the end of a line. *Part II* of the text edition includes only those verses present in two or more manuscripts. In the synopsis,

---

12 P.C. Beentjes, 'Hermeneutics in the Book of Ben Sira. Some Observations on the Hebrew Ms. C.', *EstBib* 45 (1988) 45-60; M. Zappella, 'Criteri antologici e questioni testuali del manoscritto ebraico C di Siracide', *RivB Italiana* 38 (1990) 273-300.

an asterisk (*) before a verse number indicates that such a verse is present at that place in the Hebrew manuscript, e.g. Sir 33,1 is between Sir 32,21 and 32,24 in both MS E, and MS F. For details of such matters, one must look up the relevant verse in Part I of the text edition.

1.2 A new type of synopsis

Surprisingly, this is in the first time an attempt has been made to compile a *synopsis* in the sense of those passages in which the Hebrew Ben Sira text is available in more than one manuscript. The material will be presented in a more convenient and functional way than in former editions.

The 'synoptic' systems used so far for the Ben Sira texts can be assigned to three categories.

(1) The *diplomatic* model, in which a single Hebrew manuscript serves as the basic text. The variant readings of the remaining manuscripts are placed in a text-critical apparatus. This pattern was followed, for instance, by the editions of Knabenbauer, Smend, and Vattioni.

(2) The *interlinear* model. If a text is extant in more than one Ben Sira manuscript, all textual forms that have been recovered of a verse are printed one after another, before moving to the next. This system was used by Ben-Hayyim.

(3) The *'block'* model. A quite extensive passage from MS X is printed as a whole and is then followed by the corresponding part(s) from MS Y (and Z). The textual evidence is presented in this way in the editions by Lévi, Strack, Segal and Boccaccio-Berardi.

I have attempted to combine the qualities of the interlinear and the block model, to enable the user to read the several Hebrew texts of the Book of Ben Sira more easily than in the extant editions. Each colon (or line) has been printed on the same horizontal line as the corresponding colon or line from other manuscripts. This is the only presentation that guarantees that each verse is preserved in its context. The synopsis gives no information about the dependence or the age of one text in relation to any other.[13]

---

13 This problem has been discussed in detail by H.-P. Rüger, *Text und Textform im hebräischen Sirach*, BZAW 112, Berlin 1970. Recently, fresh arguments have been introduced into this discussion by L. Schrader, *Leiden und*

1.3 Risks and danger of a 'synchronic' presentation

Presentation in one overall view of all available synoptic Ben Sira material involves problems. Everyone who uses this synopsis must realize that it raises linguistic and hermeneutic difficulties. The synopsis at the same time presents both a diachronic and a synchronic text. Hebrew manuscripts originating in quite different eras are printed here side by side. MSS A and D are dated almost unanimously in the 11th Century and MS B in the 12th Century, whereas the anthological MS C is considered to be (much ?) older.[14] Unfortunately MS E has not been dated by J.Marcus nor to my knowledge by any other scholar. The recently recovered MS F has been left undated by A. Scheiber, who published the text of the manuscript in 1982. However A.A. Di Lella, in his circumstantial description of MS F, concluded that the writing seems to be 11th or 12th Century.[15]

Whereas MSS A - F originated in the Middle Ages or were copied at that time, the provenance of the remaining Ben Sira manuscripts is entirely different. Fragments of the Book of Ben Sira recovered at Qumran have been dated either in the second half of the 1st Century BCE (2Q18) or in the first half of the 1st Century CE (11QPsª).[16] The 26 leather fragments of the Ben Sira Scroll from Masada, discovered in 1964, have been set in the first half of the 1st Century BCE.[17] The interval between the Scroll and Ben Sira himself, who composed his work about 190-180 BCE, is very small indeed.

When all this Hebrew evidence has been put together in a synopsis, the reader is faced at a glance with a millennium or even more. One should always bear this huge interval in mind. Though reckoned among the 'outside books' (ספרים החיצונים),[18] we should realize that the Hebrew

---

Gerechtigkeit. Studien zu[r] Theologie und Textgeschichte des Sirachbuches (BET 27) Frankfurt a.M. 1994, 13-57.

14 M. Gaster, 'A New Fragment of Ben Sira', *JQR* XII (1900), 688-702.

15 Di Lella, 'The Newly Discovered Sixth Manuscript', *Bib* 69 (1988) 227.

16 P.W. Skehan - A.A. Di Lella, *The Wisdom of Ben Sira* (AB 37), New York 1987, 53.

17 Y. Yadin, *The Ben Sira Scroll*, 4 (see his note 11 too).

18 S.Z. Leiman, *The Canonization of Hebrew Scripture: The Talmudic and Midrashic Evidence*, Transactions of the Connecticut Academy of Arts and Sciences 47 (1976), 86-102; R. Beckwith, *The Old Testament Canon of the*

text of Ben Sira was sometimes treated as reasonably authoritative, so that a reasonably reliable text was preserved through the ages.[19]

1.4 The synopsis: a weapon against 'parallelomania'

Putting all the parallel Ben Sira texts together into a synopsis can, paradoxically, protect the reader from an exegetical preoccupation that S. Sandmel called 'parallelomania'.[20] A synopsis can make scholars look at texts more carefully, instead of postulating dependance on other writings. Two examples may illustrate the point.

The Hebrew text of Sir 40,15b in MS B runs: כי שורש חנף על שן סלע. The colon therefore seems a close parallel to Job 39,28b: על שן סלע ומצדה. Though the text of Sir 40,15b is heavily damaged in the Masada Scroll, the final word of the colon has fortunately been preserved: צר. This synonym of סלע seems to represent the older textual form and is transmitted also as the marginal reading in MS B itself: ושורש חנף על שן צור. It looks as though somebody altered the original expression על שן צור /צר into על שן סלע in MS B to create a close parallel to the Biblical wording of Job 39,28b. However the copyist of MS B drew attention to another textual form, which seems closer to the original reading, in the margin of the manuscript.[21]

A similar instance is in Sir 42,15b. The poem on the Works of God in Creation (42,15-43,33) in MS B opens with the wording אזכר נא מעשי אל וזה חזיתי ואספרה. The second colon is particularly puzzling, as its Hebrew text completely coincides with the text of Job 15,17b. In both texts, the formula וזה חזיתי ואספרה functions as an introductory call to attention ('Lehreröffnungs-formel'). The reader could easily be misled

---

New Testament Church and its Background in Early Judaism, London 1986, 281 f.; 366 f.; 377.380.

19 The fact that MS B, and MS D, in their respective margins embodied each others variant readings is strong evidence that there was a great respect for the Hebrew Ben Sira text.

20 S. Sandmel, 'Parallelomania', *JBL* 81 (1962) 1-13.

21 The margin of Ms. B. often reproduces a textual form that coincides with the Masada text. Yadin, *The Ben Sira Scroll*, Hebrew Section, 7 [Table 1] has collected about 50 examples of this kind. See, however, his cautious comment on this (*The Ben Sira Scroll*, 9).

to assume that Sir 42,15b was a deliberate parallel to the book of Job.[22]
The second colon of Sir 42,15b in the Masada Scroll (which text was
not discussed or even mentioned by Snaith) runs as: וזה חזיתי ואשננה.
With the very rare verb שׁנן II (only Deut 6,7), the Masada text again
represents the older textual form.[23] In MS B, it was probably a copyist's
familarity with the scriptural passage of Job 15,17b that caused altera-
tion of the original Ben Sira text to a more common synonym.[24]

1.5 Marginal readings

Among all Hebrew Ben Sira manuscripts hitherto recovered, MS B is
distinguished not only by its *length* (21 folio's written on both sides),
but also by the number of marginal readings that have been incorporated into this manuscript. Four times in MS B (in the margins of 32,1;
35,20; 40,22-26, and 45,8), a special kind of marginal reading is met,
because at these points *Persian glosses* have been inserted in the margin. From what they say[25], one can infer that someone working on MS
B had several Hebrew Ben Sira manuscripts at his disposal. The textual
differences between these manuscripts and his 'Vorlage' were accurately noted in the margins of MS B. That this procedure was indeed
put into practice is proved by MS D which has handed over a Hebrew
text form that is nearly always reflected in the marginal readings of MS

---

22 Even J.G. Snaith, who for the rest is cautious in assuming parallels between
    Ben Sira and the Hebrew Bible, has supposed one here : '... the combination of
    the comparatively rare חזתי with the cohortative ending of אספרה is sufficiently
    distinctive to suggest certain dependence ...'; J.G. Snaith,'Biblical Quotations
    in the Hebrew of Ecclesiasticus', *JThS* 18 (1967), 1-12 (6).

23 Cfr. Yadin, *The Ben Sira Scroll*, 26; Th. Middendorp, *Die Stellung Jesus Ben
    Sira zwischen Judentum und Hellenismus*, Leiden 1973, 96.

24 However G.L. Prato, *Il problema della teodicea in Ben Sira* (AnBib 65) Rome
    1975, 122, here favours the text of MS B on account of the Greek and Syriac
    versions.

25 For the *text* of these Persian glosses, see Lévi, *Hebrew Text*; R. Smend, *Die
    Weisheit des Jesus Sirach, Hebräisch und Deutsch*, Berlin 1906. In Vattioni's
    edition, the Persian gloss in the margin of 32,1is missing. A *translation* of all
    Persian glosses is offered by Is. Lévi, *L'Ecclésiastique* I-II, Paris 1898-1901.
    For *linguistic* pecularities relating to the Persian glosses in Sir 32,1 and 35,20,
    see Schechter-Taylor, *Wisdom*, 56.59; W. Bacher, 'Die persischen Randnoti-
    zen zum hebräischen Sirach', *ZAW* 20 (1900) 308-309.

B.[26] The large number of marginal readings in MS B suggested to Eduard König his hypothesis in 1899 that several recensions of the Hebrew Ben Sira must have circulated,[27] a conviction that has been confirmed and elaborated by the circumstantial publications of Segal and Rüger.[28]

Let us now have a further look into the intriguing phenomenon of MS B's marginal readings. As to their nature, the following distinction can be made.

1. A first group consists of merely *orthographic* readings, which for the greater part add or suppress *matres lectionis*, for example in Sir 39,31b (פיהו / פין), Sir 40,22b (שדי / שדה), Sir 42,12b (תסתויד / תסתיד), Sir 43,26a (למענהו / למענו).

2. Marginal readings that pay attention to *scribal errors*, such as the transposition of *daleth* and *resh* (Sir 40,29d; 44,3a), of *beth* and *kaph* (Sir 41,10b; 45,7c), of *cheth* and *he* (Sir 43,5b), or the *metathesis* of consonants within the same word, for example in Sir 43,4a (מצוק / מוצק), Sir 43,4b (שלוח / שולח), Sir 43,13a (בקר / ברק), Sir 43,18a (יגהה / יהגה), Sir 44,3a (רודי / דורי).

3. Some marginal readings offer *synonyms*, for example עליון for אל (Sir 40,1a), נׄבׄרׅאׄו for נׄוׄצׄרׄו (Sir 39,28a), דׄופׅי for מום (Sir 44,19b). In type 3, we find a stereotyped pattern: the main text of MS B proves to accommodate a notable number of Biblical quotations and expressions, whereas the marginal readings quit often give a synonym which is more original, as is demonstated by the Masada Scroll. Consequently, parallels between Ben Sira and the Hebrew Bible are much fewer than is suggested by reviews of Ben Sira, especially older ones.[29] Only a few

---

26 After the Persian gloss in the margin of Sir 45,8 ('This copy goes no further'), there are no further Hebrew marginal readings in MS B.with the exception of 47,8-10.

27 Ed. König, *Die Originalität des neulich entdeckten hebräischen Sirachtextes*, Freiburg 1899, 8.

28 M.H .Segal, 'The Evolution of the Hebrew Text of Ben Sira', *JQR* 25 (1934-1935) 91-149. H.-P. Rüger, *Text und Textform im hebräischen Sirach* (BZAW 112) Berlin 1970. The doctoral thesis of Lutz Schrader, *Leiden und Gerechtigkeit*, should be mentioned here, because the conclusion of his investigation is almost the opposite of Rüger's.

29 This aspect has been thoroughly investigated in the doctoral thesis of P.C. Beentjes, *Jesus Sirach en Tenach*, Nieuwegein 1981, 107-173.

marginal readings suggest the opposite, where a variant reading creates a biblical expression.[30]

4. A fourth group of marginal readings in MS B produces an obvious change of meaning. Most offer a good alternative to the puzzles of the main text. However there are examples where the marginal reading produces a Hebrew text with no sense at all (e.g. Sir 40,18a; 41,12b; 43,8d).[31]

2. Traces of dictation in MS B and the Masada Scroll

While preparing the synoptic text of MS B and the Masada Scroll to be incorporated into the new text edition, I of course noticed all aspects relating to the marginal readings. At a certain moment, however, a phenomenon was encountered which, to the best of my knowledge, has never been systematically described for the Hebrew Ben Sira manuscripts. I would therefore like to introduce this phenomenon as a serious aspect for future textual criticism of the Hebrew Book of Ben Sira.

2.1 Sir 42,6b

MS B : ומקום ידים רפות תפתח
Mas. : ומקום ידים רבות מפתח

Even before the discovery of the Masada Scroll, all commentators agreed, on the basis of κλεῖσον in the Greek translation, that תפתח of MS B must be considered a misreading of מַפְתֵּחַ ('key') which is required by the parallel חותם ('seal').[32] More interesting is the difference

---

30   E.g. Sir 35,11b // Prov 6,31a; Sir 35,18f // Isa 14,5; Sir 38,23 // Prov 22,29b).
31   As far as the present author is aware, a systematic and complete outline of the four types does not exist. A small inventory relating to marginal readings of the *first* and *fourth* category is offered by Lévi, *L'Ecclésiastique* I, xii-xvi. The relation between the Masada scroll, MS B and the marginal readings of MS B is discussed by Yadin, *The Ben Sira Scroll*, 7-13 (Hebrew section).
32   N. Peters, *Der jüngst wiederaufgefundene hebräische Text des Buches Ecclesiasticus*, Freiburg i.Br. 1902, 197; I. Lévi, *L'Ecclésiastique* I, 48; R. Smend, *Die Weisheit des Jesus Sirach*, Berlin 1906, 390.

between רבות (Mas.) and רפות (MS B). Yadin[33] considers the latter reading 'a copyist's error prompted by the frequency of the phrase ידים רפות, as earlier suggested by N. Peters in 1902.[34] This in itself seems a reasonable solution. However precisely the same phenomenon shows up a couple more times within the Book of Ben Sira and those instances of *beth - resh* interchange cannot be explained as referring to standard formulae or to typically biblical language. So another explanation should be sought. Before offering a fresh explanation of such consonantal interchange, let us compare some more Ben Sira texts from MS B and Mas.

2.2 Sir 43,2a

MS B : שמש מביע בצרתו

Bm. : מופיע

Mas. : שמש מופי[ן] [.] בצאתו

At the outset, it is obvious that the context ('the sun at its rising') requires the verb יפע ('to shine') as reflected in Masada, and Bm, and not the verb נבע ('to pour out') of MS B.

2.3 Sir 43,14a

MS B : [למען ברא אוצן]

Mas. : למענו פרע אוצר

Although the verb ברא ('to create') of MS B is possible here, it is both the context ('storehouse'), the parallelism, and the Greek translation ἠνεῴχθησαν that make the verb פרע ('to let loose') more plausible. But in what way should the reading of MS B be interpreted? (1) As a move to replace a verb that was difficult to understand (פרע) by a more 'common' verb (ברא). (2) As a scribal error. (3) Or as originating from

---

33 Yadin, *The Ben Sira Scroll*, 23.

34 'Die nicht seltene Phrase ידים רפות hat den Fehler veranlasst'; Peters, *Der jüngst*, 197. In the Hebrew Bible, 'nicht selten'refers to only *two* occurrences: Isa 35,3; Job 4,3!

yet another direction? Before trying to answer this question, some other
texts should be outlined.

2.4 Sir 43,7a

MS B : בם מעוד וזמני חוק
Bm. :   בו מו׳ וממנו
Mas. :   לו מֹ[...] וממנו חג

2.5 Sir 43,12a

MS B : חוק הקיפה בכבודה
Bm. : הוד הקיפה בכבודו
Mas. : חֹוֹג [.....] בכבודה

On חוק (MS B) in Sir 43,7a, Yadin and Schrader suggested that it could
be a 'mishearing of חג'.[35] For the differences between MS B and Mas.
in Sir 43,12, Yadin refers to Prov 8,27 (בחקו חוג) and Job 26,10 (חק־חג).
As for Sir 42,6b, a Biblical wording could be the origin of the change
of Sir 43,12a in MS B.

That Sir 43,7 and 43,12 in MS B have a different wording from the
Masada Scroll could also be considered conversely as a *qoph - gimel*
interchange. This option is advocated by Sir 43,20b.

2.6 Sir 43,20b

MS B : וכרקב יקפיא מקורו
Mas. : וכרגב יקפיא מקור

As can be verified in all Ben Sira commentaries, the wording of MS B
is obscure, whereas the Masada Scroll offers a meaningful text: 'and He
has congealed the source like a clod'. The question again arises whether

---

35   Yadin, *The Ben Sira Scroll*, 29; Schrader, *Leiden und Gerechtigkeit*, 32.

there is any pattern in the interchange of consonants. That there is indeed a pattern can be deduced from another group of Ben Sira texts.

2.7 Sir 43,11b

MS B :   כי מאד נאדרה [...]וד

Bm. :   נהדרה

Mas. :   כי מ[.]ד נהדר[.....]

This example by no means can be considered an interchange of consonants caused by a biblical wording, as might be the case in two occurrences mentioned above (Sir 42,6b; 43,12a).

An interesting case of consonantal interchange[36] is provided by Sir 31[34],14, because two instances are found in one line.

2.8 Sir 31[34],14a

MS B :   מקום יביט אל אל תושיט יד

Bm. :   תשית

Of course, one can assume that the creator of the marginal reading תשית did not recognise the rare verbal form תושיט, which in the Hebrew Bible is only found in the Book of Esther.[37] So he altered it into a verbal that is reminiscent of the Biblical wording שׁית יד (Gen 46,4; Job 9,33). However the change in Sir 31[34],14a between תושיט (MS B)[38] and תשית (Bm.) could be explained in quite another way. The consonantal interchange of the second half of this verse suggests a surprising solution.

---

36   The monograph by A. Minisalle, *La versione greca del Siracide* (AnBib 133), Roma 1995, 165-168 provides an alphabetic and systematic classification of consonantal interchanges. However one should be aware of that Minisalle's point of view starts from the *Greek*.

37   As a matter of fact, the combination ישׁ יד is handed down both by MS A (4,31) and MS C (7,32)!

38   Segal, *Seper ben-Sira'*, 192 has vocalized as תּוֹשִׁיט.

2.9 Sir 31[34],14b

MS B : ואל דיחד עמו בטנא
Bm. :   תיחד

Within the syntax of Sir 31[34],14b the word דיחד must be a *verbal*
form. However the existence of a verbal root דחד has not been attested
in (late) biblical Hebrew. So there is a serious problem. Of course, one
could assume, as commentators do, that דיחד is a slip of the pen[39] but
nobody has ever explained this clerical error.

Whereas the copyist's familiarity with Biblical phraseology in the
first colon of Sir 31[34],14 could have produced the marginal reading,
an explanation of another kind is required for the second colon, as the
main text of MS B makes no sense at all. Instead of arguing here that
the main text of Sir 31[34],14b in MS B is the result of a clerical error,
the question should be posed whether it would not be better to assume
'a slip of the ear', namely an error caused by dictation.[40] Our list relating to MS B suggests the existence of what I would call *phonetic errors*[41] as a result of scribal methods. The most obvious way of explain-
ing such *beth - pe* / *qoph - gimel* / *aleph - he* interchanges would be to
assume that either the 'Vorlage' from which MS B was copied, or even
MS B itself, was produced by *dictation*. After the main text had been
completed, either the copyist himself, or someone after him, compared
this (first or second degree) dictated text with other Hebrew Ben Sira
manuscripts that were to hand, as we know with absolute certainty from
the Persian glosses handed down in MS B. Variant readings that were
found in those other manuscripts were added into the margins of MS B.

---

39 N. Peters, *Das Buch Jesus Sirach oder Ecclesiasticus* (EHAT 25) Münster
    1913, 256: 'Schreibfehler'.
40 'Les scribes ne copiaient pas toujours les manuscits en jetant les regards sur le
    manuscrit modèle, mais parfois s'en fiaient à la dictée'; Lévi, *L'Ecclésiastique*
    I, xii.
41 In the discussion following the presentation of this paper, Mr Joseph E. Jensen
    wondered if the examples of consonantal interchange, as offered by me, could
    be caused by dyslexia. It is my conviction that the phenomenon described by
    me is in the hearing, not in the reading of texts!

3. Traces of dictation in other Ben Sira manuscripts

Since I am convinced 'phonetic errors' would not be confined to MS B, some other Hebrew Ben Sira texts will now be tested on this hypothesis.

As within the context of this contribution, interdependences between Hebrew Ben Sira manuscripts is not the issue in question, there is no need to re-open here the scholarly debate whether MS A or MS C has handed down the older textual form of the Book of Ben Sira.[42]

3.1 Sir 3,14b

MS A : ותמור חטאת היא תנתע
Am. : תנטע

On Sir 3,14b, the text of MS C can even be left out of consideration, as it is an instance of 'dictation error' within MS A itself.[43]

Though a verbal form of נתע does occur in the Hebrew Bible, albeit only once,[44] within the context of Sir 3,14, its meaning ('to knock out') makes no sense at all. The marginal reading תנטע, on the contrary, gives good sense: 'instead of sin, it (i.e. צדקה) will be planted'. The only reasonable explanation for the change of consonants between the text of MS A (ת) and the marginal reading of MS A (ט) is a 'dictation error', most probably caused by the very rare niph'al form of נטע, which is found only once in the Hebrew Bible.[45] That there must have been something special in Sir 3,14b seems to be confirmed by the Hebrew text of Sir 3,9b, as the copyist had no problems there with the noun נטע ('planting') !

---

42 Rüger, *Text und Textform*, 27-28 is favouring MS C, whereas Schrader, *Leiden und Gerechtigkeit*, 39-57 is adducing evidence that it must be exactely the other way round: in almost every case should MS A be considered the older textual form.

43 Relating to Sir 3,14 Rüger's hypothesis is followed by R. Bohlen, *Die Ehrung der Eltern bei Ben Sira. Studien zur Motivation und Interpretation eines familienethischen Grundwertes in frühhellenistischer Zeit* (TTS 51) Trier 1991, 58-59.

44 Job 4,10 (נִתָּעוּ).

45 Isa 40,24 (נִטָּעוּ); its pronounciation hardly differs from נִתָּעוּ in Job 4,10!

3.2 Sir 5,13b

MS A : ולשון אדם מפלתו

MS C : ולשון אדם מפליטו

In Sir 5,13b there is also an interchange of *taw* and *thet*. The usual explanation for מפליטו in MS C is that this reading should be considered a 'writing error' ('Verschreibung').[46] On account of the Greek (πτῶσις αὐτῷ) and the Syriac (ܘܬ ܡܦܠܬܗ), the reading מפלתו of MS A is to to considered the best textual form. However as the verbal form מפליטו of MS C makes sense ('bringing him to safety'), albeit opposite to the meaning of מפלתו ('his fall') of MS A, it can hardly be attributed to just a 'writing error'. It would be more appropriate to characterize this feature as a *dictation error*. For how else could be explained that a copyist changed a *taw* into both a *yod* and a *thet* at the same time?

A similar case of such a *taw* / *thet* interchange is found in 11QPs^a, where the verbal form תמוט of Ps 93,1 has been handed down with a *thet* as the opening consonant (טמוט).[47]

4. The provenance of the Ben Sira manuscripts

4.1 Sir 5,13a

MS A : כבוד וקלון ביוד בוטא

MS C : כבוד וקלון ביד בוטה

Finally, an interesting case is offered by the first half of Sir 5,13. The qualification 'interesting' does not so much refer to the curious shape of ביוד[48] which, on account of MS C (ביד) and Syriac (ܒܝܕ), has to be

---

46   Rüger, *Text und Textform*, 40. Schrader, *Leiden und Gerechtigkeit*, 49: 'ist offenbar ... verschrieben worden'.

47   J.A. Sanders, *The Psalms Scroll of Qumran Cave 11 (11QPs^a)*, DJD IV, Oxford 1965, 43.

48   This colon has partially been misquoted (ביד instead of ביוד) in D.J.A. Clines (ed.), *The Dictionary of Classical Hebrew*, Vol. II, Sheffield 1995, 139

considered a writing error[49] (or even a mishearing!). Much more significant might be the morphological distinction between בוטא (MS A) and בוטה (MS C).[50] If these words should be read as a participle masculine singular of the *Qal*, as the Syriac translator did by rendering a participle masculine singular of the *Pe'al* (ܡܢ ܡܠܠ ܕܡܡܠܠ), then MS C has exactly the same verbal form as in Prov 12,18 (יש בוטה).[51] Perhaps Sir 5,13 has been composed as a kind of allusion to Prov 12,18, the more so as both lines open their second colon with לשון.[52] However the Greek text of Sir 5,13a has rendered בוטא / בוטה as a *noun* (ἐν λαλιᾷ), a choice that has good backing, considering the word-pair חכם בוטה in Sir 9,17b-18a, where it is again combined with לשון.[53]

A question relating to Sir 5,13a still remains, namely the *aleph - he* interchange between MS A and C. Intriguingly enough, the same *aleph - he* interchange shows up in Prov 12,18a, where the *Occidentales* (or Western Masoretes) have transmitted the reading בּוֹטֶה (with *he*), whereas the *Orientales* (or Eastern Masoretes) handed down the reading בּוֹטֵא (with *aleph*).

I hope that this example from Sir 5,13a can serve as a pointer in efforts to trace the provenance of the Hebrew Ben Sira manuscripts. As we all know, this aspect of Ben Sira research has been almost completely neglected. Perhaps more thorough *synoptic* research of all extant Hebrew Ben Sira manuscripts can bring out further data, which will soon enable Ben Sira scholars to draw more specific conclusions about the provenance of the Mediaeval Hebrew Ben Sira manuscripts from the Cairo genizah.

---

49 See F. Delitzsch, *Die Lese- und Schreibfehler im Alten Testament.* Leipzig/Berlin 1920, 103.

50 In his analysis of Sir 5,13 (A - C), Schrader is victim of a *taw* and *thet* interchange himself. Instead of בוטה (MS C) and בוטא (MS A) he he has written בותה and בותא! Schrader, *Leiden und Gerechtigkeit*, 49.

51 Prov 12,18 and Sir 5,13 are the only two known verbal forms of the *Qal* of this verb.

52 Only Eberharter has listed a reference to Scripture in relation to Sir 5,13b; however it is Prov 18,21, and not 12,18! A. Eberharter, *Der Kanon des Alten Testaments zur Zeit des Ben Sira* (ATAbh III/3) Münster 1911, 27.

53 Gr σοφὸς ἐν λόγῳ. Smend, *Die Weisheit*, 51 therefore suggests that the Hebrew word in Sir 5,13a be vocalized *bôt'* or *bête'*.

Fear of the Lord as Wisdom: Ben Sira 1,11-30

By Alexander A. Di Lella O.F.M., Washington

Introduction

Ben Sira has much to say about fear of the Lord as well as wisdom. Some scholars have argued that fear of the Lord is the fundamental theme of Ben Sira.[1] Indeed, the expressions 'fear of the Lord [or God]' and 'to fear the Lord' or their equivalent appear some 55 to 60 times in the Wisdom of Ben Sira.[2] Others have insisted that wisdom is the primary theme.[3] In fact, the words σοφία, σοφός, and various forms of the root σοφίζειν occur more than 90 times in the grandson's translation.[4] Thus, arguments exist for each opinion.

---

1   E.g., J. Haspecker, (*Gottesfurcht bei Jesus Sirach. Ihre religiöse Struktur und ihre literarische und doktrinäre Bedeutung* [AnBib 30; Rome 1976] 87-105 defends the thesis that fear of the Lord is "the total theme" (*Gesamtthema*) of the book.

2   So Haspecker, *Gottesfurcht*, 82.

3   See, eg., G.von Rad, *Wisdom in Israel* (tr. J.D. Martin; Nashville 1972) 242; J. Marböck, *Weisheit im Wandel. Untersuchungen zur Weisheitstheologie bei Ben Sira* (BBB 37; Bonn 1971).

4   Throughout this article I cite the chapter- and verse-numbers in Ben Sira as given in their proper order in J. Ziegler, *Sapientia Iesu Filii Sirach* (Septuaginta 12/2; Göttingen 1966), which I used for the Greek textual criticism of the poem. For the Syriac, I used the facsimile of A.M. Ceriani, ed., *Translatio Syra Pescitto Veteris Testamenti ex codice Ambrosiano sec. fere VI photolithographice edita* (2 vols; Milan 1876-1883); P.A. de Lagarde, *Libri Veteris Testamenti aporyphi Syriace* (Leipzig-London 1861), an important diplomatic edition of a 6th-century codex, British Library 12142; and *Biblia Sacra iuxta Latinam vulgatam versionem, 12: Sapientia Salomonis, Liber Hiesu Filii Sirach* (Rome 1964), and W. Thiele, ed., *Vetus Latina: Die Reste der altlateinischen Bibel nach Petrus Sabatier neu gesammelt und in Verbindung mit der Heidelberger Akademie der Wissenschaften hg. v. der Erzabtei Beuron*

Many years ago R. Smend suggested a different approach when he wrote, "Subjectively, wisdom is fear of God; objectively, it is the law book of Moses (chap. 24)".[5] Going beyond this suggestion, I would argue that Ben Sira's fundamental thesis is the following: Practical wisdom (the discipline and perfection of the will that enables one to make right moral choices), which Ben Sira identifies with the Law in chap. 24, and theoretical wisdom (the education and perfection of the intellect that result from personal study as well as experience)[6], which also has its origin from the Lord (1,1.9-10.14.26), become possible only when one fears the Lord by keeping the commandments, refraining from sin, loving the Lord, and fulfilling all the other Deuteronomic requirements about which I will have more to say in the commentary. In the elegantly crafted poem, 1,11-30, appearing right after the introductory poem (1,1-4.6.8-10ab)[7], Ben Sira explains this thesis at length, for he will come back to it time and time again throughout his book.

Text and Structure of 1,11-30

The Hebrew original of this poem, unfortunately, is not extant. Hence, I have used and analyzed the text of the grandson's Greek and consulted

---

(Band 11/2: *Sirach[Ecclesiasticus]*, fasc. 3: Prologue and 1,1-3,31; Freiburg 1989). For the concordance work of the MT, I used the elegant and powerful Macintosh computer program called acCordance/GRAMCORD MT Research Module (Version 1.1.1; Vancouver, WA 1994); and for the LXX (Rahlfs' text forms the data base, which gives GI but not GII of Sirach) I used acCordance/GRAMCORD Septuagint Research Module (Version 1.1.1; Vancouver, WA 1995). For the Hebrew of Ben Sira, I consulted D. Barthélemy - O. Rickenbacher, eds., *Konkordanz zum hebräischen Sirach mit syrisch hebräischem Index* (Göttingen 1973). All translations of Ben Sira and other biblical texts are my own.

5   R. Smend, *Die Weisheit des Jesus Sirach erklärt* (Berlin 1906) xxiii. This work is still among the best commentaries dealing with the text-critical questions of Ben Sira's book.

6   A.A. Di Lella, "The Meaning of Wisdom in Ben Sira", *In Search of Wisdom: Essays in Memory of John G. Gammie* (ed. L.G. Perdue et al.); Louisville 1993) 135-145

7   The GII additions (vv. 5.7.10cd) are glosses, and not original material.

as well the Syriac and Latin versions. I have made no attempt at retro-version into Hebrew, for that can be a rather subjective enterprise. The poem is a non-alphabetic acrostic of 22 lines or bicola, divided into two equal parts, each of 11 bicola. It is probably significant that each part has exactly the same number of words, 121, for a total of 242 words. It is possible that the grandson saw an equal number of words in each part of the Hebrew text before him, in which case he copied his grandfa-ther's technique. In Part A there are 3 + 2 + 2 + 2 + 2 bicola, and in Part B, 3 + 3 + 3 + 2 bicola. Thus the poem has nine strophes the structure of which I will explain below. Interestingly, Part B begins with οὐ, לא in Ben Sira's original, the beginning of the second half of the Hebrew alphabet.

The Greek Text

Part A

Strophe I

1,11 φόβος κυρίου δόξα καὶ καύχημα
    καὶ εὐφροσύνη καί στέφανος ἀγαλλιάματος.
1,12 φόβος κυρίου τέρψει καρδίαν
    καὶ δώσει εὐφροσύνην καὶ χαρὰν καὶ μακροημέρευσιν[8].
1,13 τῷ φοβουμένῳ τὸν κύριον εὖ ἔσται ἐπ' ἐσχάτων,
    καὶ ἐν ἡμέρᾳ τελευτῆς αὐτοῦ εὐλογηθήσεται[9].

---

8   For v. 12b the *O* MSS read: εὐφροσύνην δὲ καὶ χαράν καὶ μακροημέρευσιν
    περιποιεῖ, "for it brings about gladness and joy and length of days". Instead of
    'length of days', Syr reads ܚܝܐ ܕܠܥܠܡ, 'eternal life', the exact phrase found in
    the Peshitta of, e.g., Matt 19,16. 29; 25,46; such a concept Ben Sira did not
    share. GII MSS *O* (sub * Syh) 493-672-743 679 add 12cd: φόβος κυρίου
    δόσις παρὰ κυρίου, καὶ γὰρ ἐπ' ἀγαπήσεως τρίβους καθίστησιν, "The fear
    of the Lord is a gift from the Lord, for it puts [people] on paths of love". This
    addition is a gloss; see 1:9-10; Wis 8:21.
9   MSS B *l b* as well as Malachias Monachus read: εὑρήσει χάριν, "will find
    grace".

Strophe II

1,14 ἀρχὴ σοφίας φοβεῖσθαι τὸν κύριον,
     καὶ μετὰ πιστῶν ἐν μήτρᾳ συνεκτίσθη αὐτοῖς.
1,15 μετὰ ἀνθρώπων θεμέλιον αἰῶνος ἐνόσσευσεν[10]
     καὶ μετὰ τοῦ σπέρματος αὐτῶν ἐμπιστευθήσεται.

Strophe III

1,16 πλησμονὴ σοφίας φοβεῖσθαι τὸν κύριον
     καὶ μεθύσκει αὐτοὺς ἀπὸ τῶν καρπῶν αὐτῆς·
1,17 πάντα τὸν οἶκον αὐτῶν[11] ἐμπλήσει ἐπιθυμημάτων
     καὶ τὰ ἀποδοχεῖα ἀπὸ τῶν γενημάτων αὐτῆς.

Strophe IV

1,18 στέφανος σοφίας φόβος κυρίου
     ἀναθάλλων εἰρήνην καὶ ὑγίειαν ἰάσεως[12].
1,19 ἐπιστήμην καὶ γνῶσιν συνέσεως ἐξώμβρησεν
     καὶ δόξαν κρατούντων αὐτῆς ἀνύψωσεν.[13]

Strophe V

1,20 ῥίζα σοφίας φοβεῖσθαι τὸν κύριον,
     καὶ οἱ κλάδοι αὐτῆς μακροημέρευσις.[14]
1,21·φόβος κυρίου ἀπωθεῖται ἁμαρτήματα,
     παραμένων δὲ ἀποστρέψει πᾶσαν ὀργήν.[15]

---

10 The text of this colon is difficult, as commentators have noted; but it is trans-
    latable and consistent with the imagery of the strophe. Syr reads: "She is with
    the man of truth and she has been established from the ages".
11 The reading of MSS *O* L-694 and Armenian, preferred by Rahlfs and Ziegler,
    which I also have adopted, for it conforms better to the conceptual imagery.
    The other MSS and Versions read αὐτῆς.
12 Some GII MSS add v. 18cd: ἀμφότερα δὲ ἐστιν δῶρα θεοῦ εἰς εἰρηνην,
    πλατύνει δὲ καύχησις τοῖς ἀγαπῶσιν αὐτόν, "Indeed both are gifts of God
    for eace, and exultation opens up for those who love him".This is another
    gloss; see 1,9-10 and the gloss in v. 12cd.
13 Omit v. 19a = 1,9b: so *O* 248-694 785 Lat^MSS Sahidic.
14 Syr reads, "Her roots are eternal life [see Syr of 1,12b above], and her
    branches length of days [cf. G of 1,12b]. Blessed is the one who meditates on
    her, for she is better for him than all treasures". In place of 1,21-27, Syr has 12
    bicola that are completely different from G.

Part B

Strophe VI

1,22 οὐ δυνήσεται θυμὸς ἄδικος[16] δικαιωθῆναι·
ἡ γὰρ ῥοπὴ τοῦ θυμοῦ αὐτοῦ πτῶσις αὐτῷ.
1,23 ἕως καιροῦ ἀνθέξεται μακρόθυμος
καὶ ὕστερον αὐτῷ ἀναδώσει εὐφροσύνη·[17]
1,24 ἕως καιροῦ κρύψει τοὺς λόγους αὐτοῦ,
καὶ χείλη πολλῶν[18] ἐκδιηγήσεται σύνεσιν αὐτοῦ.

Strophe VII

1,25 ἐν θησαυροῖς σοφίας παραβολαὶ[19] ἐπιστήμης,
βδέλυγμα δὲ ἁμαρτωλῷ θεοσέβεια.
1,26 ἐπιθυμήσας σοφίαν διατήρησον ἐντολάς,
καὶ κύριος χορηγήσει σοι αὐτήν.
1,27 σοφία γὰρ καὶ παιδεία φόβος κυρίου,
καί ἡ εὐδοκία αὐτοῦ πίστις καὶ πραΰτης.

Strophe VIII

1,28 μὴ[20] ἀπειθήσῃς φόβῳ κυρίου
καὶ μὴ προσέλθῃς αὐτῷ ἐν καρδίᾳ δισσῇ
1,29 μὴ ὑποκριθῇς ἐνώπιον[21] ἀνθρώπων
καὶ ἐν τοῖς χείλεσίν σου πρόσεχε.
1,30 μὴ ἐξύψου σεαυτόν, ἵνα μὴ πέσῃς
καὶ ἐπαγάγῃς τῇ ψυχῇ σου ἀτιμίαν.

---

15 This verse, found only in GII MSS O (sub * Syh) L´ -672-694-743 768, is an essential part of the structure of strophe V that now matches the pattern of strophes II-IV. Lat [v. 27] has v. 21a only.

16 The L' MSS read θυμώδης ἀνήρ, and O ἀνὴρ θυμώδης, "a wrathful man".

17   Many good MSS read εὐφροσύνην, taking ἀναδώσει as a transitive verb with presumably the Lord as the implied subject; but this verb may also be intransitive, as I have translated it.

18 MSS B V and two Greek fathers read πιστῶν, "of the faithful". One Lat MS reads iustorum.

19 The variant παραβολή, a reading that Ziegler prefers, is equally well attested.

20 Syr begins the verse with "My son".

21 So O Lat Coptic Armenian; cf. Syr.

Strophe IX

καὶ ἀποκαλύψει κύριος τὰ κρυπτά σου
καὶ ἐν μέσῳ συναγωγῆς καταβαλεῖ σε,
ὅτι²² προσῆλθες φόβῳ κυρίου
καὶ ἡ καρδία σου πλήρης δόλου.

*Translation*²³

Part A

Strophe I

1,11 The fear of the Lord is glory and exultation
       and gladness and a crown of rejoicing.
1,12 The fear of the Lord delights the heart,
       and gives gladness and joy and length of days.
1,13 For the one who fears the Lord it will be well at the end;
       on the day of his death he will be blessed.

Strophe II

1,14 The beginning of wisdom is to fear the Lord;
       indeed with the faithful she is created in the womb.
1,15 Among human beings she built a lasting foundation,
       and among their descendants she will abide faithfully.

Strophe III

1,16 The fullness of wisdom is to fear the Lord;
       indeed she intoxicates them with her fruits;
1,17 she fills their whole house with desirable things,
       and their storehouses with her produce.

Strophe IV

1,18 The crown of wisdom is the fear of the Lord,
       making peace and perfect health to flourish.
1,19 Knowledge and discerning comprehension she rained down,
       and the glory of those who held her fast she heightened.

---

22   Omit οὐ: so Lat.
23   Note: In my translation I have tried to follow the Greek word order and to ren-
     der whenever possible in idiomatic English (the few) repeated expressions in
     the same way.

Strophe V

1,20 The root of wisdom is to fear the Lord,
        and her branches are length of days.
1,21 The fear of the Lord drives away sins,
        and where it abides it will turn aside all wrath.

Part B

Strophe VI

1,22 Unjust anger cannot be justified,
        for the weight of one's anger is one's downfall.
1,23 Until the right moment the patient person will stay calm,
        and afterwards gladness wilburst forth for him.
1,24 Until the right moment he will hold back his words;
        then the lips of many will tell of his good sense.

Strophe VII

1,25 In the treasuries of wisdom are the models of learning,
        but godliness is an abomination to the sinner.
1,26 If you desire wisdom, keep the commandments;
        then the Lord will lavish her upon you.
1,27 For the fear of the Lord is wisdom and discipline,
        faithfulness and humility are his delight.

Strophe VIII

1,28 Do not disobey the fear of the Lord;
        nor approach him with a double heart.
1,29 Do not be a hypocrite before other people,
        and over your lips keep watch.
1,30 Do not exalt yourself lest you fall
        and bring dishonor upon yourself.

Strophe IX

        Then the Lord will reveal your secrets,
        and in the midst of the assembly he will cast you down,
        Because you approached the fear of the Lord,
        but your heart was full of deceit.

As regards the structure I have proposed above, Part A is clearly a dis-
crete unit that contains the expression 'the fear of the Lord', or equivalent, eight times, at least once in each strophe. In strophe I (1,11-13)
'the fear of the Lord' occurs at the beginning of each bicolon, signaling
unity of subject matter. Strophes II to V have an identical rhetorical
pattern that establishes the limits of each, the first two words of the
opening cola (1,14a.16a.18a.20a) form an *a:b::b':a'* pattern:
ἀρχὴ σοφίας : πλησμονὴ σοφίας :: στέφανος σοφίας : ῥίζα σοφίας.

The subject matter of Part B develops the truths and aphorisms
enunciated in Part A. The noun θυμός in 1,22a, the opening colon of
strophe VI, is a semantic *mot crochet* with ὀργήν in the final colon of
strophe V (1,21b), thus connecting the two parts. In 1,22 Ben Sira articulates a principle regarding unjust anger; the other two bicola (1,23-
24), both of which begin with the same expression ἕως καιροῦ, explain
the benefits of patient behavior. The unifying element of strophe VII is
the noun σοφία appearing in each bicolon (1,25a.26a.27a). The syntax
of 1,28-30ab, μή plus a 2d person singular volitive verb, demonstrates
the unity of strophe VIII. In strophe IX, a concluding couplet warning
against insincerity, the phrase 'the fear of the Lord' in 1,30e, in the final bicolon, forms an inclusio with the same expression in 1,11a, in the
opening bicolon of strophe I.

Commentary and Intertextual Analysis

Part A

Strophe I (1,11-13)

The opening words of each bicolon mention the fear of the Lord
(1,11a.12a.13a) and state the theme of the poem. Fear of the Lord forms
the basis of biblical faith; see, e.g., Exod 14,31; Deut 6,2; 10,12; 17,19;
31,12.13; Josh 24,14; 1 Sam 12,14; Prov 14,2; Ps 66,11; 112,1; 128,1.
The greatest blessings result from the fear of the Lord: glory, exultation, gladness, a crown of rejoicing, delight for the heart, joy, and
length of days (1,11-12) — everything the faithful Jew of that day
could ever hope for. Best of all, those who fear the Lord will have a

happy end and will be blessed on the day of their death (1,13), a thought Ben Sira develops further in 11,22-28. Thus, the opening strophe provides pragmatic motivation to practice the fear of the Lord. Such advice was timely for the Jews of that day who lived in a society that was permeated with Hellenism and its alluring culture, not to mention its economic advantages.[24] As C. Spicq correctly observes, Ben Sira in 1,11-13 emphasizes two essential aspects of Judaism: (1) the close connection of moral conduct and religion, i.e., virtue is the fruit of fear of the Lord; and (2) the utilitarian idea of this moral conduct, i.e., virtue brings its own immediate reward. Thus, to acquire wisdom is to one's advantage whereas sinners are fools who do not understand their own interests.[25] See 3,14-16.25-31; 16,14; 17,22-23.

Nowhere else either in the earlier or later parts of the OT or in the rest of Ben Sira do we find in so few verses such a concatenation of blessings flowing from the fear of the Lord. To be sure, each of these blessings echoes a passage of the earlier biblical books. Ben Sira as well as his grandson read in Prov 22,4, e.g.: "The reward for humility and fear of Yahweh is *riches and honor and life* [πλοῦτος καὶ δόξα καὶ ζωή in the LXX]". Also in Sir 9,16; 10,22; and 25,6 the grandson has καύχημα connected with φόβος κυρίου; but nowhere else in the LXX do these words occur in the same verse. In the LXX the expressions φόβος κυρίου and εὐφροσύνη occur together only in Sir 1,11-12. The expression στέφανος ἀγαλλιάματος recurs in 6,31 and 15,6, but not even once in rest of the LXX. The nouns εὐφροσύνη and ἀγαλλιάματος occur as a stereotyped pair also in LXX Isa 16,10; 22,13; 35,10; 51,3.11; 60,15; 65,18 [*bis*]. The noun μακροημέρευσις of 1,12b is repeated in strophe V (1,20b); the noun recurs only one more time in the LXX, in Sir 30,22, where it follows εὐφροσύνη and ἀγαλλιάματος: εὐφροσύνη καρδίας ζωὴ ἀνθρώπου καὶ ἀγαλλίαμα ἀνδρὸς μακροημέρευσις, "Gladness of heart is life itself for a person,/ and rejoicing is length of days for a person". The notion of 'length of days', or long life, in recompense for fearing the Lord and keeping the com-

---

24   See P.W. Skehan and A.A. Di Lella, *The Wisdom of Ben Sira* (AB 39; New York 1987) 16.

25   C. Spicq, "Ecclésiastique", in SB 6 (ed. L. Pirot and A. Clamer; Paris 1951) 565.

mandments derives from Deut 5,33; 6,2; 11,9; and 32,47 where the
LXX employs not the noun but the related verb μακροημερεύειν. [26]

A good *end* and *blessing* on the day of death are in store for *the one
who fears the Lord* (1,13); no other single text of the OT makes those
promises in quite that way. The promise of a happy future occurs again
in 2,3: κολλήθητι αὐτῷ καὶ μὴ ἀποστῇς, ἵνα αὐξηθῇς ἐπ᾽ ἐσχάτων
σου, "Cling to him [the Lord] and do not fall away, so that you may increase at your latter end". Ben Sira learned, of course, about the blessings listed in 1,11-12 as well as others from the Deuteronomic theology
that permeates his teachings and aphorisms. He echoes repeatedly what
I call the great Deuteronomic equation found in such texts as Deut 4,5-
6; 6,1-5.24; 8,6; 10,12.20; 13,5; 17,19; 31,12-13: to fear the Lord = to
love the Lord = to serve the Lord = to walk in his ways = to keep the
commandments/Law = to worship the Lord = to be wise. Elements of
this equation can be found in such passages as Sir 2,7-10.15-17; 4,11-
16; 15,1.13; 19,20; 21,11; 23,27; 25,6.10-11; 27,3; 32,14.16; 33,1;
34,14-18; 40,26-27. Among the rewards of fidelity are earthly proper-
ity, a long life, and a good name memorialized by virtuous children; see
Deut 28,1-14; Sir 30,4-5; 41,11-13. Failure to observe the Deuteronomic demands will result in personal and national disaster; see Deut
28,58-68; Sir 41,7-9.

Strophe II (1,14-15)

Strophes II to V give further details about the fear of the Lord. "The
beginning of wisdom is to fear the Lord" (1,14a) summarizes Ben
Sira's thesis; he quotes these words from Ps 111,10 and Prov 1,7; 9,10
the LXX of which has in each case ἀρχὴ σοφίας φόβος κυρίου, which
the grandson has adapted slightly.[27] The noun ἀρχή (MT ראש or תחלה,
as in Prov 9,10) has three meanings: (1) point of departure, as in 15,14;
(2) the most important part of something, as in 29,21; 39,26; and (3) the
best part or essence of something, as in 11,3. In 1,14a ἀρχή has all

---

26 This verb occurs only two other times in the LXX: Judg 2,7 and Sir 3,6.
27 This is one of the rare cases where Ben Sira quotes Scripture (virtually) verba-
tim; he of course constantly refers to other parts of the OT but mostly by way
of allusion.

three meanings.[28] The truth of this thesis dominates Ben Sira's thought; there simply can be no authentic theoretical or practical wisdom without the fear of the Lord. The idea that wisdom for the faithful was created *in the womb* (1,14b) is an allusion to Jer 1,5. In fact, Ben Sira writes of Jeremiah, "For they had mistreated him,/ who even *in the womb* had been consecrated a prophet,/ to pluck up and ruin and destroy,/ and likewise to build and to plant" (49,7). Ben Sira seems to say that like life itself wisdom is an infused gift granted to the faithful in the womb.[29]

The text of 1,15a is difficult, as noted above. But I believe the meaning is clear, wisdom has laid [lit., has nested] a lasting foundation among human beings. Ben Sira probably derived the content of 1,15 from Prov 8,30-31: "Then I [personified Wisdom] was beside him as a master worker,/ and I was his delight day by day,/ Rejoicing before him always,/ rejoicing on the surface of his earth;/ and delighting in human beings". This passage seems to be the basis also of the Syriac, "She [wisdom] is with the holy person [lit., man of holiness], and she was formed from the ages, and with their seed her mercy [or kindness] has been established".

In 4,16 Ben Sira expresses similar ideas: "If he remains faithful, he will inherit her [Wisdom];/ and his descendants will also obtain her". What Ben Sira alludes to briefly in 1,15 he gives fullest expression to in 24,7-9:

> Among all these I [Wisdom] sought a resting place;
> in whose inheritance should I dwell?
> Then the Creator of all gave me a command,
> and my Creator chose the place for my tent.
> And he said, "In Jacob make your encampment,
> and in Israel receive your inheritance".
> Before the ages, in the beginning, he created me,
> and for all the ages I shall not cease to be.

---

28   Skehan and Di Lella, *Wisdom of Ben Sira*, 144.
29   See Spicq, "Ecclésiastique", 566.

Strophe III (1,16-17)

The imagery of 1,16-17 has as its starting point the noun πλησμονή, 'fullness'. Ben Sira insists in 1,16a that there can be no fuller or more complete wisdom, both theoretical and practical, than that which comes from fear of the Lord. Yet as desirable as wisdom may be, the fear of the Lord has pride of place: "How great is the one who finds wisdom!/ But none is superior to the one who fears the Lord./ The fear of the Lord surpasses everything;/ to whom can we compare the one who holds it fast"? (25,10-11).

In 1,16b-17 wisdom is now personified. She gives so lavishly of her fruits (see Prov 8,19; 11,30; Jas 3,17) that she intoxicates (μεθύσκει) those who fear the Lord (1,16b). In 32,13 Ben Sira says that God is the one who intoxicates: καὶ ἐπὶ τούτοις εὐλόγησον τὸν ποιήσαντά σε καὶ μεθύσκοντά σε ἀπὸ τῶν ἀγαθῶν αὐτοῦ, "But above these things bless the One who made you/ and who intoxicates you with his good things".

Then the images change, Wisdom "fills *their* [αὐτῶν, O L-694] whole house with desirable things,/ and their storehouses with her produce" (1,17). I accept this minority reading because it is more in keeping with the thrust of the strophe. Since in 1,16b Wisdom intoxicates *them* (i.e., those who fear the Lord), it seems more consistent that in 1,17a she should fill *their* whole house, and not her own house, and *their* storehouses, and not her own storehouses. As noted above, most of the Greek MSS and versions read αὐτῆς instead, "fills *her* whole house", a reading I reject, as do Rahlfs and Ziegler. This reading most likely came about because an early scribe was thinking of Prov 9,1-6, which speaks of Wisdom's house and her food and drink.

Strophe IV (1,18-19)

The image of 'crown' (1,18a), an adornment for the head, further specifies the fullness of wisdom that is the fear of the Lord. The wisdom meant here is again primarily practical wisdom. The phrase στέφανος σοφίας occurs nowhere else in the LXX; here it harks back to the expression στέφανος ἀγαλλιάματος of 1,11b. Presumably, wisdom's crown is made of leaves (see 1 Cor 9,25). The plant imagery continues in 1,18b with the verb ἀναθάλλειν, "to shoot up, sprout afresh, make flourish", the fear of the Lord makes peace (εἰρήνη) and perfect health (ὑγίειαν ἰάσεως [lit., health of healing]) flourish. The nouns εἰρήνη and ὑγίεια appear together only one other time in the LXX, Isa 9,5. The phrase ὑγίειαν ἰάσεως is peculiar, occurring nowhere else in the LXX. The *O* MSS make some attempt at improving the text by reading: ἀναθάλλει δὲ ἐν αὐτοῖς κύριος εἰρήνην μεστήν, "The Lord makes flourish in them full peace". Syriac also differs, "and it [fear of the Lord] increases peace and life and healing". Whatever the case, the meaning of 1,18b is clear: fear of the Lord brings with it 'peace' (i.e., well-being, prosperity, proper horizontal and vertical relationships, safety, tranquility) and 'health', an essential ingredient of a good life; see 34,17-20 and Prov 3,7-8.

Continuing with the agricultural imagery, 1,19a now speaks of Wisdom raining [or showering] down "knowledge and discerning comprehension [lit., comprehension of discernment]", i.e., theoretical wisdom. Because of such knowledge-laden rain Wisdom raises up "the glory of those who hold her fast". The message is unmistakable: the possession of theoretical wisdom, which also comes from fear of the Lord, is indeed a person's true glory.

Strophe V (1,20-21)

Agricultural imagery continues in 1,20. The phrase ῥίζα σοφίας recurs in 1,6, the only other time in the LXX: ῥίζα σοφίας τίνι ἀπεκαλύφθη; καὶ τὰ πανουργεύματα αὐτῆς τίς ἔγνω; "The root of wisdom, to whom has it been revealed? And her subtleties, who has known them"? Ben Sira answers his own questions in 1,8-9: Only One is wise, awe-inspiring and seated on his throne —the Lord, who created wisdom and saw her and apportioned her out and pours her out on all his works. The nouns ἀρχή (1,14a) and ῥίζα (1,20a) are in synonymous parallelism.

The use of ῥίζα recalls the noun θεμέλιον, 'foundation', in 1,15a. In fact, the expression 'root of the mountains' in Job 28,9 and Jdt 6,13; 7,12 appears with virtually the same meaning as 'foundations of the mountains', or 'of the earth' in 2 Sam 22,16; LXX Pss 17,16; 81,5; Prov 8,29; Sir 10,16; 16,19; Isa 44,23. But ῥίζα in 1,20a is a tree image[30] as is obvious from the noun κλάδοι, wisdom's 'branches', which are μακροημέρευσις, 'length of days' (1,20b), the same word found in 1,12b, thus forming an inclusio between the first and last strophe of Part A. The repetition of μακροημέρευσις, a noun that recurs only once more in the LXX (Sir 30,22), emphasizes the importance of this concept in Ben Sira's moral teaching. This point becomes even more forceful in Syriac that renders the verse: "Her [wisdom's] branches are eternal life, and her flowers length of days".

The fear of the Lord performs another vital function in the life of the believer, it drives away sins (1,21a). And where it abides (παραμένων, present participle, denoting continual action), it "will turn aside all wrath" (1,21b), presumably God's wrath because one has avoided sin.

Part B

Strophe VI (1,22-24)

After detailing the many blessings of wisdom as fear of the Lord, Ben Sira now gives his observations and warnings about how to live out the fear of the Lord. As noted above, the noun θυμός in the opening colon of Part B forms a semantic *mot crochet* with ὀργή in the final colon of Part A. Anger is a topic of grave concern to Ben Sira and the other sages of Israel; see, for example, Sir 27,30; 28,3-11; Prov 10,18; 12,16; 14,29; 15,1.18; 16,32; 20,3; 29,11. The nouns ὀργή (found 21 times in the grandson's Greek) and θυμός (19 times) occur together in a single verse 108 times in the LXX ; in Sirach, these nouns appear in a single verse seven times, 5,6; 10,18; 28,10; 36,8 (36,6 in Rahlfs' edition); 45,18.19; 48,10. The phrase θυμός ἄδικος, however, occurs only here in the LXX. A similar expression appears in the pseudepigraphical Psalms of Solomon 15,4: ὁ ποιῶν ταῦτα οὐ σαλευθήσεται εἰς τὸν αἰῶνα ἀπὸ κακοῦ φλὸξ πυρὸς καὶ ὀργὴ ἀδίκων οὐχ ἄψεται αὐτοῦ, "The one who does these things will never be shaken by evil; the flame of fire and *the anger of the unjust* will not touch him".

---

30   The imagery of wisdom as a tree is more fully developed in 24,13-14.16-17.19-21.

The imagery in 1,22b is graphic: ἡ ῥοπὴ τοῦ θυμοῦ αὐτοῦ, "the weight of one's anger". This phrase is a *hapax legomenon* in the LXX. The noun ῥοπή is itself rare[31], found only six other times in the LXX. The use of ῥοπή, however, lends force to the point being made: anger is so heavy it leads to a person's 'downfall', πτῶσις.

The sayings of 1,23-24 suggest the remedy for unjust anger. The patient person keeps his composure "until the right moment" (1,23a), i.e., the time when he can react calmly to what occasioned the anger in the first place. The result of such self-control is the bursting forth of εὐ-'φροσύνη, 'gladness' (1,23b), one of the blessings of the fear of the Lord (1,11-12). The clear implication is that the opposite of εὐφροσύνη, viz., sadness, comes from unjust anger in the impatient person. The thought of the verse derives from Prov 15,18, which reads in the LXX, ἀνὴρ θυμώδης[32] παρασκευάζει μάχας . . . μακρόθυμος ἀνὴρ κατασβέσει κρίσεις, "The wrathful man makes battles . . . but the patient man will quench judgments".

The patient person will also remain silent, keeping his comments to himself "until the right moment" (1,24a); he will not speak out of turn, a characteristic of the wise. Ben Sira expands on this thought in 5,11-13:

Be swift to hear,
but slow to give answer.
If you are able, answer your neighbor;
but if not, place your hand over your mouth!
Honor and dishonor through speaking!
And a person's tongue is his downfall[33].

The patient person who controls his anger and speaks only at the right moment will receive the coveted reward of public acclaim for 'his good sense' (1,24b); see 39,9.

---

31 Perhaps that is why Codes S* and Lat read ὀργή, a reading preferred by Smend, *Die Weisheit des Jesus Sirach erklärt*, 15.

32 As noted above, instead of θυμὸς ἄδικος (1,22a) in the best witnesses, MSS O 694 read ἀνὴρ θυμώδης and L' read θυμώδης ἀνήρ, clearly based on LXX Prov 15,18.

33 For a study of this poem, see A.A. Di Lella, "Use and Abuse of the Tongue: Ben Sira 5,9-6,1",'*Jedes Ding hat seine Zeit...* '. *Studien zur israelitischen und altorientalischen Weisheit* (FS D. Michel; ed. A.A. Diesel a.o.) (BZAW 241; Berlin - New York 1996) 33-48.

Strophe VII (1,25-27)

Ben Sira now returns to wisdom, a major theme of the poem. In 1,25-27 he alludes to a major portion of the great Deuteronomic equation I mentioned above, wisdom (1,25a.26a.27a) = fear of the Lord (1,25b.27a) = keeping the commandments (1,26a) = gift of the Lord (1,26b) = discipline (1,27a). The expression ἐν θησαυροῖς σοφίας occurs only this once in the LXX. But in composing 1,25, Ben Sira had in mind Isa 33,6 the LXX of which has the following three italicized nouns that appear in the grandson's Greek: ἐν νόμῳ παραδοθήσονται, ἐν θησαυροῖς ἡ σωτηρία ἡμῶν, ἐκεῖ σοφία καὶ ἐπιστήμη καὶ εὐ-σέβεια πρὸς τὸν κύριον, οὗτοί εἰσιν θησαυροὶ δικαιοσύνης, "In the Law there have been handed over, *into treasuries* our salvation, there *wisdom* and *learning* and fear toward the Lord; these are the treasuries of righteousness". The grandson may even have chosen the noun θεο-σέβεια (instead of his usual φόβος κυρίου) on the basis of the Isaiah passage's use of εὐσέβεια (a noun that occurs only once in Ben Sira, 49,3).

The expression, 'In the treasuries of wisdom', refers primarily, though not exclusively, to theoretical wisdom in which are found 'models of learning' (1,25a). The noun παραβολαί translates of course מְשָׁלִים, the singular of which means, 'saying, proverb', hence, 'an example, illustration'. The context here requires the translation 'models'. Because the sinner finds the fear of the Lord an abomination (1,25b), however, he will never attain wisdom, which is a gift from the Lord (1,1.9-10); see also Prov 1,29-30. The noun θεοσέβεια (a *hapax* in Ben Sira) is very rare in the LXX, recurring only six other times three of which are in 4 Maccabees (7,6.22; 17,19). Θεοσέβεια translates MT יראת אלהים ('the fear of God') in Gen 20,11 and יראת אדני ('fear of the Lord') in Job 28,28.

One must desire and will wisdom in order to attain her; a mere wish will not do. And one can come to wisdom only by keeping the commandments (1,26a). Ben Sira expresses the same thought in 15,15a: "If you choose, you can keep the commandments". Then in 23,27bc, he states: οὐθὲν κρεῖττον φόβου κυρίου καὶ οὐθὲν γλυκύτερον τοῦ προσέχειν ἐντολαῖς κυρίου, "Nothing is better than the fear of the Lord,/ and nothing sweeter than to heed the commandments of the Lord". When you desire wisdom by keeping the commandments, then the Lord "will lavish [χορηγήσει] her upon you" (1,26b). The verb χορηγεῖν recurs also in 1,10b: "The Lord lavished her [wisdom] on those who love him". Ben Sira articulates an important theological truth: though wisdom is indeed a gift of the Lord (1,26b; 1,10b), one must also freely choose to keep the commandments (1,26a).

The grandson's translation of 1,27a is simply a rewording of LXX Prov 15,33a: φόβος κυρίου [some MSS θεοῦ] παιδεία καὶ σοφία. Ben Sira again categorically affirms that the fear of the Lord alone is wisdom, adding that discipline is an essential part of wisdom. Πίστις, 'faith, fidelity, firmness, contancy', in the service of the Lord and πραΰτης, 'humility', in the face of the transcendent Lord are 'his delight' (1,27b). The nouns πίστις and πραΰτης recur together only one other time in the LXX, Sir 45,4 (for which Geniza MS B is extant, אמונה and ענוה, respectively): God chose Moses from all flesh because of his אמונה and ענוה. The noun πίστις will lead into the idea of the next strophe, "Do not disobey [μὴ ἀπειθήσῃς] the fear of the Lord" (1,28a). Disobedience is the ultimate form of infidelity. Humility, πραΰτης, will become the subject of the poem in 3,17-24.

Strophe VIII (1,28-30ab)

In the penultimate strophe Ben Sira warns against infidelity to the fear of the Lord and against a double heart in serving the Lord (1,28). He will hark back to this verse in the concluding bicolon of the poem (1,30ef) where he speaks of "your heart full of deceit". The expression ἀπειθεῖν φόβῳ κυρίου (1,28a) occurs nowhere else in the LXX. The verb ἀπειθεῖν, however, recurs five more times in GI of Ben Sira[34] as well as six times in LXX Deuteronomy and twice in LXX Proverbs, two of his favorite books. In three texts, LXX Deuteronomy has ἠπειθήσατε τῷ ῥήματι κυρίου, or equivalent: 1,26; 9,23; and 32,51. It is probable that Ben Sira (and the grandson) had these passages in mind when composing 1,28. In fact, we read the equivalent expression from Deuteronomy elsewhere in Ben Sira: οἱ φοβούμενοι κύριον οὐκ ἀπειθήσουσιν ῥημάτων αὐτοῦ καὶ οἱ ἀγαπῶντες αὐτὸν συντηρήσουσιν τὰς ὁδοὺς αὐτους, "Those who fear the Lord will not

---

34   Sir 2,15; 16,28; 23,23; 30,12; 41,2.

disobey his words,/ and those who love him will keep his ways" (2,15); ἕκαστος τὸν πλησίον αὐτοῦ οὐκ ἐξέθλιψεν καὶ ἕως αἰῶνος οὐκ ἀπειθήσουσιν τοῦ ῥήματος αὐτοῦ, "Each [of the Lord's works] did not crowd its neighbor,/ and they will never disobey his word" (16,28).

The exhortation in 1,28b employs the verb προσέρχεσθαι, which recurs also, by way of inclusio, in 1,30e; this is the only verb, except for φοβεῖσθαι (four times), that recurs more than once in the entire poem. Interestingly, the grandson uses the same verb as a *mot crochet* in 2,1, the opening bicolon of the following poem that deals with fear of the Lord and belief and hope in him amid trials: τέκνον εἰ προσέρχῃ δουλεύειν κυρίῳ, ἑτοίμασον τὴν ψυχήν σου εἰς πειρασμόν, "My child, when you come to serve the Lord,/ prepare yourself for testing".

The thought of 1,29b is a type of synthetic parallelism to 1,29a. Approaching the fear of the Lord 'with a double heart' is condemned also in the final bicolon (1,30ef) that speaks of 'the heart full of deceit'. The concept of ἐν καρδίᾳ δισσῇ, a phrase which is unique in all of the LXX, probably derives from Ps 12,3: "They tell lies to one other;/ with flattering lips and a double heart they speak". The LXX (Ps 11,3) renders that second colon: χείλη δόλια ἐν καρδίᾳ καὶ ἐν καρδίᾳ ἐλάλησαν, lit., "With deceitful lips, a heart here and a heart there they speak". The text of 1,28 calls to mind 'the two paths', which Ben Sira condemns in 2,12: οὐαὶ καρδίαις δειλαῖς καὶ χερσὶν παρειμέναι καὶ ἁμαρτωλῷ ἐπιβαίνοντι ἐπὶ δύο τρίβους, "Woe to cowardly hearts and drooping hands,/ and to the sinner who walks on two paths"! In both 1,28 and 2,12 Ben Sira condemns those Jews who have lost their hope in the Lord and as a result have compromised their faith by approaching the fear of the Lord 'with a double heart' because they attempted to walk on 'two paths', viz., of their ancestral religion and of the Hellenistic culture and life-style of the day[35].

The thought of 1,29 is expressed in an *a:b::b':a'* rhetorical chiasm with a nicely balanced antithetic parallelism: μὴ ὑποκριθῇς : ἐνώπιον ἀνθρώπων :: καὶ ἐν τοῖς χείλεσίν σου : πρόσεχε. In OT thought, the heart (1,28b) is the seat of thought and free will; the lips (1,29b) express externally what the heart conceives and chooses. Having a double heart, therefore, makes one a hypocrite (1,29a). Thus, there is a progression of thought in 1,28-29, from not disobeying the fear of the Lord

---

35   Skehan and Di Lella, *The Wisdom of Ben Sira*, 151-152.

and approaching it with a double heart to not becoming a hypocrite by watching over one's lips. Later Ben Sira will warn his students against the 'double tongue', δίγλωσσος, in 5,9.14; 6,1; 28,13. This imagery is reflected in the Letter of James that speaks of ἀνὴρ δίψυχος, 'the double-minded man' (1,8), and then warns: ἀγνίσατε καρδίας, δίψυχοι, "purify your hearts, you double-minded ones" (4,8).

Warnings against pride appear frequently in the Bible (e.g., Sir 10,15; Ezek 17,24; Dan 4,34; Job 22,29; Prov 11,2; 16,18; 18,12; 29,23; Matt 23,12; Luke 1,52; 14,11; 18,14). The exhortation in 1,30a, however, may again be directed against Jews who were tempted to exalt themselves by giving in to the blandishments of Hellenistic culture and religion that superficially seemed superior to the ancestral faith. If this be the case, then the point of 1,30b is that such Jews will bring dishonor upon themselves — something that is the reverse of the exaltation they were led to expect from following Greek ways.

Strophe IX (1,30c-f)

In the final couplet of the poem, Ben Sira summarizes the dire consequences that will come upon those who compromise their Jewish faith by failing to observe the negative injunctions he gives in 1,28-30ab. I understand the καɩ, at the beginning of 1,30c as emphatic; hence, my translation, "Then. . . ". Note the use of the future indicative verbs in 1,30cd, suggesting the certainty of the Lord's action. These verbs may even be understood as prophetic futures—a point that receives some support from the phrase πλήρης δόλου (1,30f), which recurs only one other time in the LXX, in Jer 5,27: ὡς παγὶς ἐφεσταμένη πλήρης πετεινῶν, οὕτως οἱ οἶκοι αὐτῶν πλήρεις δόλου, "Like a trap that has been set is full of birds,/ so are their houses full of deceit". Thus, Ben Sira hurls a prophetic denunciation at anyone who ignores his commands in 1,28-30ab.

The 'secrets' the Lord 'will reveal' (1,30c) are the wicked thoughts and desires of those who do not fear the Lord. The verb ἀποκαλύπτειν and the neuter plural adjective κρυπτά, used as a noun, recur only one other time in a single verse in the LXX, in Sir 4,18, a context totally different from the present: καὶ πάλιν ἐπανήξει κατ᾽εὐθεῖαν πρὸς αὐτὸν καὶ εὐφρανεῖ αὐτὸν καὶ ἀποκαλύψει αὐτῷ τὰ κρυπτὰ αὐτῆς,

"Then she [Wisdom] will come straight back to him again and gladden him,/ and will reveal her secrets to him". To be cast down 'in the midst of the congregation' was a public disgrace—one of the results of the dishonor you bring upon yourself when you exalt yourself (1,30ab). Ben Sira borrowed the ideas here from Prov 5,12-14: "Oh, how I hated discipline, and my heart despised reproof!/ I did not listen to the voice of my teachers and to my instructors I did not incline my ear./ Now I have come to the point of utter ruin in the public assembly". The 'assembly', συναγωγή (עדה in the MT and Heb. MSS of Ben Sira), played an important role in the life of the Jew.[36]

The important ὅτι-clause in 1,30ef now explains why the Lord punishes so severely. You ignored the exhortation in 1,28b not to 'approach', προσέλθῃς (aorist subjunctive), the fear of the Lord with 'a double heart'. Instead, you 'approached', προσῆλθες (aorist indicative), the fear of the Lord hypocritically (1,30e) with a heart full of deceit. Note the inclusio of the verb προσέρχεσθαι in 1,28b and 1,30e as well as of the noun καρδία in 1,28b and 1,30f; these words connect strophes VIII and IX.

Two texts in LXX Proverbs probably occasioned the grandson's use of καρδία and δόλος in 1,30f: δόλος ἐν καρδίᾳ τεκταινομένου κακά, "Deceit is in the heart of the one who plans evil" (Prov 12,20); χείλεσιν πάντα ἐπινεύει ἀποκλαιόμενος ἐχθρός, ἐν δὲ τῇ καρδίᾳ τεκταίνεται δόλους, "With his lips a weeping enemy assents to everything,/ but in his heart he plans deceits" (Prov 26,24).

Conclusion

In this programmatic poem at the beginning of his book, Ben Sira has indeed made his position clear. He employs the expression, 'the fear of the Lord', or equivalent a total of twelve times (about 20 percent of the occurrences), and the noun 'wisdom' seven times (about 13 percent of the occurrences) to underline the connection between the two. Additionally, Ben Sira probably used those expressions the significant bibli-

---

36   See Sir 4,7; 7,7; 23,24; 41,18; 42,11.

cal numbers of 'twelve' and 'seven'[37] times, respectively, in order to emphasize his thesis that 'the fear of the Lord is wisdom and discipline' (1,27a). In 1,14-21 he affirms that wisdom's beginning, fullness, crown, and root are the fear of the Lord. He teaches that the fear of the Lord, which brings many blessings (1,11-13), also involves keeping the commandments (1,26), refraining from unjust anger by maintaining one's composure (1,22-24), and avoiding disobedience, hypocrisy, and pride (1,28-30).

---

37   See M.H. Pope, "Number, Numbering, Numbers", *IDB* 3 (ed. G.A. Buttrick; Nashville 1962) 561-567; "Seven, Seventh, Seventy", *IDB* 4, 294-295.

Trial Motif in the Book of Ben Sira with Special Reference to Sir 2,1-6[1]

Núria Calduch-Benages MN, Rome

Introduction

Trial is a reality which, on the anthropological level, touches the deepest part of a person and affects continuously both his/her inner-being and daily affairs. Trial is the outcome of the tension with reality that every person experiences in life and therefore trial naturally manifests itself on all levels of human existence: physical, psychological, social, cultural, spiritual,... To understand trial as an inherent condition of human development in all its aspects does not do justice to its full meaning. Rather than an inevitable human condition, trial is a beginning of self-knowledge. A person does not know what he or she is or can become, until difficulties and conflicts, i.e. trials, reveal this to him or her. In this sense, trial is revelatory.

Human life is subject to trial from its conception in the mother's womb until death, which is the final trial. Human life is active resistance to all that constitutes a danger, an obstacle, a limitation or a threat of death. Active resistance in life actually requires three things: a real defence of the higher values; an untiring struggle to apply them in practice and constant reflection on their nature and their repercussion in history.

Trial presents a double problem. On the one hand, a human being must face all the external threats invading personal integrity. On the other hand, a person must confront the self-made limitations that derive from insufficiently or inadequately developing his or her personal powers.

---

[1] I acknowledge the help of Jan Liessen SSL, who translated the Spanish original into English.

The purpose of our study is precisely the motif of trial in this double sense in the Book of Ben Sira.[2] The sage reflects upon trial from various angles of human experience, and careful analysis shows that his perspective is always permeated with a spiritual dimension. In other words, several texts in Ben Sira conceive of a trial as a reality that concerns the most intimate level of human existence in which a personal encounter with the Creator takes place. We will embark on our study of these more significant texts of the Book beginning with Chapter 2, as the second part of the title indicates.

1. Programmatic Occurrence of Trial (Sir 2,1-6)

Thematically, Sir 1-2 develops gradually and logically. The book opens with a beautiful poem about Wisdom, which appears as God's attribute, as the world's quality and as the gift of God to those who love him. It is followed by another poem about the close relationship between Wisdom and fear-of-God. With attractive imagery the author describes fear-of-God as the beginning, fullness, crown and root of Wisdom. The presentation of the two pillars of the book (Wisdom and fear of God) is suddenly interrupted by a parenetic section. The parenesis opens with a frontal attack on impatience, and proceeds with a presentation of the necessary qualities to reach Wisdom (patience, loyalty to the Law, sincerity and humility).

At this point of the introductory chapters, the field is prepared for the first and main condition for the disciple to meet Wisdom, the fear of God.[3] The first chapter narrates in a poetic way the origin of Wisdom and her close relationship with fear of God. However in the second chapter, Ben Sira shifts to a personal level and describes the disciple's attitude towards God. In other words, Sir 2 complements the former ex-

---

2 For a general treatment of the same motif in wisdom literature, see N. Calduch-Benages, "La teologia de la prova en la tradició sapiencial de Israel", *Butlletí de l'Associació Bíblica de Catalunya* 50 (1995) 13-16.

3 See H. Irwin, "Fear of God, the Analogy of Friendship and Ben Sira's Theodicy", *Bib* 76 (1995) 551-559. Based on the points of contact between Sir 1-2 (esp. 2,1-18) and 6,5-17 (about friendship), Irwin concludes that a clear analogy exists between fear of God and friendship.

position with a deeply religious poem illustrating the relationship between God and the faithful. As the sapiential discourse progresses, the features of fear of God become more precise and its demands more explicit. What does it really mean to fear God? What are its benefits and its disadvantages? Ben Sira answers such questions in a programme of authentic spiritual life, which rounds off the presentation of Wisdom that began in Sir 1. Moral, social and cultural themes are treated throughout the book after these announcing the book's theme. The conclusion of Sir 1-2 is evident: the search for Wisdom is a religious task that has a profound impact on all aspects of life.

Sir 2,1-18 is a lively exhortation, addressed to those who come forward as disciples of Wisdom. It is organized into four sections:

the reality of trials (vv.1-6)
the divine mercy (vv.7-14)
the faithful's behaviour (vv.15-17)
'in the hands of the Lord' (v.18)[4]

In this parenetic appeal, the sage introduces the young to his programme of wisdom with an extraordinary pedagogic ability. His programme is complex, but well planned and accurately articulated. It encompasses clear objectives, strong motivations, adequate means, examples to imitate, and obstacles and difficulties to overcome. It presupposes freedom of choice; it envisages final results; it looks forward to rewards and punishments.

Ben Sira opens the speech with a peculiar invitation (Τέκνον, εἰ προσέρχῃ δουλεύειν κυρίῳ, ἑτοίμασον τὴν ψυχήν σου εἰς πειρασμόν, 'My son, if you come to serve the Lord, prepare your soul [yourself] for testing'). This peculiar initial formulation announces the Leitmotiv of his parenesis, which is the inevitable reality of trial. At first sight, this invitation seems unreasonably severe, especially if we consider the youthfulness of the hearers. However the sage's choice of words has the almost irresistible attraction of a challenge. Formulating his invitation with a conditional clause, he creates a climate of freedom, which favours the disciple's personal choice. This context of freedom is

---

4 Cf. N.Calduch-Benages, *En el crisol de la prueba*. Estudio exegético de Sir 2,1-18 (Monografías de la Institución San Jerónimo; Estella, Navarra) [*forthcoming*]. However, cf. L. Schrader, *Leiden und Gerechtigkeit*. Studien zu Theologie und Textgeschichte des Sirachbuches (BET 27; Frankfurt am Main 1994) 192.

characteristic of the Wisdom school as is explicitly stated in 6,32-33[5]
and 15,15-17. Here too, Ben Sira introduces his teaching with the typical formula 'if you want' (חפץ אם and ἐὰν θέλῃς).[6]

Therefore, we can say that the warning 'prepare your own soul for
testing' (2,1b) is a programmatic occurrence of trial in the book of Ben
Sira. From now on, the sage starts his teaching. Syntactically, the pro-
tasis ('If you come to serve the Lord') is followed by an extended
apodosis consisting of six warnings. The first four warnings ('prepare
your soul for testing; direct your heart; be steadfast; do not hurry in
time of affliction') refer to the inner life of the disciple and the last two
warnings concern his relationship with God ('cling to him and forsake
him not'). With a synthetic parallelism, the author gives a strong conclusive quality to 2,3a, while emphasizing the first imperative of the
semicolon. In other words, Ben Sira says that the main thing in trial is
to cling to the Lord.

Ben Sira interrupts the list of imperatives that make up the apodosis
and inserts a final clause in 2,3b. This clause seems to express the purpose of the whole apodosis proleptically: 'so that you grow at your
end'.[7] After the interruption, Ben Sira continues the sequence of imperatives which started in 2,1b with δέξαι('accept') and μακροθύμησον
('be patient', lit. 'be great-hearted'). First, he encourages the disciple to
accept 'whatever befalls him'. God being the implied subject of the
verb (ἐπαχθῇ), this short sentence amounts to an unconditional ap-
proval of divine designs. Second, he exhorts the disciple to μακροθυμία
and this exhortation represents a double action. On the one hand, the
disciple must practise the virtue of patience, if he wants to overcome
trials; on the other hand, trial itself becomes a teacher of patience. This
dynamic character of patience and the educational value of testing con-

---

5   A. A. Di Lella, "The Search for Wisdom in Ben Sira", *Psalms and Other
     Studies on the Old Testament* (FS. J. I. Hunt; [eds. J. C. Knight / L. A. Sinclair]
     Nashotah, Wisconsin 1990) 190.

6   Paralleled by Matt 19,17: εἰ δὲ θέλεις εἰς τὴν ζωὴν εἰσελθεῖν... ('If you
     want to enter into [eternal] life...') and 19,21: εἰ θέλεις τέλειος εἶναι... ('if
     you want to be perfect...').

7   The meaning of the expression ἐπ' ἐσχάτον σου is disputed. My view is that
     this expression does not refer to eternal life, or the day of death, or the end of
     time, but to the time after a trial, when the tribulation or affliction has been
     overcome. In Syriac ܡܛܠܬܐ ܡܬܚܟܡ ܒܐܘܪܚܬܟ ('so that you become wise in your
     ways').

trast sharply with the profane usage of μακροθυμία in some Greek authors. For example, Menander says: ἄνθρωπος ὢν μηδέποτε τὴν ἀλυπίαν αὐτοῦ παρὰ θεῶν, ἀλλὰ τὴν μακροθυμίαν ('being a person, do not ask the gods for the absence of pain, but for resignation').[8]

In order to justify the two elements of the extended apodosis ('accept whatever befalls you' and 'be patient') the passage includes a wisdom saying which functions as a clause of justification (*Begründungssatz*). At this point the passage changes strategy and allows popular wisdom to take over. An anonymous representative of the Wisdom of Israel voices a powerful message. The persuasive quality of the justification rests in its truth based on experience· ἐν πυρὶ δοκιμάζεται χρυσός ('gold is tested with fire'). The passage builds the wisdom argument by carrying over the experimental truth of nature to the human sphere: καὶ ἄνθρωποι δεκτοὶ ἐν καμίνῳ ταπεινώσεως ('and acceptable men [are tested] in the crucible of humiliation'). The result of the intertwining of experimental truth with human life is a proverb with a typically chiastic disposition of its elements.

Sir 2,5 is the only instance in the Book of Ben Sira in which the image of the crucible is used to illustrate the idea of testing.[9] This image of the melting of metals reminds of a literary motif, very common in prophetic books (Jer 6,28-30; 11,4; Isa 1,22.25; 48,10; Ezek 22,17-22; Zech 13,9; Mal 3,3). Whereas the prophetic tradition applies the metaphor of the crucible to Israel, Ben Sira and the Psalms apply it to the individual (Ps 26[25],2 and 17[16],3; 66[65],10). In Sir 2,5, the logical direct object of divine testing is not the chosen people, but the ἄνθρωποι δεκτοί ('acceptable men'). God tests them with fire (ἐν καμίνῳ ...), not to make them suffer but because they are as precious as gold for him, a noble metal of great value. A person, even when right-

---

8   *Fr.* 549 (*CAF* III, 167). In Strabo, μακροθυμία means 'tenacity' (*Geogr.* V, 4,10) and in Artemidoros, 'delay' (*Oneirocr.* II, 25,9). Other authors, on the contrary, use it to describe the positive effects of suffering: Aretaeos 3,1 (*CMG* II, 36,12); Plutarch, *Luc.* 32, I 513a; 33, I 514c and Flavius Josephus, *Bell. Jud.* VI,37. An example in the Bible is 1 Macc 8,4.

9   In 27,4-7 Ben Sira describes the human dimension of testing with the following images: a sieve (Am 9,9), the kiln of the potter (cf. Jer 18; Is 29,16; 45,9) and the cultivation of a tree (Prov 1,31; 11,30; 12,14; 13,2; 18,20; 27,18). Cf. J. Hadot, *Penchant mauvais et volonté libre dans la Sagesse de Ben Sira* (Bruxelles 1970) 141-145 and P. C. Beentjes, *Jesus, zoon van Sirach* (Cahiers voor levensverdieping 41; Averbode 1982) 80-85.

eous, has to pass through a crucible in order to be purified (as gold is purified) as described in Prov 17,3).[10]

This first section of Chapter 2 concludes with v. 6, of which the most relevant feature is the emphasis on the relationship with God (πίστευσον αὐτῷ, καὶ ἀντιλήμψεταί σου· εὔθυνον τὰς ὁδούς σου καὶ ἔλπισον ἐπ᾽ αὐτόν, 'trust God and he will help you; make straight your ways and hope in him'). Here the sage's teaching reaches a high point when he speaks of the relationship with God, which consists of two main elements. On the one hand, this relationship involves the active collaboration of the disciple both in his inner attitude and his outer actions; on the other hand, the unconditional help of God. In short, the trust and hope in God combined with particular dedication and effort opens up the way for God's intervention in favour of the disciple. When trial comes to the disciple, the helpful hand of God offers a new horizon of hope, the shape of which becomes visible in the following verses.

At this point, let us look back to where we started our analysis and try to put it together. In 2,1b, the text does not specify the origin of trial. In fact, the Lord is not the grammatical subject of the verse. The origin of trial is given later in 2,5.9 (and also in vv. 10-11). In spite of this lack of explicit information, the disciple can already infer that both trial and liberation come from the Lord. This is what Ben Sira affirms in 33[36],1 'no evil can harm the one who fears the Lord; in trial, he will deliver him again and again'. At first this affirmation appears to be a contradiction, but in fact it reveals the teaching of God (מוסר), whose method combines firmness and affection at the right moment (as in Deut 8,5).

We now know who the agent of testing is, and who is being tested, but we are still unaware of the nature of the trial. In various passages dispersed throughout his book, Ben Sira provides us with some indications of what trial consists of (4,17 [Gr] 'fear and dread, discipline and

---

10   Melting of metals as an metaphor for spiritual purification also occurs in the Qumran documents: 1QS IV,20: ואז יברר אל באמתו כול מעשי גבר וזקק לו מבני איש ('then God will purify by means of his truth all the works of man and will purify for himself the human configuration'); 1QH V,16: ותביאהו במצרף כזהב במעשי אש וככסף מזוקק בכור נופחים לטהר שבעתים ('you have brought him [the poor] to the test as gold is subjected to the action of the fire and as refined silver in the oven of the refiners so that he may be purified seven times'); VI,8: ותזקקם להטהר מאשמה ('you will refine them so that they may be purified from the offense').

requirements'; 31[34],10 'mortal dangers', 44,20 sacrifying a son). He concludes with his personal experience in 51,1-12, where he speaks of the ultimate trial of death. However in Sir 2, however, the text refrains from any explanation and only acknowledges the reality of testing.[11]

2. Testing as an educational strategy (Sir 4,11-19)

Sir 4,11-19 is the second of a series of 'wisdom poems', which are spread throughout the book.[12] For the first time, Wisdom decides to speak out (as also in Chap. 24) in order to address her sons or disciples in a beautiful composition.[13]

The poem opens with a general statement on the educational action of Wisdom (v. 11). She carries out two complementary tasks: למד ('teaching') and העיד, ('stimulating') from the root עוד. Wisdom does not limit herself to imparting instruction, but also stimulates the disciple to open his mind to new horizons. In other words, Wisdom's teaching is not academic but oriented to life.

This general opening statement is followed by three verses dealing with the different stages which the disciple has to go through in the learning process in Wisdom's school: loving, searching, persevering and serving. A gift from the Lord corresponds to each stage: life; favour; glory; and blessing. It follows that love of Wisdom and love of God are two inseparable realities for the disciple.

After this introduction, Wisdom speaks in the first person singular (the Greek version has the third person singular), in order to instruct the disciples about her method. As a skilled teacher, she begins with arousing enthusiasm in the disciple with a promise of a final reward (vv. 15-16 [Gr]). Actually, she offers a double reward: first, the disciple

---

11 Gr II, on the contrary, is much more explicit: 'In sickness and poverty put your trust in him' (Sir 2,5c).

12 Cf. J.Marböck, *Weisheit im Wandel.* Untersuchungen zur Weisheitstheologie bei Ben Sira (BBB 37; Bonn 1971) and O.Rickenbacher, *Weisheitsperikopen bei Ben Sira* (OBO 1; Freiburg Schweiz/Göttingen 1973). For this section we follow the Hebrew text of MS A in the main.

13 The principle ideas of this section are expounded in more detail in N. Calduch-Benages, "La Sabiduría y la prueba en Sir 4,11-19", *EstBib* 49 (1991) 25-48.

responding positively to Wisdom's teaching will be allowed to live in the inner rooms of her house and; second, he will be allowed to pronounce judgment in the tribunal. Thus, intimacy and familiarity as well as social responsibility will be the disciple's recompense.

In v. 17, Wisdom speaks about her method of training in wisdom using the metaphor of going on a road. Studying wisdom is like walking on a long and arduous road, as once the Israelites did in the desert (Deut 8). Formerly, YHWH walked with his people; now Wisdom walks with her disciple (עמו אלך) without him realizing it (בהתנכר). YHWH guided and protected his people in the wilderness, and, he also tested them with hard trials without withdrawing his protection (Exod 16,4; 20,20). In our text, Wisdom behaves in a similar way. She is an unusual travelling companion, who puts the disciple to the test with her strategies, without abandoning him. Testing, in fact, is presented as a necessary and painful step on the road, but never as the final goal of the road. If the disciple's heart is to be filled with Wisdom, she must make her presence known and she must reveal her secrets (v. 18) to him. However if the disciple deviates from the path set out by Wisdom to choose another direction, he will be severely punished: binding with chains and handing over to devastators (v. 19).

The four semicola of v. 17 deserve closer scrutiny. In the first semicolon, Wisdom is walking with the disciple. Every day, experience shows that walking in the company of another person favours (or even can create) a relationship, and the deeper the relationship, the more pleasant the going will be. The exchange of mutual empathy is normally expressed with words, gestures, and even silence. However v. 17a, there is a remarkable detail worth investigating. Wisdom walks with the disciple 'cunningly' (בהתנכר, in Greek διεστραμμένως, 'by tortuous roads'), or 'in disguise', using P. Skehan's translation, without the disciple realizing her presence. Wisdom transforms herself in a veiled, but very near presence that takes care of the disciple. Deliberately she renders herself invisible to the disciple's eyes, in order to probe him more easily. This sort of trial or educational strategy was used also by Jesus in the Emmaus episode: as he walked with the two disciples and explained the Holy Scriptures to them, their eyes were prevented from recognizing him (Luke 24,15-16). The hiding of Wisdom is, then, a means of submitting the disciple to a critical situation. The result of this approach is that the disciple is obliged to reflect on himself, his attitudes, and his actions, and moreover to take personal decisions.

In the second semicolon ('first I shall probe him with trials'), the explicit mention of trial (בנסיונות) reminds of 2,1-6, particularly of 2,1b (εἰς πειρασμόν), where trial makes its programmatic appearance as we have already seen.[14] The reminiscence is based on the similarity of the school of Wisdom to the school of fear of God. If disciples who are tested in their being learn to fear the Lord, they will reach the Wisdom that comes from the one who alone is wise (as 1,8). In the same way, disciples who have learned the teachings of Wisdom through being tested, actually serve the Lord (as 4,14: 'the one who serves her [Wisdom], serves the Lord'). However we notice a strange difference: whereas 2,1-6 repeats insistently that the Lord comes to the aid of a youth undergoing a trial, in 4,11-19 no mention is made of such a disposition on the part of Wisdom. Wisdom seems more exigent than God himself. However even without explicitly saying that she will help the disciple, Wisdom is already doing so by her veiled presence. In my opinion, trial is here meant as a real educational strategy.

3. Trial of Endurance (Sir 6,18-37)

The starting point for our reading of the third text about trial is inquiry as a proper human activity. In a certain sense, all human searching is motivated by a profound desire to discover. It is equally well known that discoveries do not come easily nor immediately. For any inquiry to be sustained over a longer period of time, one must be guided by a sincere motivation to meet with the desired object or person. This experience is well expressed as a proverb in several languages: 'Quien no sabe aguantar, no sabe alcanzar', 'No pleasure without pain', 'No learning without tears', 'Ohne Fleiß, kein Preis'. Ben Sira applies this fact of life to the disciple's search for Wisdom in a suggestive poem

---

14 According to J. Haspecker (*Gottesfurcht bei Jesus Sirach. Ihre religiöser Struktur und ihre literarische und doktrinäre Bedeutung* [AnBib 30; Rom 1967] 217, note 9), Sir 2,1-5; 4,17 and 6,18-22 are basically identical. The way of teaching Wisdom is the way of teaching about God and Wisdom's teaching is education in fear of God.

(6,18-37) composed of three stanzas. In this section, we will deal with only the first two of them (6,18-22 and 23-31), because of our thematic approach.[15]

After an assumedly conditional statement ('My son, if you concentrate on instruction in your youth, you will find Wisdom in your old age'), the sage describes the learning process of Wisdom with a stream of images (6,19-22).

Through the images of ploughman and sower, of fields and fruits, Ben Sira invokes the agricultural context in order to illustrate the learning process. The relationship between a farmer and his field is bipolar. On the one hand, it is characterized by love, nearness, gratitude, hope; on the other hand, it requires work, fatigue, sweat, continuous effort and patience. However the sage puts the emphasis on the first aspect with subtlety. The work is not excessive, the harvest is soon coming, and the fruits are abundant. The same is true for Wisdom and her disciple. As the farmer cultivates the land in order to eat its produce, so the disciple has to cultivate his contact with Wisdom diligently in order to enjoy her fruits.

The sage's realism comes to the surface in 6,20-21. Since he already spoke of the disciple's search for Wisdom, he now complements the scene with the disciple's counterpart, i.e. the fool. This coincides with a new set of images. In the preceding verses, he utilized agricultural images and now he shifts to mineral imagery. The insensitive fool does not bear with Wisdom: he finds her rough, burdensome, and uncomfortable. For him Wisdom is like a heavy stone, a touchstone (אבן מסא, λίθος δοκιμασίας), which bears down on his shoulders and which puts him to the test.[16] Not being able to endure it, he loses no time in shaking it off. All the wealth of vitality and fecundity that was elicited by the first group of images has now disappeared to give way to the sterility and inertia of stones.

In the second stanza of the poem (6,23-31), the sage is concerned with the difficulties of learning Wisdom and describes them with suggestive images taken from slavery, hunting, and love. The disciple is like a slave caught in a net, constrained with shackles and burdened with the yoke of Wisdom. He is like a tireless hunter, who tracks the

---

15 Our reading of these stanzas is based mainly on the Hebrew text.
16 This refers to a Greek custom, common among young men, in order to prove their virility: the sport of lifting heavy stones.

trail of his prey. He is like the lover passionately in search of his beloved (as 14,20-24).[17] Slave, hunter and lover, the disciple has to pass through many hard trials to attain his desired goal. But if he really longs for it and persistently searches for it, the moment will arrive when oppressive slavery, fatiguing pursuit, and preoccupied love stop being an unbearable weight and are transformed into a reason for peace and joy. Then, Wisdom's net is transformed into a secure refuge, her chains into a glorious robe, her yoke into a golden ornament, and her bonds into purple threads. In v. 31, the symbolism of clothing is like a golden brooch; it is the finishing touch to the exuberant series of images. With this metaphor, the sage expresses the profound harmony between the disciple and Wisdom, 'you will wear her as a splendid robe; as a wreath of honour, you will crown yourself with her'.

In this way, Ben Sira has illustrated artistically how the search for Wisdom is in fact a true trial of endurance, without speaking explicitly of trial.

4. Trial of Travelling (Sir 31[34],9-17)

Though geography does not seem to be of much interest to Ben Sira, it provides him with another occasion for divulging his concept of trial. In three instances of his wisdom book (31[34],9-17; 39,4; 51,13a), he describes travelling in a favourable way. He considers it as a fount of experience, knowledge and wisdom.[18] For the sage, the connection between travelling and Wisdom is unquestionable. Travelling is enriching in every way: the person who travels increases his cultural treasure and comes closer to Wisdom with each journey.

Of the three texts referred to above, the most significant is undoubtedly the first, i.e. 31(34),9-17. This text ingeniously contrasts with the preceding pericope (31[34],1-8), which deals with dreams and the un-

---

17 M. Gilbert, "La sequela della Sapienza, lettura di Sir 6,23-31", *ParSpV* 2 (1980) 53-70.

18 This position contrasts with the negative view of Qohelet about all that he saw and experienced in the world (e.g. Qoh 1,13-14). For a brief treatment of this subject, see the recent monography by O. Wischmeyer, *Die Kultur des Buches Jesus Sirach* (BZNW 77; Berlin – New York 1995) 96-97.

real. The vivid and realistic experience of travelling clashes with the deceiving fantasy of dreams. Our pericope consists of two clearly distinguished parts: vv. 9-12 and vv. 13-17, which are united by a link word (τούτων χάριν).[19] Both parts are subdivided, the former consists of vv. 9-10 and 11-12 , and the latter of vv. 13-15 and 16-17.

Sir 31,9-10 present us with the figure of the traveller as a man of experience (πολυπειρός), who knows many things (πολλά), increases his resourcefulness (πληθυνεῖ πανουργίαν), which enables him to overcome difficulties and to share his knowledge with others (ἐκδιηγήσεται σύνεσιν). Only one hemistich (31,10a) is devoted to the one who has not been tested (in this context, the one who has not travelled): such a person knows few things (ὀλίγα).

Unexpectedly, the author interrupts this general presentation (in 3rd pers. sg.) and starts to speak of personal experience in first person singular. It is as if the writer wanted to say, 'Listen carefully, this experienced, tested and intelligent traveller ... is me!'. For, immediately he discloses to us that he has seen many things (πολλά), that his knowledge goes beyond his words (πλείονα τῶν λόγων) and that all his vicissitudes in the world have brought him more than once (πλεονάκις) to the gates of death. So it may seem that not everything is advantageous in travelling. A traveller must always reckon with serious and unexpected circumstances that can endanger his life. The main instruction, then, he holds till last (v. 12b and vv. 13-17). He came away safely from all dangers, thanks to the Lord; for the Lord protects the pious person who respects him, puts his or her trust in him and loves him. In other words, the person who fears the Lord need not to fear anything, for the Lord watches over his or her ways. This is the lesson of the sage, in my interpretation. In this pericope about travel (31[34],9-17), fear of God and Wisdom come into contact with a cultural phenomenon

---

19   We understand τούτων χάριν ('because of these things') to refer to the following verses (13-17), which deal with fear of God and its effectiveness. Similarly, Smend, Duesberg / Fransen, Alonso Schökel and Morla Asensio. However other authors relate the expression at issue to vv. 9-12. According to them "these things" must be understood as the accumulated experience of the sage (Bretschneider, Frietzsche, Peters, Spicq, Minissale, Di Lella and the interconfessional translation of the Catalan Bible).

typical of Hellenistic culture and their meeting point is the experience of trial.[20]

Although travels are a source of wisdom and experience, they also entail many sacrifices and hard trials. And so Ben Sira speaks of the traveller who has to deal with thirst (26,12), with storms at sea (36[33],2), with unpleasant fellow travellers (42,3), with dangers that lurk on desert roads and in lonely places (8,16). Be it on land or sea, on foot or mounted, travelling is a continuous trial.

5. Trial of Abraham (Sir 44,19-21)

Just as trial is a constant reality in life for the one who is searching for Wisdom, so also the help of the Lord is never lacking for the one who fears him. In trial, the righteous reckons with the protection and help of the Lord (1 Kgs 5,18 and Job 5,19). This is what the sage affirms in 36(33),1 'no evil can harm the one who fears the Lord; in trial, he will deliver him again and again'. This general affirmation finds its application in an instructive example from tradition (44,19-21).

From the glorious past of Israel one person stands out: the figure of the patriarch Abraham, father of a multitude of nations, unblemished in his glory (v. 19). Taking his inspiration from the narrative material of the Book of Genesis, Ben Sira describes Abraham as a pious man who kept the Law of the Most High, who made a covenant with him, putting it as a seal on his flesh (circumcision), and who remained faithful in trial. It should be noted that he concludes the characterization of the Patriarch by exalting his unbreakable fidelity, even on the moment of the decisive trial: ובניסוי נמצא נאמן, 'and in trial he was found faithful' (v. 20).

Jewish tradition holds that Abraham was tested ten times during his life: in Ur of the Chaldeans, when leaving Haran, with Sara and Hagar, with King Abimelek, in making the covenant and cutting sacrificial animals, in circumcision, and with his sons Ismael and Isaac. He overcame

---

20   Cf. Philo, *De Ebr.*, 158; *De Abr.*, 65; Flavius Josephus, *De Migr. Abr.*, 216-218; Pseudo-Isocrates, *A Demon.*, 18.

them all.[21] Although our text does not specify the trial Abraham underwent, tradition suggests that the sacrifice of his son Isaac was the ultimate trial (Gen 22,1-19).[22] God demands of Abraham the greatest sacrifice that could be asked of a father. And this with the sole purpose of probing the soundness of his faith. Abraham does not waver. He is determined to put into practice the Lord's command. Abraham triumphed in the most dangerous trial of his life and becomes a model for future generations (as Judith 8,25-27; 1 Macc 2,52; Job 15,17-18; Wis 10,5). In answer to his unconditional readiness and obedience, the Lord gives Abraham the promise to bless the nations through his descendants, to multiply his offspring as the dust of the earth, to exalt his house as the stars and to give him the land as inheritance from one sea to another (v. 21).

The teaching of the sage is not the exclusive fruit of his observation, reflection and personal experience. It builds upon a long tradition that proclaims tirelessly the infinite mercy of the Lord. That is to say, the example of the ancient, in this instance the Patriarch Abraham, enforces the sage's teaching: when the Lord puts man to the test, he also helps him to overcome the trial.

6. Ben Sira, a Man of Experience (Sir 51,1-12)

The emblematic example of Israel's far past finds present-day expression in the experience of the sage. So the Patriarch Abraham now withdraws, in order to make way for Ben Sira. In the teaching of the sage, the example of tradition and personal testimony complement each other. For the disciples, the authority must be recognized of their

---

21   Cf. *Abot R. Nat.* 33,11(A) and 36,3 (B); *PRE* 26-31; *P. Abot* 5,3-4; *Jub* 17,7; 19,8. In these trials, J. H.Korn, PEIRASMOS. Die Versuchung des Gläubigen in der griechischen Bibel (BWANT 72; Stuttgart 1937) 55-56, perceives an allusion to the Hellenistic tradition of the '12 works' of Hercules.

22   J. Swetnam, *Jesus and Isaac in the Light of the Aqedah.* A Study of the Epistle to the Hebrews (AnBib 94; Rome 1981) esp. 23-80. For abundant bibliography on this passage, see C. Westermann, *Genesis* (BKAT 1/2); Neukirchen-Vluyn 1981) 429-430 and J. K. Murray, "The Trauma of Isaac", *JBL* 26 (1991-92) 96-104; I. Willi-Plein, "Die Versuchung steht am Schluss. Inhalt und Ziel der Versuchung Abrahams nach der Erzählung in Gen 22", *TZ* 48 (1992) 100-108.

anchestors, and the coherence of life must be discovered of their present teachers. Conscious of his responsibility, Ben Sira reinforces his
teaching by the testimony of his life. Such a testimony undoubtedly im-
presses his disciples, for whom their own sage is much nearer and convincing than a glorious figure of the past.

At the end of his book, Ben Sira intones a thanksgiving psalm to the
Lord (51,1-12).[23] He thanks the Lord with an almost endless series of
reasons: he was saved from death, from destruction, from She'ol, from
calumny, from deceit, from lies, from lurking enemies, from a narrow
circle of flames, from consuming fire, from the deepest abyss, from ly-
ing and insincere lips and from the arrows of a treacherous tongue (vv.
2-6). This multitude of dangers (צרות מרבות) is in fact a concatenation of
images, all of which express the frightening experience of a man ex-
posed to a deadly trial: slander from enemies.[24] Full of gratitude, the
sage recalls the desperate appeal to God in those terrible moments when
he was struggling and floating between life and death (v. 10): ומשואה
אל תרפני ביום צרה ביום שואה ('do not abandon me on the day of tribu-
lation, on the day of terror and affliction'); he remembers the merciful
intervention of the Lord on his behalf (v. 12): צרה ויפדני מכל רע וימלטני
ביום ('He saved me from every evil [G: from perdition] and he liberated
me on the day of affliction [G: of the bad moment]').

This personal testimony of the sage (for I believe the prayer is autobiographical) is fully in line with the teaching about the trial, which began in 2,1 ('My son, if you want to serve the Lord, prepare your soul
for trial') and which has developed throughout the book. We can now
affirm that the experience of Ben Sira is a vivid example of actively enduring trials. When placed alongside Old Testament tradition, such an
example dissipates any possible doubt about the intervention of the
Lord on behalf of the righteous who fears the Lord and loves Wisdom
(as Ps 34,20; 37,39). In the sage's own words: 'the Lord saves those
who take refuge in him and rescues them from all evil' (51,8cd).

---

23   M. Gilbert, "L'action de grâce de Ben Sira (Sir 51,1-12)", *Ce Dieu qui vient*
     (FS. B. Renaud; [ed. R. Kuntzmann] LD 159; Paris 1995) 231-242.
24   Alonso Schökel, *Proverbios y Eclesiástico*, 327: "La situación es el peligro de
     muerte visto como una síntesis de todos los males y como suceso humana-
     mente irremediable".

Conclusion

Speaking about the principal themes of the Book of Ben Sira, one usually refers to the famous triptych Wisdom, fear of God and the Law, to which one may add, for instance, cult, history, prayer, death and social life. Trial is not normally mentioned in such a list.[25]

We have sought to fill this omission by showing that trial is a reiterative theme in the work of Ben Sira. The reason that Ben Sira wanted to underline the presence of trial in human life is that he is concerned mainly with Wisdom as a quality of life and that he is convinced of the need of trial to attain Wisdom. Trial has the capacity to make a person grow and mature. This educational principle is well appreciated by Ben Sira and so he imparted it to his disciples throughout his teaching.

The programmatic occurrence of trial in Sir 2,1 is worked out in various ways and contexts throughout the book. However all instances, trial is associated strictly with the search for Wisdom. This search entails a long and arduous road. It is long, because it lasts for the whole of life, including the moment of death (6,18; 51,13-15). It is arduous, because it demands constant effort and improvement (6,19; 51,26). The stages of this road to Wisdom constitute a true learning experience, in which trial serves an educational function. In her school, Wisdom subjects the disciples to all sorts of trials. Only after overcoming all trials will the disciple attain the Wisdom desired and enjoy her company (6,18-22; 14,22-25). The process of going along Wisdom's road can be found in the glorious past of Israel, in the figure of Abraham, the faithful Israelite who overcame even the hardest trial sent by the Lord (44,19-21). It can also be found in the daily life of the disciple, namely in the figure of their teacher Ben Sira, who successfully underwent various mortal dangers in his life (31[34],9-13; 51,1-12).

In all these texts, the Lord and Wisdom put the disciple to the test, not to satisfy a simple whim, not to justify themselves as teachers nor to demonstrate the efficiency of their method. The Lord and Wisdom are motivated by love, and so they pursue a positive aim: purification and strengthening of the disciple's heart who wants to serve the Lord (2,1-

---

25 e.g., A. Minissale, *Siracide*. Le radici nella tradizione (LoB 1.17; Brescia 1988) and M. Gilbert, "L'enseignement des sages: le Siracide", *Les Psaumes et les autres Écrits* (dir. J. Auneau) (Petite bibliothèque des sciences bibliques. Ancien Testament 5; Paris 1990) 308-318.

6). Far from being a destructive reality with negative connotations, trial dignifies the human person. Ben Sira has demonstrated this to us.

Wisdom of the Poor: Ben Sira 10,19 - 11,6

By Maurice Gilbert S.J., Namur

1. Hebrew Text of Ben Sira 10,19-11,6

1.1 Short history of the discovery

In April 1900, Elkan Nathan Adler published an article dealing with some missing chapters of Ben Sira.[1] He gave a transcription and a photograph of the page including Sir 10,19-11,6.[2] At the beginning of his article, he explained:

> "Among the numerous fragments from the Cairo Genizah which I brought away with me in January, 1896, and which I have since acquired, I have discovered a portion of the famous Hebrew Text of Ecclesiasticus, and hasten to publish the text and translation with facsimiles. The requisite critical appendix and notes must follow, but the case containing the fragment was only opened on March 7 last, and the precious fragment itself identified two days later. This consists of a pair of leaves from the same MS. as Messrs. Taylor and Schechter's MS. A, and supplies the hiatus in their edition. [...] My fragment comprises chapter VII.29 to XII.1 [...]" (466).

In October 1900, Israel Lévi published some critical notes on Adler's article in the same periodical.[3]

For several decades, till the "golden Sixties" of this century, the Hebrew text of Sir 10,19-11,6 was only known by this fragment of MS A. The still basic commentaries of Israel Lévi (1901),[4] of Norbert Peters (1902),[5] and of Rudolf Smend (1906)[6] were based on it.

---

1   E.N. Adler, " Some Missing Chapters of Ben Sira", *JQR* 12 (1900) 466-480.
2   E.N. Adler, "Some Missing Chapters", 470-471.
3   I. Lévi, "Notes sur les ch. VII.29-XII.1 de Ben Sira édités par M. Elkan N. Adler", *JQR* 13 (1901) 1-17.
4   I. Lévi, *L'Ecclésiastique ou la Sagesse de Jésus, fils de Sira.* Texte original

Between 1904 and 1906, each of these three scholars published a manual edition with critical notes on the Hebrew texts of Ben Sira: Lévi in 1904,[7] Peters in 1905[8] and Smend in 1906.[9] For Sir 10,19-11,6, they only had access to the medieval paper of MS A, but they were already able to suggest some corrections or conjectures to give a better Hebrew text by comparing this Hebrew text with the ancient Greek and Syriac versions. Before I show it to you, let me say something about the new situation created by the publication in 1960 of the new fragment of MS B.

In 1960, then, J. Schirman, from the Hebrew University of Jerusalem, published an article in Hebrew with the first edition of some additional leaves from Ecclesiasticus in Hebrew, which had been discovered at the University Library of Cambridge amidst uncatalogued materials recovered from the Cairo Geniza.[10] The Hebrew text of Sir 10,19-11,6, transcribed by Schirman, was then reproduced the same year by Ernst Vogt[11] and by Francesco Vattioni.[12]

However on a visit to the University Library of Cambridge in August 1963, Alexander A. Di Lella "examined carefully the new leaves of Sirach. It became obvious" – he wrote – "that in transcribing the leaves of MS B Schirman often reconstructed letters or entire words on the basis of MS A; but in many such instances MS B itself contained the letters or words in question, or enough of them, so that we know with certainty what was written by the medieval scribe". So Di Lella

---

hébreu édité, traduit et commenté. Deuxième partie (BEHE.R 10,2; Paris 1901).

5   N. Peters, *Der jüngst Wiederaufgefundene hebräische Text des Buches Ecclesiasticus* untersucht, herausgegeben, übersetzt und mit kritischen Noten versehen (Freiburg im Breisgau 1902).

6   R. Smend, *Die Weisheit des Jesus Sirach erklärt* (Berlin 1906).

7   I. Lévi, *The Hebrew Text of Ecclesiasticus* (SSS 3; Leiden 1904).

8   N. Peters, *Liber Iesu Filii Sirach sive Ecclesiasticus Hebraice* (Friburgi 1905).

9   R. Smend, *Die Weisheit des Jesus Sirach hebräisch und deutsch* (Berlin 1906).

10   J. Schirmann, "Some additional Leaves from Ecclesiasticus in Hebrew ", *Tarbiz* 29 (1960) 125-134.

11   E. Vogt, "Novi textus hebraici libri Sira", *Bib* 41 (1960) 184-187.

12   Fr. Vattioni, "Nuovi fogli ebraici dell'Ecclesiastico", *RivB* 8 (1960) 172-173.

"decided to make a fresh transcription of the leaves utilizing of course the original mss themselves", and to publish them.[13] He also wrote:

> "The new leaves of Ms B, like the older ones, offer an abundance of marginal readings, variants, additions and glosses. Despite these faults, in fact because of them, the present writer considers Ms B the most valuable of the Geniza fragments of Sirach. For with the patient use of the usual critical tools plus ingenuity one can extract from the mass of material in Ms B genuine readings of Ben Sira which would otherwise be lost because of corruptions in the text of the other mss" (155).

So, with photographs of MS B, Di Lella gave the best Hebrew text, with critical notes, on the passage which here interests us. Henceforth, scholars had access to two Hebrew MSS for Sir 10,19-11,6: MS A as well as B. This new situation was exploited mainly by three scholars.

In 1970, Hans-Peter Rüger made an accurate comparison between all the Hebrew, Greek, Syriac and Latin witnesses, in order to propose a Hebrew text of Sir 10,19-11,6 which he considered the original redaction of Ben Sira (H I), distinguishing it from a later secondary and re-elaborated edition (H II).[14] In 1983, Di Lella himself published a study of Sirach 10,19-11,6, in which he gave the critical Hebrew text of that poem, divided into strophes, with an English translation.[15] Finally, in 1995, Antonino Minissale, in his doctoral thesis[16], also suggested a reconstructed Hebrew text of Sir 10,19-11,6, with an Italian translation and critical notes. Such is the context into which the present analysis fits.

1.2 Comparison between MS A and MS B

It is not my intention to compare here the texts of the three editions of the beginning of this century, those of Lévi, Peters and Smend. More

---

13 A.A. Di Lella, "The Recently Identified Leaves of Sirach in Hebrew", *Bib* 45 (1964) 153-167 (quotations taken from pages 153-154).

14 H.-P. Rüger, *Text und Textform in hebräischen Sirach* (BZAW 112; Berlin 1970), esp. 54-68,

15 A.A. Di Lella, "Sirach 10:19-11:6: Textual Criticism, Poetic Analysis, and Exegesis", C.L. Meyers & M. O'Connor (eds), *The Word of the Lord Shall Go Forth* (Fs D.N. Friedman; Winona Lake, Ind. 1982) 157-164.

16 A. Minissale, *La versione greca del Siracide* (AnBib 133; Rome), 56-65.

useful, it seems to me, is a comparison between their texts based on MS
A and those of the three recent scholars who also made use of MS B.

Starting from the two most recent studies, those of Di Lella and
Minissale, we see that both reach almost full agreement on the Hebrew
text of Sir 10,19-11,6. If we note from the start that the reconstruction
of Sir 10,19 does not distinguish them, the differences are the following. First of all, there are orthographic differences which in no way
modify the meaning:

Sir 11,1b תושיבנו   MS A, Minissale   תשיבנו MS B, Di Lella;

Sir 11,3a דברה   MS A, Minissale   דבורה MS B, Di Lella;

Sir 11,4a בעטה   MS A, Minissale   בעוטה MS B, Di Lella.

Furthermore, some discrepancies of letters or words exist, but again
without any serious change of meaning:

Sir 10,22a וזר   MS A[17], Minissale זר MS B, Di Lella;

Sir 10,26a לעבד   MS A, Minissale   לעושת MS B, Di Lella;

Sir 10,31a נכבד   MS A, Minissale   הנכבד MS B, Di Lella;

Sir 11,5b עלו   reconstruction by Minissale, with Lévi and Peters;

עלים   reconstruction of Di Lella, with Smend.

Only two differences concern the meaning:

Sir 10,20b בעיניו   Minisalle's reconstruction , with the Greek and with
Peters;   בעמו   reconstruction of Di Lella, with Smend.

Sir 11,2b אדם without מכוער (?) Minissale, with the Greek;

אדם משבר   MS B (?), Di Lella.

Now, if we compare this general agreement between Di Lella and
Minissale with the propositions of Rüger, we observe that most of the
choices made by Rüger, who was in fact the first in time, are also those
of Di Lella and Minissale. Furthermore, I note the following occurrences where Rüger did not decide between two readings or between
two reconstructions:

Sir 10,22a וזר or זר.

Sir 10,22b אלהים, MS A, or יהוה, MS B, Di Lella and Minissale.

Sir 11,4d מאדם, MS A, Di Lella and Minissale, or מאנום, MS B.

Sir 11,5b reconstruction of עלו or of עלים.

On the other hand, Rüger made his choice in the following verses:

Sir 10,20b בעיניו reconstructed with the Greek, as Minissale.

Sir 10,26a לעשות דרכך MS B with Bmg.

---

17   After correction.

Sir 10,30b   ויש איש reconstructed with the Latin.

Sir 10,31a   נכבד : MS A, as Minissale.

Sir 11,2b   אדם with the Greek, as Minissale.

Sir 11,4a   במעוטף בגדמי אל תחפאר, with MS B and the Greek.

Sir 11,4b   כמרירי with MS B.

For the meaning, only the readings chosen by Rüger in 10,26a and in particular in 11,4ab differ from those where Di Lella and Minissale agree. But in these two verses, agreement between MS A and MS B allows us to exclude the readings chosen by Rüger. This is to say, the texts of Sir 10,19-11,6 proposed by Di Lella and by Minissale are acceptable. Only two readings divide them, in Sir 10,20b and in 11,2b.

So we can now see all the benefit provided by the edition of MS B to establish the Hebrew text of Sir 10,19-11,6. For this purpose, let us compare the edition of Di Lella and that of Minissale with those of Lévi, Peters and Smend:

Sir 10,19, MS B gives 10,19cd at the top of the page, and therefore 10,19b can surely be reconstructed as suggested by Smend.[18]

Sir 10,23, MS B gives the entire verse and confirms the reconstructions of Peters and Smend, but not that of Lévi.

Sir 10,24a, MS B gives the full stich and is preferable to MS A.

Sir 10,25a, the third line of MS B now gives the full text.

Sir 10,25b, the third and the fourth lines of MS B allow the reconstruction of the stich, in disagreement with Lévi, Peters and Smend.

Sir 10,28b, MS B confirms the reading of Smend, in disagreement with Lévi and Peters.

Sir 10,30b, MS B gives the word עשיר and therefore י ש איש is to be omitted.

Sir 10,31, MS B gives the full verse, which is now intelligible.

Sir 11,3a, MS B gives קמה, which is now accepted.

Sir 11,6b, the first line in MS B omits גם and gives זעירים at the end.

The discovery of MS B therefore allows construction of an almost complete Hebrew text of Sir 10,19-11,6, when the only one provided by MS A is incomplete and partly corrupted. Even with its various readings, MS B, when it differs from MS A, is "the most valuable", as Di Lella remarks.

---

18   Cf. A.A. Di Lella, "Authenticity of the Geniza Fragments of Sirach", *Bib* 44 (1963) 184-187.

We can then follow the edition of Sir 10,19-11,6 given by Di Lella and by Minissale, in spite of their disagreement about 10,20b and 11,2b. However, we must observe that P.W. Skehan[19] anticipated the choices of Minissale; still more, in the same commentary (230 and 233), Di Lella does not retain the two readings chosen by him in 1983. So there is now agreement between Di Lella and Minissale and we can therefore go on with analysis of the text.

2. Literary structure of Sir 10,19-11,6

2.1 Di Lella's structure

In order to establish the literary structure of our text, it is better to use the reconstructed text published after the discovery of the new leaves of MS B. This is to say that the structures suggested at the beginning of the 20th century are of little interest here. The strophic structure of our poem proffered with arguments, by Di Lella in 1982 must retain our attention, more perhaps than that of Minissale, who did not elaborate his analysis.

To be brief, I will quote the exact words with which Di Lella presents each strophe of the poem.

Strophe I (Sir 10,19-23: 5 bicola). "The opening stanza contrasts the God-fearing wise man, who is often poor or disadvantaged (10:22a-23a), with the lawless man (10:23b), who transgresses the Law (10:19d). The expression 'fear of YHWH/God' occurs three times (10:19b, 20b, 22b) to emphasize the centrality of this concept in the poem. ... Sir 10:19 gives the principal idea of the poem: people are honorable only when they fear the Lord; they are dishonorable when they transgress the Law" (160).

Strophe II (Sir 10,24-27: 4 bicola). "This stanza describes different classes of people - prince, judge, ruler (10:24a), the one who fears God

---

19   P.W. Skehan - A.A. Di Lella, *The Wisdom of Ben Sira* (AB 39; New York 1987) 227-228.

(10:24b), the wise slave (10:25a), the conscientious worker (10:26-27a), and the idle boaster (10:27b)" (161).

Strophe III (Sir 10;28-29: 2 bicola). "The opening of this stanza is clearly indicated by *benî*. The stanza, which contains the two middle bicola of the poem, has as subject matter the need for proper self-esteem. ... One can achieve proper self-esteem only when one thinks of oneself with humility, and not with pride. [...] In 10:29, Ben Sira excoriates self-depreciation, which, contrary to popular opinion then and now, is not what humility is all about" (161).

Strophe IV (Sir 10,30-11,2: 4 bicola). "This stanza contrasts the poor man and rich man and gives the reason why each is honored (10:30-31). It also describes the happy fate of the wise poor man (11:1) and urges against reacting to a man solely on the basis of his appearance (11:2). The opening verse (10:30) has the verb *kbd* in both cola, as do the opening verses of the first three stanzas (10:19, 24, 28)" (162).

Strophe V (Sir 11,3-6:5 bicola). "The final stanza has as its theme how mysterious are God's ways and how God can reverse human expectations. Note how the stanza begins with *qetannâ,* 'least', and ends with *ze'erîm,* 'few'. ... In the context of the poem, the verse [10,6] implies that the 'many exalted' [11,6a] and 'the honored' [11,6b] do not fear the Lord (10:19; cf. 10:20, 22, 24); hence, their fate is to become 'dishonored completely' (11:6a) and to be 'given into the power of the few', i.e. the Jewish remnant who remain stead-fast in their service of the Lord (11:6b). ... As I indicated above, this verse [11,6] also contains the same two verbs *kbd* and *qly* found in the opening verse (10:19)" (162-163).

2.2 Minissale's structure

According to Minissale too, the poem is structured into five strophes.

Strophe I (Sir 10,19-24). The verb כבד occurs in each verse, except in 10,22, where the word that is semantically close is תפארת. The theme is that only the God-fearing man merits honour.

Strophe II (Sir 10,25-27). The root עבד occurs in each verse. Working without pretension is recommended and the merits of the intelligent 'servant' are exalted.

Strophe III (Sir 10,28-29). This central strophe, introduced with בני,
recommends correct self-esteem, which does not contradict humility.

Strophe IV (Sir 10,30-11,1). This strophe apposes the honour due to
the poor man to the honour given to the rich: so the theme goes back to
the first strophe.

Strophe V (Sir 11,2-6). This final strophe concludes with the pare-
netical application. The imperatives of 11,2.4 are justified by new reasons (11,3.4cd.5.6), which recall the changes of social condition either
for better or for worse.

2.3 New suggestion

The literary structure I suggest will try to respect not only verbal recur-
rences of the same words, but also the development of Ben Sira's
thought which alternates statements and precepts.

The general theme is that of honor and contempt towards human
beings. This antithetical pair appears in 10,19.29b.31;11,6. This fact
seems to suggest a division of the poem into two main parts: 10,19-29
and 10,30-11,6. But the first verse 10,19 "gives the principal idea of
the poem", or "is the topic sentence of the whole poem", as Di Lella
wrote (1983, 160, and 1987, 229). However in the same verse 10,19,
Ben Sira considers that only the God-fearing can be in honour, and this
secondary theme of the fear of God or fear of the Lord only comes
again explicitly in 10,20.22.24. Therefore, I propose that there is a strophe in 10,20-25. In fact, 10,20 and 22 are echoed in 10,24-25: surely
10,20 and 10,24 put the God-fearing man above all people who hold
power, and then the fact that the last word of 10,20b is unknown is not
really important: 10,24b is not explicit either. Verses 10,22 and 10,25
are complementary: there is mention of those who have no power in
contrast to those who have it (10,20a.24a): the glory of the former is the
fear of the Lord (10,22b), and the 'clever servant' of 10,25a is one of
them; in the same verse 10,25a, there is a contrast between servants and
nobles: the cleverness of a servant, which means his wisdom (as 11,1),
comes from his fear of God, and if a man of a higher class has the same
cleverness (10,25b), he will agree to see the social order inverted, when
'nobles serve the clever servant'. In other words, the fear of God, giv-

ing cleverness and wisdom, establishes an order of social values that differs from the social order regulated by power.

At the center, 10,23 is the first precept of the poem: a negative attitude must be avoided, i.e. 'to despise the clever poor man', exactly as we must avoid an antithetical positive attitude, i.e. 'to honour any unjust man'. In other words, honour or contempt must not be bestowed on anybody according to his power or his lack of power.

Now, I am aware that I will cause astonishment if I say that, in my opinion, 10,26-29 is a unit. I am fully aware, of course, that בני is at the beginning of 10,28, and I shall come back on it. But first I will explain why these verses could be united. These are grouped two by two, with a precept and an explanation in each group. The two precepts (10,26 and 10,28) exclusively concern the disciple, specifying an attitude he has to take towards himself: not to boast (10,26) and to have correct self-esteem (10,27): a negative precept, then, followed by a positive one. The explanations of 10,27.29, respectively correspond to each precept.

But, there is a problem: the meaning of 10,26a is not clear. The reading of MS A לעבד or that of MS B לעשות does not make the difference. Among the scholars at the beginning of this century, neither Lévi nor Smend made any comment. Only Peters in his commentary wrote: "V. 26-27 wollen sagen: alles zu seiner Zeit, Weisheitswort und Arbeit!".[20] In 1912, W.O.E. Oesterley explained the Greek version, "Do not play the wise man" as "Do not affect the style of a rich man when your condition is that of a poor one. Both clauses are protests against pretending to be what one is not".[21] G.H. Box on the Hebrew text: "Do not make a show of superior wisdom - do thy work quietly and honourably; do not pose as being superior to thy work (for then the work will suffer). Such superior wisdom is an excuse for idleness".[22] But in 1929, Gottfried Kuhn proposed the reading "מִלְּעֲבֹד halte dich nich für zu klug, deine Arbeit zu tun".[23] This proposal was accepted explicitly

---

20 N. Peters, *Das Buch Jesus Sirach oder Ecclesiasticus* übersetz und erklärt (Münster in Westf. 1913) 94. But on p. 91, for *kein* read *dein* : cf. N. Peters, *Der jüngst Wiederaufgefundene hebräische Text des Buches Ecclesiasticus* (Freiburg im Breisgau 1902) 344.

21 W.O.E. Oesterley, *The Wisdom of Jesus the Son of Sirach or Ecclesiasticus* (Cambridge 1912) 75.

22 *APOT* I, 351.

23 G. Kuhn, "Beiträge zur Erklärung des Buches Jesu Sira I", *ZAW* 47 (1929) 293.

by Duesberg and Fransen in their Italian commentary[24] and implicitly by John G. Snaith: "Do not pretend to be 'too clever' for manual 'work' 'when you have nothing to live on' !".[25]

The Israeli scholars do not change the text, keeping the reading לעבד of MS A. Moshe Segal wrote: "If your material condition requests that you should do a physical work, do not say: 'I am wise and honorable, and of that work I am ashamed'".[26] And A.S. Hartom: "The meaning is apparently this one: At your time of need, when you must do your business [...] to supply your need, [...] do not consider that such a work will not be conformable to your wisdom or to your honor".[27]

More recently, Di Lella, who reads לעשות [28] comments: "Do not show off in doing the daily work required to sustain yourself; rather, do your job quietly and competently. The precept of v. 26b then follows: 'and boast not [i.e. do not make extravagant claims about what you might have done]in your time of need'".[29]

For all these scholars, there is agreement on the following three points:

1. The verb חכם Hitp. means "to make a display of wisdom", with a nuance of excess, i.e. here "in doing your business". This meaning only appears in Qoh 7,16 and Sir 32,4. Elsewhere in the book of Ben Sira, the Hitp. of חכם means "to show himself wise", "to prove his own wisdom", or even "to become wise" (6,32, 38,24-25). In Exod 1,10, it means more or less the same: "to be shrewd (ל, with somebody)".

2. The preposition ל, with constructed infinitive, corresponds to the Latin gerundive: "in doing ...".

3. The noun חפץ does not mean "what you please", as translated P.W. Skehan[30], even if that meaning appears with the verb עשה in 1 Kgs 5,22-23; Isa 46,10; 48,14. Rather, it means "business, work, trade";

---

24   H. Duesberg - I. Fransen, *Ecclesiastico* (La Sacra Bibbia; Torino-Roma 1966) 138-139.

25   J.G. Snaith, *Ecclesiasticus or the Wisdom of Jesus Son of Sirach* (Cambridge 1974) 57-58.

26   M.H. Segal, *The Complete Book of Ben Sira* [Hebr.] (Jerusalem 1958) *ad loc.*

27   A.S. Hartom, *Ben Sira* [Hebr.] (Tel Aviv 1969) *ad loc.*

28   Di Lella, "Sirach 10:19-11:6 ...", 1983, 158.

29   Skehan - Di Lella, *The Wisdom of Ben Sira* (AB 39; New York 1987) 231.

30   Skehan - Di Lella, *The Wisdom of Ben Sira* (AB 39; New York 1987) 227.

this meaning appears in Isa 58,13 and, according to Smend[31], in Sir 11,23, a text which is badly transmitted.

We could therefore translate, as do Di Lella and Minissale, "do not show off your wisdom in doing your business", or "make not a display of wisdom ...". Or, in Italian: "non atteggiarti a saggio nel fare tuo lavoro", or again "Non far sfoggio di saggezza quando attendi al tuo mestiere".[32]

It seems also correct to consider that Ben Sira thinks of manual work, as Segal and Snaith explain (see also Prov 31,13): Sir 38,24-25 also emphasizes the opposition between the professional sage and manual trade.

Therefore, when you do a manual trade, which gives you resources to live (Sir 10,27), "do not make a display of wisdom": the two are incompatible, because to make a display of wisdom in doing your work prejudices your work.

The meaning of 10,26b also needs to be discussed. The Hebrew text of MS A is already clear. But, according to Oesterley, it means: "Do not affect the style of a rich man when your condition is that of a poor one" (75); according to Box, "Viz. as to what thou mightst have done. The fact remains that all that thou couldst have done has not availed to keep off want" (351); according to Peters, "Rühme dich nicht, sc. deiner Weisheit";[33] and according to Di Lella, following Box, "do not make extravagant claims about what you might have done".[34]

It seems to me that the explanation of Peters is the best one: in making a display of wisdom when you have to practise a manual trade, you put in danger the quality of your work, and when your time of need arrives, your display of wisdom is in fact out of season.

Therefore, Sir 10,27 concludes in a positive way, with a "Better Proverb": "Better the worker" who works correctly without making a display of wisdom, but has "goods in plenty, than the boaster" who makes a display of wisdom, but "who is without sustenance".[35]

---

31 R. Smend, *Die Weisheit des Jesus Sirach erklärt* (Berlin 1906) 109.
32 *Siracide (Ecclesiastico)* (Nuovissima Versione della Bibbia 23; Roma 1980) 75.
33 N. Peters, *Das Buch Jesus Sirach oder Ecclesiasticus* (Münster 1913) 94.
34 Skehan - Di Lella, *The Wisdom of Ben Sira* (AB 39; New York 1987) 231.
35 Sir 10,27 is a "Tôb-Spruch", like in the Hebrew text of Sir 16,3; 30,14,17; 33,22; 40,28b; 41,15; 42,14. The Greek text of Sir adds 18,16b; 19,24; 20,31

Sir 10,28-29 is concerned with the opposite excess: namely, self-discredit. Ben Sira formulates his precept in a positive way, introducing it with בי. In his Hebrew texts, if one includes 10,28, there are, at the beginning of a verse, 14 occurrences of בי that are considered authentic. Where the Hebrew text is lacking, we find 3 other Greek occurrences in the same position. Of all these 16 occurrences, 10,28 being excluded, 9 introduce a positive precept, and 7 of them (2,1; 3,17a; 4,20; 11,20; 14,11; 37,27; 38,9) a positive precept which concerns only the disciple in respect of himself. In 2,1; 3,17 and 4,20, בני is at the beginning of a new development. In 11,20; 14,11 and 38,9, בני opens a sub-development. But in 37,27, בני opens the conclusion of 36,18-37,31. About 4,1, there is a discussion whether that verse opens a new development: Skehan and Di Lella answer no. In 42,11, בני opens precepts which follow statements. So בני is not always at the beginning of a development.

In 10,28, בני opens a positive precept which only concerns the disciple, but it comes after a negative precept that also concerns only the disciple (10,26), and both the negative precept and the positive one are complementary: make not a display of wisdom nor glory (10,26), but give yourself, with humility, the esteem you deserve (10,28).

Sir 10,28 certainly invites the disciple to avoid self-depreciation, as 10,29 clearly explains. Therefore, I consider that 10,26-29 is a unit. For Ben Sira, the first context in which his teaching, given in 10,20-25, has to be applied is about yourself.

2.4 Second part of the poem

Sir 10,30-11,6 no longer concerns the attitude of the disciple towards himself, but towards others. These nine verses are divided into three groups of three verses each.

(= 41,15); 29,22. On the preceding tradition, see G. Bryce, "'Better'-Proverbs: An Historical and Structural Study," *SBL Seminar Papers*, 108 (1972) 2. 343-354; G.S. Ogden, "The 'Better'-Proverb (Tôb-Spruch), Rhetorical Criticism, and Qoheleth," *JBL* 96 (1977) 489-505; H.C. Washington, *Wealth and Poverty in the Instruction of Amenemope and the Hebrew Proverbs* (SBLDS 142 ; Atlanta, Georgia, 1994) 102-104, 190-191. Sir 19,24; 29,22; 30,4 give advantage to the poor man.

In the first group of three verses, 10,30-11,1, without any precept, the first stich and the last verse, 10,30a and 11,1, are inclusive: "The poor man is honoured on account of his wisdom", and "The wisdom of the poor man lifts up his head and makes him sit among princes". On the other hand, 10,30 and 31 are both antithetical: honour to the wise poor man and honor to the rich man, but 10,31 also poses a question about a change in the social order: if a poor wise man is honoured, how much will he be when he becomes rich? The parallel question arises about a despised rich man: how much will he be despised when he becomes poor? These changes in the social order will be explained at the end of the poem (11,4c-6).

In the mean time, Ben Sira takes the opportunity to give a new teaching to the disciple: if there are changes in the social order, avoid any evaluation of anybody according to his looks (11,2 and 4ab), but in this second group of three verses, he emphasizes what concerns the poor, exactly as he did in 10,30-11,1. Sir 11,2b and 4ab are parallel and inclusive. At the centre of this second group of three verses, the observation made about the bee means that to judge according to squalid appearance or poor look is sometimes a mistake: even if a bee is so small, honey is fabulous (11,3).

The last group of three verses (11,4c-6) does not give any precept, but justifies the precepts of the second group by an explanation of the facts observed in the first group. If there are changes in the social order, the reason for which you must not evaluate people, especially a poor man, according to their appearance, is that the Lord himself often changes this social order: he makes us marvel in exalting certain poor men and in humiliating certain powerful people. In this last group of three verses, the two last verses (11,5-6) have two parallel stichs each, and both verses are antithetical.

In short, do not judge anybody according to appearance, because the Lord so frequently does wonderful things, hidden from man, in changing the social order by exalting a wise poor man.

2.5 Text as a whole

Now, if we look at the text of Sir 10,19-11,6 as a whole, we can read it in two parts, with two statements in 10,19 that function as a general introduction. The next nine verses, 10,20-29, are considering the social order as it is. Ben Sira presents two ways of reflection.

According to him, it is true that the human society is divided into two groups, powerful people and powerless people. But it is also true, in such a society, that the true value is not power but fear of God and wisdom, which are acknowledged as greater values, at least by educated people, who do not complain to see noble people serving a clever or wise servant (10,25). So nobody has to be evaluated otherwise than by those greater values of wisdom and fear of God (10,23).

In this context, the disciple himself must have correct self-esteem. He has not to boast, pretending to be what he is not (10,26) but must appreciate himself as he is, with humility and measure (10,28), without any abusive self-depreciation (10,29).

The last nine verses, 10,30-11,6, start with what was said in the first half of the poem. It is true that the social order invites us to honour a rich man because he is wealthy (10,30b), and it is also true that a poor man is at times honoured on account of his wisdom (10,30a and 11,1). But in human society, there are sometimes changes to the social order. A poor wise man who is honoured can become rich, just as a rich man who is despised can become poor, and then the first will still receive more honour and the second more contempt (10,31). The social order changes. So the disciple has not to evaluate people by their present and external appearance. Do not praise the splendor of a rich man and do not disparage or mock anybody who is broken or poor. As for the bee and her honey, you do not know what they really produce, what they will become (11,2-4ab).

The social order changes. The Lord, in fact, changes it and man does not understand His action (11,4cd). As is so frequently said in the Bible, "He has deposed the mighty from their thrones and raised the lowly to high places" (Luke 1,52), and "The Lord makes poor and makes rich, he humbles, he also exalts" (1 Sam 2,7).

The poem, then, can be divided into two parts, both having nine verses; the two statements of 10,19 are introductory, but they are also an enigma presented under the wisdom's topic of question and answer. The whole poem illustrates this enigma.

3. Context

The last two verses of our poem, 11,5-6, remind us of 10,14-15, at the end of another poem that immediately precedes ours. According to Joseph Haspecker, Sir 9,17-10,18 is the first part of a diptych to which 10,19-11,6, our poem, is the second. These two poems constitute a "Traktat über die falsche und wahre Ehre" (139). The first poem gives a "negative prologue" in 20 verses (138). Haspecker rejects 10,15, while the second poem, 10,19-11,6, which also contains 20 verses, gives the positive teaching of Ben Sira. Furthermore, both poems elaborate on the last sentence that precedes them, in 9,16b: "in the fear of God be your glory". The same words occur again in our poem about the foreigner or the poor man: "his glory is the fear of the Lord" (10,22b).

The theme of the first poem, 9,17-10,18, is that of pride, גאוה (10,6b.7a.8b) or גאון (10,12a); the verb גאה occurs in 10,9a; the plural of גֵּאֶה, 'proud', occurs in 10,14a and in the Greek text of 10,15a, a verse which, against Haspecker, has to be retained as authentic. The synonymous noun זדון, 'pride', occurs in 10,13a.18a. These words do not occur in our poem, 10,19-11,6, where the roots כבד and קלה, expressing honour and contempt, are frequent, as we saw, and these two roots do not occur in the first poem.

The first poem, 9,17-10,18, is a treatise on the government, as Gian Luigi Prato explains in his book.[36] Prato analyses the structure of this treatise. There are good and bad leaders, but in any case, "Sovereignty over the earth is in the hand of God" (10,4a). About bad leaders, Ben Sira states that pride is "odious to the Lord and to humans" (10,7a). Pride is odious, because it is contrary to human nature: human beings are "dust and ashes" (10,9a). Pride is also a sin (10,13a), which God has punished, "overturning the thrones of proud leaders and enthroning the humble" (10,14). Historical experiences implicitly justify such a statement, as Prato illustrates. So the conclusion is a "peremptory affirmation" (370): "Pride is not for man" (10,18). On the contrary, our poem (10,19-11,6) describes the right way to be honoured, which is the

---

36 G.L. Prato, *Il problema della teodicea in Ben Sira*, (AnBib 65; Rome 1975) 369.

fear of God and wisdom. But the first poem of this diptych undeniably throws light on the second.[37]

4. Greek version

In his book on the Greek version of Ben Sira, Minissale analyses the textual discrepancies between the Hebrew text of Sir 10,19-11,6 and its Greek version.[38] Here I do not discuss the corruption of the Greek MSS in Sir 10,22, a verse which had already been partly restored with the help of the Sahidic version.[39] Furthermore, the secondary addition in Sir 10,21 is ignored in the present inquiry.

My purpose is to analyse again some changes of meaning we find in the Greek version of Sir 11,4-6.

In 11,4b, the translator modified or read differently the Hebrew text. The *New English Bible* gives this translation of the Greek: "Do not pride yourself on your fine clothes / or be haughty when honours come to you".

To arrive at this version, the so-called grandson of Ben Sira confused three things: he read אֶדֶר (cf. Mic 2,8, which Peters already referred to), instead of אזור ; then, under the influence of 11,2a (תהלל), he read the verbal form תתהלל, instead of תהתל ; thirdly, he understood the verb קלס, *to scoff*, in its post-Biblical meaning, *to glorify*, as Lévi has already remarked. And "with the greatest flippancy", Lévi wrote (72), he made his own version of the two last words of the stich. "At a man's bitter day" became "in glorious days", or he perhaps read something like בהדרי יום, "in the splendours of a day", as Peters suggested, but Minissale disagreed, or במרומי יום, "in the exaltations of a day", as proposed by Smend and accepted by Minissale.

In any case, it is remarkable to discover that the first reading of 11,4a in MS B exactly corresponds to the Greek! Rüger (65) considered this first Hebrew reading of 11,4a to be original. But the other reading, "The one who wears a loincloth mock not" (Di Lella) better fits this

---

37   G.L. Prato, *Il problema della teodicea in Ben Sira*, 369-372.
38   A. Minissale, *La versione greca del Siracide*, 62-65.
39   Cf. for Sir 10,30-11,6, N. Bosson, "Un palimpseste du Musée Copte du Caire", *Le Muséon* 109 (1991) 25-26.

context, where Ben Sira is no longer teaching the disciple in respect of himself, as he did in 10,26.28. So the question arises, Could the first reading of 11,4a in MS B be a Hebrew retroversion from the Greek?

For the grandson of Ben Sira, the text of 11,4ab gives another precept to the disciple in respect of himself and, in the context, the new Greek meaning can be: do not judge anybody (11,2), not even yourself (11,4b), by appearances. Furthermore, when the grandson reverses the sense of 11,4ab, speaking now about glory, instead of misery, he seems worried about this idea of a changing social order, not so much by the promotion of a poor wise man, but by those who have been honoured and now lose their glory under the pressure of people who are not honourable.

This new direction of teaching, which is not that of 10,26, where boasting is only inappropriate, has to be understood in the light of the two last stichs of 11,4: if the disciple does not have to be haughty when he gains success, the reason is that the Lord can perform among men some hidden, unexpected works.

But again, according to the grandson,these hidden works of God, are more the decline and dispossession of many powerful and honoured people. In 11,5a, instead of "Many oppressed have sat on a throne" (Di Lella), he reads: "Many rulers (נדיבים, instead of נדכאים) have sat down upon the ground", again with great flippancy in translating the last word.

Finally, the last word of this poem: זעירים, in MS B, which seems to be original, was translated into ἑτέρων by the grandson. This Greek word here means a group of people which is the opposite of the group referred to at the beginning of the stich, the renowned men. So זעירים means *vulgus pecus,* or the lower classes, humble folk, powerless people.[40]

---

40   This meaning is better than "the few" (Di Lella) or "i piccoli" (Minissale). It appears in the Aramaic *Ahiqar,* 114, 145; see A. Cowley, *Aramaic Papyri of the Fifth Century B.C.* (Oxford 1923) 216-217. It is also accepted by *HAL³,* 265: "Von niederem Stand".

Honor and Shame in Ben Sira:
Anthropological and Theological Reflections

By Claudia V. Camp, Fort Worth

The underlying question of this paper is a particular variant of a larger one that has driven much of my work for the past several years. The big question has to do with the relationship of rhetorically powerful language – especially the language of metaphor – to configurations of social status and power. My particular concern has been with the relationship of powerful female images in biblical literature to women's power in both ancient and modern times. As you may be aware, the focus of my interest has been on the figures of Woman Wisdom and the Strange Woman in Proverbs, with only one significant foray into the book of Sirach.

Sirach is interesting to me because, with respect to its treatment of women, it seems to me to be both similar to and different from Proverbs which, following Burton Mack, we might think of as one of its "precursor texts".[1] Undoubtedly the most significant similarity is Ben Sira's adoption of the female personification of Wisdom, a move which might augur some hope for the feminist heart, were it not for this later sage's virulent attacks on real women, compared to which Proverbs' occasional snipes at the nagging wife sound like gurgles of affection.[2] Where, then, does this leave us with respect to understanding Ben Sira's gender ideology? And where does it leave us with respect to understanding the place of female imagery and gender consciousness in his larger theo-ideological system?

The concepts of honor and shame constitute an essential part of Ben Sira's ideological matrix. In an earlier paper, I used analysis of the so-

---

1   B. Mack, *Wisdom Myth and Hebrew Epic* (Chicago, IL 1985) 111-171.
2   On the other hand, although Ben Sira expresses deep fear of various sorts of "other women", he does not pick up Proverbs' well-developed symbol of the Strange Woman as the antithesis of Woman Wisdom. This issue deserves more attention than the scope of this paper allows.

called "honor-shame complex" from contemporary Mediterranean anthropology to try and elucidate aspects of the particular form of patriarchy one encounters in this book; to try to analyze, that is, the place of
women in the system of signs Ben Sira used to encode and thereby
create his world.[3] The present paper retains this interest in a reading of
Sirach that is nuanced by the overlapping perspectives of gender and
the anthropology of honor and shame.[4] Here, however, I would like
also to bring God into the picture. How do these perspectives color our
understanding of Ben Sira's theology? Such a question is validated, indeed, demanded, by Ben Sira's own lexicon, specifically, his reliance
on the vocabulary of honor and glory to designate essential attributes of
both God and man.

> Nominal and verbal forms of the Greek δόξα occur no fewer than 85 times,
> along with τιμή (14x) and ἔντιμος (3x). In the Hebrew manuscripts, these
> three words translate a variety of roots, most often כבד (21x) and הדר (7x).
> The honor concept itself can refer to the Lord, the stars, wisdom, and one
> who fears the Lord . . . ; it can also refer to a human status, recognized by
> other humans . . . . Δόξα is, then, a quintessential ideological term serving
> not only as a religious symbol valorizing the worshipper and the object of
> worship in the cultic context, but also as a cultural symbol defining the
> worshipper's status goals within society.[5]

This intersection of terminology for both deity and male humanity requires a theological analysis that does not lose sight either of anthropology or of gender.

Guided, then, by the conceptual framework of honor and shame, we
shall here consider two of Ben Sira's crucial theological topoi: the glory
of priest and cult and the personification of Wisdom.

Let me first summarize some of the arguments and conclusions of
my work on honor and shame and the profound effects of this ideology

---

3   C. Camp, "Understanding a Patriarchy: Women in Second Century Jerusalem
     Through the Eyes of Ben Sira", *Women Like This: New Perspectives on Jew-
     ish Women in the Greco-Roman World* (ed. A.-J. Levine) (SBL 01; Atlanta,
     GA 1991) 1-39. For the concept "system of signs" as applied to Ben Sira, see
     Mack, *Hebrew Myth*, 5-6.
4   Although I had completed my first literary-anthropological analysis of Ben
     Sira before encountering the work of K. Stone, I have found his notion of
     "anthropological reading" quite helpful. K. Stone, "Sexual Power and Political
     Prestige: The Case of the Disputed Concubines", *BR* 10 (1994) 28-31, 52-53.
5   Camp, "Understanding", 6.

on the place of women in Ben Sira's ethos and worldview. One way of thinking about honor is as the ability of a man to control the defining attributes of his life over against the challenge of others to subvert that control. These defining attributes may be seen as socially determined signs of value and power: one's women, one's property (i.e., one's household in both personal and impersonal dimensions), one's political influence, one's body, one's reputation or name. In another sense these defining attributes *are* oneself, for the self and its worth are, in this ideological system, publically rather than privately defined and evaluated. Shame, then, is the loss of control over these extensions of self.

The interrelationship of economic and gender issues are central to the way in which honor and shame play out in Ben Sira. Gender has long been significant in Mediterranean anthropologists' explication of the honor-shame system. Anthropologist David Gilmore summarizes the traditional view in three points[6]: (1) Honor and disgrace are acquired by men through women, especially through women's sexual misconduct. Women are, therefore, both a "weak link" in the chain of honor, but also powerful because of their "potential for collective disgrace." (2) Shame is mainly a property of women, but it governs the relationship between the sexes. (3) Honor is a zero-sum game: a man gets it by taking it from others. More recently, Gilmore and others have noted in field studies less aggressive aspects of honor such as economic success, family autonomy, hospitality, generosity, physical prowess, and integrity. Though honor and shame are not, then, defined exclusively in *sexual* terms, Stanley Brandes maintains the broader *gender* basis of much of the system:

> The connection between honor or esteem, on the one hand, and social masculinity on the other, is also an inescapable part of the Mediterranean value system. . . . [E]ven where the concern for expressing virility and masculine prowess coexists with other evident aspirations . . . a man's performance in the non-sexual domain confers upon him a coveted manliness. *To be respected is to achieve gender-specific goals.*[7]

---

6 D. Gilmore, "Honor, Honesty, Shame: Male Status in Contemporary Andalusia", *Honor and Shame and the Unity of the Mediterranean* (ed. D. Gilmore) (Washington, DC 1987) 90.

7 S. Brandes, "Reflections on Honor and Shame in the Mediterranean, *Honor and Shame* (ed. Gilmore) 122 (my emphasis).

To phrase this in terms of my earlier remarks, one's selfhood is co-terminous with one's manliness, in its multi-faceted dimensions. A threat to manhood is a threat to personhood.

Consideration of Gilmore's list of "less aggressive" aspects of honor and shame highlights the economic basis of many of them: family autonomy, hospitality and generosity are closely related to economic success. It is not surprising to find, then, that crucial within the web of connected values that comprise male honor in the Mediterranean world is the "rather unusual [ethnographically speaking] connection between erotic and economic power, the latter being largely contingent on the former".[8] Gilmore describes as "an almost universal thread in the [anthropological] literature" the "organic connection between sexuality and economic criteria in the evaluation of moral character".[9] He notes further D. O. Hughes' terms "economics of shame" and "fiscal sexuality," which refer to "the conceptual identification of erotic with tangible resources and correlative belief that sexual access represents a convertible or 'marketable' commodity".[10]

I have, in light of such conceptions, tried to argue that Ben Sira's book is deeply marked by the concern for honor and shame, played out in a dovetailing of sexual and economic issues and rhetoric that would be remarkable, if it were not so utterly predicted by the honor-shame model. The economic issues are on one level independent of the sexual issues, but in other ways closely linked to them, both practically and rhetorically. The book evidences, first of all, a great ambivalence about wealth and its accompanying social status that is different in attitude from its wisdom literature companions, Proverbs and Qohelet. While Proverbs is certainly capable of noticing exceptions to the rule, the retribution theory lends the book optimism: good things in life are available to those who seek wisdom. Qohelet, of course, sees the cup half-empty rather than the cup half-full, and responds with resignation. Ben Sira, however, vacillates dramatically between these two poles, sometimes insisting on God's ultimate reward of the just, elsewhere observing the clear evidence to the contrary. The contradiction between belief

---

8   Gilmore, "Introduction", *Honor and Shame* (ed. Gilmore) 4.
9   Gilmore, "Introduction", 6.
10   Gilmore, "Introduction", 6, citing D. O. Hughes, "From Brideprice to Dowry in Mediterranean Europe", *Journal of Family History* 3 (1978) 285.

and perception leads to confusion of values: how can one claim honor if wisdom brings poverty rather than wealth?[11]

This was not an abstract philosophical question for Ben Sira but was, rather, indicative of an existential dilemma for men of his social class in his particular historical context. Wealthy enough to give alms and sinful enough to feel that he needs to; capable of making loans and going surety, but financially insecure enough to lose his shirt on a bad deal; carrying enough social weight to be a patron to some but still needing patronage himself – Ben Sira is a man in a dangerous middle, in both practical and moral terms, a middle-class speculator in the high-risk market of honor.[12]

The first court of appeal for relief from the tension of contradiction in values and behavior lies in the idea of one's name. A man's name is, in effect, the ideological basket containing that sense of self we have designated materially as control over the signs of value and power, particularly his women and his household. Because it is immaterial, the name is more susceptible to the ideological manipulation necessary to deal with the contradictions of economic life: wisdom may not bring one wealth, but one can depend on its eternally honorable status in the eyes of God. Unfortunately, one's name provides no such bulwark against the threat to honor presented by women and, indeed, needs constant protection from them.

Wives, daughters, slave women, strange women, singing girls, virgins, prostitutes, other men's wives. I have detailed the multitude of ways all these women threatened male honor, both sexually and economically, and I will not repeat that here.[13] What I would emphasize is what I have called the psychology of weakness in Ben Sira's relationships with women that both reinforces and is reinforced by the threat to honor presented by other men in the economic arena. While women do not present the conflict of values occasioned by the need to reconcile wisdom and righteousness with wealth and social status, they present two other kinds of challenge: first, to a man's control of his physical

---

11   This connection of honor and shame to difficulties with the theory of retribution suggests that anthropological analysis of Ben Sira's treatment of the problem of theodicy would also prove fruitful.

12   For further discussion of the relationship of honor-shame ideology to Ben Sira's social location, see Camp, "Understanding", 7-18, 38.

13   Camp, "Understanding", 20-39.

self, his body; second, to the point of vulnerablity through which other men can dishonor that body: as Leviticus makes so clear, exposing the nakedness of a man's wife exposes his own nakedness. It is the ultimate form of dishonor and a perpetual threat to his name.

In an ethos so dominated by the problematic of male honor and shame, it is not surprising to find a theology articulated in terms of God's honor or glory. In his work on the hymn to the fathers, Burton Mack turns our attention to the theme of glory in Ben Sira in a way that sets the stage for the next part of my discussion. Mack's larger thesis is that this hymn provides a mythic rationalization for the social structure of Second Temple Judaism, a social structure centered in and deter- mined by the Temple cult, with the high priesthood manifest in Simon as "climax and fulfillment of Israel's glorious history as a whole".[14] I shall argue that, while Mack's discussion of glory, in the context of his larger agenda, provides many helpful insights, it ultimately presents only half the picture insofar as it defines this term in strictly theo- religious ways, without attention to its anthropological connotations so evident elsewhere in the book.[15] Mack notes that

> The theme of glory is one of the most consistently encountered and striking characteristics of the hymn. Its source is surely to be found in the priestly traditions of scripture and Second Temple theology, where "glory" (*kabôd*) is used as a term for the majesty and manifestation of God. . . . [I]ts special locus in the priestly theologies was understood to be in the cult, especially as a term for the divine presence in the tent or temple (52).

Precisely these traditional associations, however, make Ben Sira's use of the term in his hymn to the fathers all the more remarkable, for here the term is applied to the illustrious leaders of Israel's past – and one of

---

14 Mack, *Wisdom Myth*, 36. In the following summary of Mack's argument, I shall, for the sake of simplicity, indicate the page numbers of direct quotations in the body of my text.

15 My thinking about the book of Sirach actually parallels closely that of Mack, and I am indebted to him for the basic structure of my argument. Mack's dis- cussion of the book's semiotic system, however, often tracks its generation of myth at the level of the "intention" of the author, whereas I am reading more as an ancient reader, tracking how "he" might have read/felt himself into the text, based on culturally shared assumptions. My claims about "Ben Sira" as an author tend to be at the level of the un/subconscious rather than at the level of intention.

the present, i.e., Simon – who are thus deserving of praise in the assembly (52, 82, 167).

Indeed, Mack argues, it was probably precisely his reflection on the contemporary cult – the locus of correlation of glory, blessing and praise – that allowed Ben Sira to use the term "glory" to mediate the divine and the human. "The hymnic description of Israel's leaders as glorious would have been possible . . . as projections upon them of the glories of the high priest himself in his performance of high liturgical functions" (82). Notably, however, although the hymn's use of "glory" does evoke the presence of God in the sanctuary, it is "not used expressly of the presence of God, but of a quality of the presence of the human figure who performs perfectly his high office" (168). But this only moves the problem back one level. What allows this ascription of glory even to one human?

To answer this question, Mack moves in two directions (168-171). The first appeals to his argument about the relationship of the hymn to the Hellenistic encomium, whose purpose is to assign glory to its subject. The second, more relevant for our purposes, is the wisdom tradition itself, particularly as mythicized by Ben Sira.

> Respect, honor, and glory are deeply rooted in traditional wisdom and mark a major value and motivation for the teaching-learning enterprise. Glory also becomes the sage, and wisdom coming to speech is said to praise herself and receive honor both among the people and in the presence of the Most High (Sir 24,1) (169).

Mack's connection of wisdom and glory is particularly important because it demonstrates that, although the *term* "wisdom" is entirely missing from the hymn to the fathers, its *presence* is not. Wisdom receives constant evocation in the idea of "glory".

Mack argues, finally, that the term "glory" provides a focal point for Ben Sira's recasting of his precursor texts into a new vision.

> The vision is tensive and dialectical with respect to exactly whose glory is manifest or on what basis the human figures actually may be said to be worthy of glorification. The mediation of the glory of the radically transcendent God on the one hand and that of the man of superior achievement on the other, a mediation made possible by the wisdom anthropology of the sage, leaves little room for questions about the conditions and possibilities of glory. . . . [L]ike the term "wisdom," it has no content of its own, depending for that upon its context (169).

It is at this point I believe Mack's analysis requires the nuancing of anthropology. To the extent "glory" is understood strictly as a theologumenon, what he says is accurate. If we look back, however, to the many uses of כבד in the earlier portions of Ben Sira's text, a field of connotations is marked out by the ideology of honor and shame that cannot be ignored, even in the more elevated realm of the hymn to the fathers. I would suggest that the contentless term "wisdom" has in fact been as profoundly specified by its connection to the ethos of honor and shame as it has by association with the glory of the cult. These two understandings of honor/glory must be put in conversation with each other in order to understand the wisdom of Ben Sira.

To recover this conversation, we must return women to the scene of glory from which they have been displaced; return them, that is, to the hymn of the fathers and its location in the cult. We shall do this by tracing the process of their displacement, a process that includes three movements: abstraction, demonization, and erasure.

1. Abstraction

Abstraction begins with the personification of wisdom in Proverbs and works in two ways: both wisdom and women are affected by this move. Mack argues that Proverbs 1-9 is an effort to rethink conventional wisdom, which, with the crisis of exile, had become "dysfunctional in the wake of destruction of its assumed social stabilities" (145). Because "the social arena had lost its capacity for conventional wisdom discourse," the figure of Wisdom had to be imagined as outside that discourse, located "in the divine ordering of the natural world" (145). I believe Mack is correct in part: Prov 8,22-31 certainly supports his case. I have also argued, however, that it is precisely the *female* personification of Wisdom that maintains the figure's dialectical anchoring in the social world: this elevated female figure remains literarily tied to positive figurations of real women, both directly (through the inclusion of the erotic poem of 5,15-19 and the wise women of Ch. 31) and indirectly (by allusion to various female character types familiar from bib-

lical narrative).[16] The pendulum swings both ways, however. Just as
Wisdom is socially grounded by being imaged as woman, woman is
also abstracted by the metaphorical connection to Wisdom, now divinely construed. It is a moment of dangerous opportunity as far as
women are concerned. The canonical tradition knows no higher elevation of the feminine than that of Woman Wisdom. But it is an elevation
achieved by male hands, and thus subject to gender distortion as well.
Paradoxically, I think, it is at least to some degree Proverbs' main-
tainance of divine Wisdom's connection to the realia of women's lives
that allows the figure to valorize real women's status and power.

The danger of the female abstraction in Proverbs is increased to the
degree that this male vision of female goodness is accompanied, rather
predictably, by the embodying of female evil as well. I'll say more
about the Strange Woman shortly, but for now let me note simply that,
in Proverbs, female evil is located in a figure encountered outside a
man's own house. It is, therefore, still escapable by knowledge of his
own proper location at home with his good wife, with whom he can
take his proper pleasure. We need to notice here the valuation of
sexuality as good within the proper confines of marriage.

Ben Sira, of course, is also capable of envisioning a good wife. She
shares with her sister in Proverbs the ability to add substance to her
husband's house-hold (Prov 31,10-31; Sir 26,13b). Her physical charm
(חן) is a delight to her husband (Sir 26,13a), but is superseded (חן על
חן)[17] by her (proper sense of) shame (בי״שׁת; 26,15a).[18] Shame is defined
in two ways by the double entendre of 26,15b: ואין משקל לצרורת פה, literally something like "There is no weight like her bound-up mouth".
The "binding up" or "narrowing" of her mouth most obviously refers
to the desirability of wifely silence, the first meaning of proper shame.
Skehan and Di Lella note, however, that "mouth" can be a euphemism

---

16   C. Camp, *Wisdom and the Feminine in the Book of Proverbs* (Bible and Litera-
     ture Series 11; Sheffield - Decatur GA 1985).

17   Note double meaning of חן where women are concerned. A woman's
     "graceful" behavior receives the same commendation as a man's. The potential
     danger of woman's physical "charm", however, has no male gender parallel.
     See further the discussion of Sir 9,8 below, and Prov 31,30, where the good
     wife's fear of YHWH is valued over her חן.

18   The form בי״שׁת is unknown in the Hebrew Bible, and occurs elsewhere, disput-
     edly, only in Sir42,1c(Mas; בי״שׁ? בושׁ?). The Greek in both cases, however, is
     αἰσχυντηρ-, and there is no reason to translate other than "shame".

for "vagina," and that David's concubines are similarly "shut up" after Absalom's liaison with them (cf. the daughter's "open quiver" in Sir 26,12). Thus, in their re-euphemized translation: "priceless is her chaste person".[19] However, משקל, while it may connote value, is literally "weight," which, we might note, is the material meaning of כבוד as well. As such, משקל makes a nice, though subtle, antithetical parallel with בוש in the first colon of the verse. It seems likely that we should consider sexual "weight" as one of the underlying connotative associations of both משקל and כבוד:[20] Sir 26,15 becomes, then, a bald statement of honor-shame thinking: a man's manliness in a world of sexual contest is determined by his control over his wife's sexuality.

Ben Sira thus expresses interest in his wife's physical beauty or sexuality primarily in terms of anxiety about keeping it for himself, an anxiety that tends to keep his expressions of appreciation for his wife rather closely tied to ruminations about women's evil. The one apparent exception to this rule occurs in 26:16-18, where Ben Sira uses a series of what Skehan and Di Lella rightly call "daring metaphors"[21] to compare the beauty of the wife to the splendor of the Temple, with its lamp, lampstand, and pillars (cf. 50:1-21). One might, indeed, go further. Most English translations follow the Greek in 26:16b, with its reference to the woman's "well-ordered home" (κόσμω οἰκίας). The Hebrew, however, is דביר בחור.[22] In the Hebrew Bible, however, דביר always refers to the holy of holies of the Temple. In its only other appearance in Ben Sira (45,9), דביר refers at least to the Temple precincts, if not to its inner chamber. Understanding a cultic allusion in this description of the wife's beauty in her "chosen sanctuary" provides a fitting comparison to the preceding colon: she is "like the sun rising in the heights on

---

19 P. W. Skehan - A. A. Di Lella, *The Wisdom of Ben Sira* (AB 39; Garden City, NY 1987) 345, 350.

20 Cf. the stain on Solomon's כבוד from sexual misbehavior (47,20).

21 Skehan - Di Lella, *Wisdom*, 351.

22 In discussion following the presentation of this paper, Alexander Di Lella observed that, given the correspondence of the Syriac with the Greek, the Hebrew may reveal a *Tendenz* of MS C, presently our only source for the Hebrew. Originality is difficult to determine here; given present knowledge, we must simply attend to the varied claims of the textual traditions.

high" (cf. 50,7).[23] Two things have happened here. On the one hand, the value of the wife has been exalted to the highest level Ben Sira knows: the woman is brought inside the holy of holies.[24] This exaltation, however, occurs at the price of abstraction: her body is displaced by the light of God. Bathed in its glow, the sage can find a rest from the anxiety of honor and shame that he cannot find elsewhere, even in the house of his good wife. To this I would contrast the confidence Proverbs expresses in the woman of worth (31,10-31) who is very much the embodiment of Wisdom.

Ben Sira retains on one level Proverbs' figure of personified Wisdom, but, especially in Ch. 24, increases the level of abstraction by reducing its personal and, thus, female qualitites. As we have just observed, the connection between Wisdom and the good wife is already more attenuated in Sirach than in Proverbs. Now, moreover, instead of the dramatic metaphor of Wisdom being conceived and brought to birth by YHWH, as in Prov 8, Ben Sira has her coming forth mist-like from the mouth of the Most High. In addition, the tree imagery that forms a small part of her picture in Proverbs dominates it in Sir 24. Most notably, "she" becomes a book! Outside Ch. 24, Wisdom sometimes retains more personal traits. However, although the image is occasionally cast in specifically female terms, "her" main role as a rigorous disciplinarian sounds more like the attitude of a father/teacher than a loving wife or even mother (e.g., 4,11-19; 6,18-31).[25] Sir 14,20-27, on the other hand, foreshadows Ch. 24: it begins with animal imagery for Wisdom, shifts to Wisdom as house (though not without sexual innuendo!), then concludes with the metaphor of the tree.

---

23 Reading MS C's מעל rather than the Greek κυρίου. I thank Ben Wright for the text-critical judgment for preferring MS C over the Greek, the latter having read אל for על.

24 The Hebrew thus reminds us of P. Skehan's proposed "Temple structure" of the book of Proverbs, which literarily "builds" a cella for Woman Wisdom. P.W. Skehan, "Wisdom's House", *Studies in Israelite Poetry and Wisdom* (CBQMS 1; Washington, DC 1971) 27-45. It is tempting, however, to ponder MS C's choice of adjective: בחור can also be a noun, in which case the woman's designated space becomes "the chamber of the young man"!

25 These characterizations begin the process of erasure by masculinization that I will discuss further below.

2. Demonization

If abstraction begins the displacement of women from Ben Sira's ideal cultic world, demonization continues it. Demonization begins, of course, with the creation of the Strange Woman in Proverbs. There has been much debate as to whether the Strange Woman should be understood simply as the sage's representation of his experience of "real women," whether she is a cipher for false worship, or, as I have argued elsewhere, whether she is a multi-faceted symbol of evil comprised by a hyperbolic caricature of the dangers presented by women to men: she is prostitute *and* adulteress *and* purveyor of cultic impurity.[26] To the extent our understanding moves in the latter direction, one could make the case that the sage of Proverbs attacks the perceived evil of *real* women less than he adulates their perceived good. Most significantly, as we have already noted, Proverbs excludes the bad from the man's household domain.

In Ben Sira, however, two important changes occur.[27] First, the possibility of having an *evil wife* is not just raised, but given rather extensive treatment. The real possibility of women's evil, defined repeatedly as sexually transmitted shame, has moved from the streets of Proverbs into the heart of the man's home. Proverbs' sense of safety in the prescriptive force of marriage – its capacity to control women's shame – is absent in Sir 25-26, as it is in 9,1-9, which registers so little distinction between the sexual dangers presented by different kinds of women.[28]

---

26 C. Camp, "What's So Strange About the Strange Woman?", *The Bible and the Politics of Exegesis* (FS. N. Gottwald; [ed. D. Jobling, P. L. Day, and G. T. Sheppard] Cleveland, OH 1991) 17-32.

27 There is, in fact, a third change – the erasure of the symbol of the Strange Woman –that requires an extensive disussion of its own, beyond the limits of present space.

28 Sir 36,24-28, which I do not discuss here, has a rhetoric of its own. The effort in this case seems to be to persuade young men to marry by showing the drawbacks of bachelorhood, as well as the delights of marriage. Naturally, there is no "evil wife" polemic here! It is replaced by concern for what happens (to other men!) when the single man is not "fenced in." Honor-shame ideology involves intergenerational issues – the control of fathers over sons – as well as gender issues. Camp, "Understanding", 25-26, and cf. C. Newsom, "Wisdom and the Discourse of Patriarchal Wisdom: A Study of Proverbs 1-9", *Gender and Difference in Ancient Israel* (ed. P. Day) (Minneapolis, MN 1989) 142-160, on intergenerational discourse in Proverbs.

One blurs into another, as "the woman of your bosom" (that is, your wife) in v. 1 becomes simply the woman to whom one "gives oneself" in v. 2, who, in turn becomes the harlots to whom one also "gives oneself" in v. 5. Similarly, one should not "look at" a virgin (v. 5) or at beauty not belonging to oneself (v. 8b), but rather "turn one's eyes" from a "shapely woman" (v. 8a). But a man's own daughters are virgins and, if he's fortunate, his own wife is "shapely" (חן; 26,13). That the "shapely woman" in 9,8a represents a wife is made clear in 8b, where she is placed in parallel with "beauty not belonging to oneself" (cf. the "beauty of one's wife"; 26,16). The implicit concern, then, is not just for a man's own behavior when he's out, but for the actions of other men he invites in (cf. 11,29-34, which barely conceals reference to sexuality).

A second change from Proverbs' depiction of female evil comes in Ben Sira's close connection of the imagery for Wisdom in Ch. 24 with that of the adulteress in 23,22-27. While previous scholars have noted this connection[29], I don't think its full effects on Wisdom have been reckoned with. The adulteress in her "disgrace" (ὄνειδος; 23,26) provides an "heir" (κληρονόμον) by a stranger (23,22), while YHWH, Wisdom and Torah are the "inheritance" (κληρονομία) of "honored" (δεδοξασμένῳ) Israel (24,12. 20-23). Disgrace is the antithesis of honor and, if a woman's adultery is its definitive moment, the fruit of her liaison its enduring legacy, as is evident in the allusions to heirs and inheritance in chs. 23 and 24. Thus, in contrast to the offspring of the adulteress, those who inherit Wisdom will not be put to shame (24,20-22). The verbal connections continue: the adulteress' children will not "take root" (23,25), though Wisdom does (24,12). The woman's "memory" will be a curse (23,26); that of Wisdom "sweeter than honey" (24,20). "Sweetness" is also the experience of those who follow the commandments of the Lord as an antidote to the adulteress (23,27) and, of course, Wisdom finally is identified this selfsame Torah (24,23).

I certainly agree with Prof. Beentjes, who has argued that the reference to "the law of the Most High" in 23,23 should be construed broadly, as parallel to "the book of the covenant of the Most High" in 24,23: these rhetorical connections between the adulteress and Woman

---

29   J. Marböck, *Weisheit im Wandel. Untersuchungen zur Weisheitstheologie bei Ben Sira* (BBB 37; Bonn 1971) 42; P. Beentjes, "Full Wisdom is Fear of the Lord," *EstBib* 47 (1989) 32-33.

Wisdom are hardly accidental, and are related to "the book"[30]. But think now about what we have just said! At the very least, Woman Wisdom been tarnished by association. While the Wisdom figure might possibly be seen as the antithesis of the adulteress, the instruction on good and bad wives in the immediately succeeding chapters clouds this straightforward reading by its implication that even marriage provides no haven from the evil woman. If wives can be tainted, no female image is any longer safe. On one level, female Wisdom cannot escape the possibility of shame posed by all women.

But the problem goes further even than this. For it seems at best that the exalted Woman Wisdom - and, with her, the book of the covenant itself - has been reduced to a defense mechanism against the crudities of a shameful wife. The only way, I think, to save Wisdom and Torah from such an apparent reductionism in the thought of Ben Sira is to elevate sufficiently the fundamental threat posed by the shame of women to his construction of an ideal world.[31] The cosmic force of this threat is signified once more by both the content and location of the bitter invectives against daughters and all women in 42,9-14.[32] Why else introduce the magnificent hymn to God as creator with verses on the danger to men of women's shame? Surely one needs all the power of creation against a force such as this.

3. Erasure

Demonization requires destruction. Women and their shame are now not just a problem men must overcome in the social world; they are a threat to the ideal world that must be erased from its authorizing model and context, that is, the Temple cult as schematized in the hymn to the fathers. The erasure must take place at the levels of both ethos and

---

30   Beentjes, "Full Wisdom", 33.
31   My argument on the cosmic status of Wisdom and Torah parallels that of R. Hayward, "Sacrifice and World Order: Some Observations on Ben Sira's Attitude to the Temple Service", *Sacrifice and Redemption: Durham Essays in Theology* (ed. S. W. Sykes) (Cambridge 1991) 29, who insists on the cosmic role played by Wisdom and Torah. Whereas Hayward formulates their world-constructing function unproblematically, however, the lens of honor and shame limns the contest and polemic in this rhetoric.
32   Camp, "Understanding", 35-36.

world view, that is, there must be erasure of both woman and Woman Wisdom, a feat more easily accomplished by virtue of the rhetorical interweaving of the adulteress and Wisdom in chs. 23-24.

The primary way a man can be shamed is, as we have noted, through failure to control the sexual behavior of his wife. Striking, then, are the connections between the castigation of the adulteress in 23:22-27 and the hymn to the fathers, especially but not exclusively in the prologue of Chapter 44. Both pericopes are dotted by references to "children" (τέκνα; 23,23.24.25; 44,9.12), though the latter, with its male subject, also uses "seed" (σπέρμα; 44,11.12.13). In 23,22-23, the woman's τέκνα are identified by chiastic structure with the "heir" (κληονόμον) she presents her husband, who is really the son of a "stranger".[33] In 44,11, the reference is not to the heir, but the inheritance (κληρονομία), which is, nonetheless, said to be guaranteed to the pious man's posterity (ἔκγονα). One wonders, however, where the emphasis of this latter promise falls. Is it simply (à la Qohelet) that the wealth of one generation will not be dissipated in future ones? Or, with reference to the danger suggested in Ch. 23, is there also the assurance that the children to whom a man passes on his property will indeed be his own? Other verbal resonances require that we not ignore the latter possibility. The hymn to the fathers reflects briefly on men who perished without honor or name. These leave no "memorial/memory" (μνημόσυνον), a fate comparable to the cursed "memory" of the adulteress (23,26; 44,9). On the other hand, neither the "honor/glory" (δόξα) of the pious nor the disgrace (ὄνειδος) of the adulteress will be "blotted out" (ἐξαλειφθήσεται; 23,26; 44,15). Finally, just as the adulteress will be brought before the "assembly" (ἐκκλησία) for condemnation, this same body will forever proclaim the praise of the pious (23,24; 44,15). The issue at stake, then, is the honor of the pious, vested in the purity of their seed. By reproducing the language of the adulteress pericope, while eliminating the adulteress, Ch. 44 in effect rhetorically guarantees the seed of the pious from all potential shame.[34]

---

33   καὶ παριστῶσα κληρονόμον ἐξ ἀλλοτρίου . . . καὶ ἐξ ἀλλοτρίου ἀνδρος τέκνα παρέστησεν. (23,22b.23d)

34   For a thorough discussion of the concern with pure seed in the Hebrew Bible priestly writings and Mishnah, and the ideological contradiction this creates vis-à-vis women, see H. Eilberg-Schwartz, *The Savage in Judaism* (Bloomington - Indianapolis, IN 1990) 115-234.

Many of these verbal links of the hymn's prologue and the adulteress pericope are, of course, precisely the links between the adulteress and Woman Wisdom and, thus, between Wisdom and the honored fathers. On one level, the prologue draws a contrast between the adulteress and the fathers identical to that between the adulteress and Wisdom. The shame of the former is overcome in each case by the honor/glory of the latter. There is also a difference, however, for, as we observed, Wisdom in Ch. 24 is literarily enfolded and thus ideologically tainted by the shame of women, a problem whose solution begins with the masculinization of glory/honor in Ch. 44.

The process by which women and their shame are erased and replaced by an ideal cosmos constituted entirely of men finds completion in the depiction of Simon's glory in Ch. 50.[35] Simon replaces Woman Wisdom as the one who ministers (λειτουργειν; 24,10; 50,14, 19) before YHWH in the holy place, assuming from her the sensual imagery of plants and fragrant incense, along with her honor. Nor does Simon stand alone. Wearing "garments of splendor" (בגדי תפארת), he is encircled by a "crown of sons" (עטרת בנים; 50,12), "all the sons of Aaron in their כבוד" (50,13), who have replaced Woman Wisdom's "crown of splendor" (עטרת תפארת; 6,31; cf. 15,6). Women and their shame have been erased by transformation into the glory of a perfectly male world. Here the contradictions and anxiety wrought by an ethos of honor and shame receive their eternal resolution.

Conclusion

I have argued that Ben Sira's interpretive transformation of the wisdom tradition happens on more than one front. While we are accustomed to commentators' observations about his connection of female personified Wisdom with Torah, as well as his association of wisdom and cult, I have tried to make a case complementary to these: not only has Ben Sira linked wisdom to Torah and cult, he has also anchored wisdom, Torah, and cult in the ideology of honor and shame. This move has as

---

35   See Hayward, "Sacrifice", 24-28, for a detailed discussion of the corresponding imagery for Simon and Wisdom.

many ramifications for his work as the others. Honor-shame anthropology informs a literary analysis of the relationship of the female images within chs. 23-26, as well as with the priestly imagery in Ch. 50, in such a way as to highlight the cultic need for control of the feminine, whose traces nonetheless still mark the holy place. The processes of control I have described – abstraction, demonization, and masculinizing erasure – were not, I should add, necessarily intentional. Like any good ideology, the honor-shame system works implicitly as much as explicitly. Indeed, ideologies are most effective when people habitually resort to them without intention. By elucidating the work of female imagery in Ben Sira's semiotic system, honor-shame anthropology not only nuances his view of cultic glory, but also highlights the symbolic shifts from his precursor text in Proverbs. If, as some have argued, Sir 51 replicates the acrostic of Prov 31,10-31, then the house of the good wife has been masculinized as the sage's house as well, a re-gendering prefigured in Sir 24, where the voice of Woman Wisdom melts seamlessly into the voice of the teacher in (24,30). In sum, one might say that the linkage of wisdom and cult in Ben Sira takes place by means of the gendered logic of honor and shame.

"Fear the Lord and Honor the Priest"
Ben Sira as Defender of the Jerusalem Priesthood*

By Benjamin G. Wright III, Bethlehem (USA)

From the early years after the people of Israel returned from exile in Babylon to the land of their forefathers, the conduct of the priesthood that served in the Temple constituted the principle reason for the dissatisfaction of some Jews with the worship of God in Jerusalem, and it became a lightening rod for criticism. Upon his return to Palestine, for example, the scribe Ezra in the fifth century BCE found that the priests and the Levites, as well as ordinary Israelites, had married foreign women, and stopping this practice became one of the cornerstones of his religious reforms (Ezra 9-10). The post-exilic prophet known as Malachi excoriated the priests for offering defective animals as sacrifices in the Temple cult (Mal 1,6-14). He further indicted them for divorcing their wives and producing polluted offspring with other women (2,13-16).[1]

---

* I presented some preliminary thoughts on these issues in a paper entitled "Seeking the Sublime: Aspects of Inner Jewish Polemic in the Wisdom of Ben Sira" to the Hellenistic Judaism Section of the 1993 Annual Meetings of the Society of Biblical Literature in Washington, D. C. The general argument given here can also be found in my paper "Putting the Puzzle Together: Some Suggestions Concerning the Social Location of the Wisdom of Ben Sira", *SBL Seminar Papers 1996* (Atlanta 1996) 133-149. In several places here, I have adapted and revised portions of that paper.

1 On priests in general, see Lester L. Grabbe, *Priests, Prophets, Diviners, Sages: A Socio-historical Study of Religious Specialists in Ancient Israel* (Valley Forge 1995) 41-65 and M. Stern, "Aspects of Jewish Society: The Priesthood and Other Classes", in S. Safrai and M. Stern, eds. *The Jewish People in the First Century* (*CRINT* I.2; Philadelphia 1976) 561-630.

In the turbulent political world of the late third to early second
century BCE, it should not be a surprise to see that the priesthood and
thus the Temple are still seen by some as corrupt institutions that God
would punish or replace. The discovery and publication of the literature
of the Qumran *yahad* brought into bold relief a group that rejected the
Jerusalem priesthood.[2] But already for several decades before the
Maccabean Revolt, prior to the composition of the sectarian literature
from Qumran, there was a lively, oftentimes acrimonious, war of words
being waged in Palestine over the legitimacy of the Jerusalem
priesthood. Some of the critical voices from this period, like the
anonymous authors/compilers of *The Book of the Watchers* (*1 Enoch* 6-
36), the *Astronomical Book* (*1 Enoch* 72-82) and the *Aramaic Levi
Document*, have been identified and their criticisms outlined by
scholars.[3]   Other Jews, however, did not see the priesthood in such a
negative light, but, in fact, believed that God's approbation rested on
those who served in the Jerusalem Temple.

In the early second century BCE, perhaps the most prominent of
those who supported the Jerusalem priests was a Jerusalemite named
Jesus ben Eleazar Ben Sira. Indeed, many scholars of the Wisdom of
Jesus Ben Sira have commented on his positive valuation of the
Jerusalem priests and cult.[4] One scholar, Helge Stadelmann, has tried

---

2   On the origins of the Qumran community and its relationship with the priests in
     Jerusalem, see James C. VanderKam, *The Dead Sea Scrolls Today* (Grand Rapids
     1994) 101-102 and Lawrence H. Schiffman, *Reclaiming the Dead Sea Scrolls*
     (Philadelphia 1994) 87-89.

3   See, for example, David Suter, "Fallen Angel, Fallen Priest: The Problem of
     Family Purity in 1 Enoch 6-16", *HUCA* 50 (1979) 115-135; George W. E.
     Nickelsburg, "Enoch, Levi and Peter: Recipients of Revelation in Upper Galilee",
     JBL 100 (1981) 575-600; *idem, Jewish Literature Between the Bible and the
     Mishnah* (Philadelphia 1981) 52-54; Michael Stone, "Enoch, Aramaic Levi and
     Sectarian Origins", *JSJ* 19 (1988) 159-170; Robert A. Kugler, *From Patriarch to
     Priest: The Levi-Priestly Tradition from Aramaic Levi to Testament of Levi*
     (Early Judaism and Its Literature 9; Atlanta 1996).

4   See, for example, T. Maertens, *L'éloge des pères* (*Ecclésiastique XLIV-L*)
     (Bruges 1956) 121, 156; G. Maier, *Mensch und freier Wille: Nach der jüdischen
     Religionsparteien zwischen Ben Sira und Paulus* (WUNT 12; Tübingen 1971) 52-
     54.

to make the case that Ben Sira was himself a priest.[5] In this paper, however, I want to go another step. I believe that a case can be made on the basis of certain pieces of circumstantial evidence, that Ben Sira's positive view of the Jerusalem priesthood did not take shape in an ideological vacuum, but that he was deeply engaged in that ongoing war of words as one who actively took the side of the Temple priests in polemical opposition against those who criticized them.

The argument of this paper is that Ben Sira was aware of and intended some passages to respond polemically to complaints that had been lodged against the Jerusalem priestly establishment and those who supported it. These complaints can be found in the works mentioned above, which are roughly contemporary to Ben Sira.[6] He had a strategy for addressing these concerns that consisted of (1) writing positively about the priesthood and encouraging Jews to pay the priests in the Temple the honor due them and (2) confronting some of the means by which the communities who produced and used these works that opposed the Temple priests legitimated or gave authority to their criticisms. I believe that Ben Sira knew the specific criticisms of those whom he supported and came to their defense.

This last claim highlights the inevitable circumstantial character of this argument. Ben Sira does not mention the targets of his polemic, but embeds his remarks against them in the middle of other discussions. Likewise, some of the critics of the Jerusalem establishment couched their criticisms in the heavily symbolic language of apocalyptic without

---

5   H. Stadelmann, *Ben Sira als Schriftgelehrter: Eine Untersuchung zum Berufsbild des vor-makkabäischen Sofer unter Berücksichtigung seines Verhältnisses zu Priester-, Propheten- und Weisheitslehrertum* (WUNT 2/6; Tübingen 1981).

6   The *Book of the Watchers* and the *Astronomical Book* probably date to at least the third century BCE. J. T. Milik, *The Books of Enoch* (Oxford 1976) dates the Qumran manuscripts of these sections to the second century BCE. Since they are surely not the autographs, the composition of the books must be earlier. On the dating of the Enochic corpus, see Nickelsburg, *Jewish Literature*, 46-55, 150-151. On a third century BCE date for Aramaic Levi, see Stone, "Enoch, Aramaic Levi", 159 note 2 and Kugler, *From Patriarch to Priest*, 222-224. Sirach is usually dated to somewhere around 180 BCE. See P.W. Skehan and A.A. Di Lella, *The Wisdom of Ben Sira*, (AB 39; Garden City, NY 1987) 8-10. On the relationship between the Aramaic Levi Document and the Greek Testament of Levi which used Aramaic Levi see H. W. Hollander and M. de Jonge, *The Testaments of the Twelve Patriarchs: A Commentary* (Leiden 1985) and also Kugler's discussion and the literature cited therein.

any specific references to their contemporary agenda. Consequently, the social situations reflected in these documents must be reconstructed from precious few clues, which present a difficult obstacle. Do the literary devices, themes and issues provide a firm enough basis to reconstruct a social world where real people and communities are struggling to realize their own visions for the Israel of God? Can we see here communities of Jews in conflict with each other? In other words, even though Ben Sira and the communities represented in the Enochic works and *Aramaic Levi* may be contemporary and even treat the same themes and issues, can we move from those "facts" to envisioning a social world in which these people know about one another and attack or respond to one another? Given the indirect and ambiguous nature of the evidence can one move from literary theme to social reality? I think that the cumulative effect of all the pieces of evidence when they are drawn together will enable a plausible scenario to emerge of a continuing confrontation among different Jewish groups over what they consider to be foundational issues for Jews in the period before the Maccabean Revolt.

1. Ben Sira's Support of the Jerusalem Priesthood and Temple

Sirach contains several passages that demonstrate the author's out-spoken enthusiasm regarding the Jerusalem priesthood and the Temple cult. Since these have been treated in detail elsewhere, I will outline only the most important passages in this section.[7] I cannot review in detail in this paper the problem of whether Ben Sira is simply giving lipservice to the importance of the cult while really being concerned about ethical living or whether he does think that the cult is important in and of itself. Saul Olyan has provided a good summary discussion of these issues and concludes that for Ben Sira the cult really matters. I am convinced by his overall argument and his conclusion that "Ben Sira's

---

7   See especially Stadelmann, *Ben Sira als Schriftgelehrter*; Saul Olyan, "Ben Sira's Relationship to the Priesthood", *HTR* 80 (1987) 261-286 and the literature cited in these studies.

positive view of the cult is as obvious as are his ethical concerns. There is no conflict between the two".[8]

Ben Sira expresses his views on the priesthood most succinctly in the critical passage 7,29-31.[9] Here he adapts the language of Deut 6,5, part of the Shema, in order to encourage giving the priests their due. "With all your heart (כבל לכב) fear the Lord and regard the priests as holy (הקדיש). With all your might (מאודך) love your maker and do not forsake his servants. Give glory to God and honor the priest, and give their portion as you are commanded". As Olyan remarks, "the parallelistic structure of this passage is striking".[10] Each action intended for God is paralleled by one intended for the priests. Ben Sira's use of Deuteronomy lends tremendous symbolic and rhetorical weight to how important honoring the priests is. Giving the priests honor is the symbolic equivalent of fearing and loving God. Thus, the command to give the priests their portion of the sacrifices (which are listed in v. 31) also takes on greater rhetorical importance in the context. Performance of the cult and giving the priests their due is elevated to the level of extending to God his proper honor.

Sir 34,21-35,12 deals more specifically with the performance of the cultic sacrifices.[11] In this passage, Ben Sira contrasts the abuse of the cult with its proper performance. What distinguishes the one from the other is proper ethical conduct. Ben Sira states forthrightly that God does not accept the sacrifices of the ungodly (34,23) and that "the sacrifice of the righteous is acceptable" (35,9). But his other comments about the cult in this passage do not seem to spiritualize it in favor of ethics.[12] In 35,1-12 Ben Sira repeatedly notes the importance of performing the sacrifice. The sacrificial offerings "fulfill the commandment". Sir 35,1-2 connect intimately the cult with righteousness. "The one who keeps the law makes many offerings; one who heeds the commandments makes a peace offering".

---

8   Olyan, "Ben Sira's Relationship to the Priesthood", 263. The full discussion can be found on pp. 261-263, 265 note 13, 266-267.

9   For a full discussion of this passage, see Stadelmann, *Ben Sira als Schrift-gelehrter*, 56-68.

10   Olyan, "Ben Sira's Relationship to the Priesthood", 264.

11   On this section, see Stadelman, *Ben Sira als Schriftgelehrter*, 68-138.

12   See Stadelmann, *Ben Sira als Schriftgelehrter*, 119, who compares his under-standing of Ben Sira's position to the one later found at Qumran.

Although Ben Sira in this passage stresses the importance of the relationship between ethics and sacrifice, he does not do so to the diminution of the sacrificial system practiced in the Temple. Proper sacrifice "enriches the altar" (35,8). The Jew who fulfills the law, a matter of crucial importance to Ben Sira, acts properly and performs the necessary sacrifices in the Temple.[13]

Returning to the priesthood, many have remarked on the greater amount of attention that Ben Sira devotes to Aaron as compared to his more famous brother Moses. The long section on Aaron (45,6-22) is followed by one on Phinehas (45,23-25), and later in Chapter 50 Ben Sira closes the Praise of the Ancestors section by glorifying the high priest Simon II. God makes an eternal covenant both with Aaron and with Phinehas, the everlasting covenant being mentioned twice in Aaron's case. Olyan notes that in these passages Ben Sira "alludes to P passage after P passage ... ignoring for all intents and purposes other Pentateuchal narrative".[14] He goes on to argue that Sirach reflects a position in which, like the Priestly narrative in the Pentateuch, Aaron and his descendents are the true priests. According to Olyan, Ben Sira maintains a "pan-Aaronid" view of the priesthood, while at the same time neglecting the Levites entirely and never mentioning the sons of Zadok.[15] Since Ben Sira's praise of Simon II harks back to that of Aaron, Simon becomes the epitome of the high priest who fulfills the covenant made with Aaron and Phinehas.[16] Ben Sira's pan-Aaronid views find further confirmation in the description of Simon exiting the Temple and blessing the people in which those priests who accompany

---

13 Sir 38,9-11 also enjoins the offering of sacrifices, in this case in time of illness. One should offer sacrifice and then call a doctor.

14 Olyan, "Ben Sira's Relationship to the Priesthood", 270.

15 Olyan, "Ben Sira's Relationship to the Priesthood", 275, implies that Ben Sira's "pan-Aaronid" views may also account for the absence of Ezra from the Praise of the Ancestors since he was a Zadokite, and that balancing the absence of Zadokites in Sirach might explain the addition of the hymn after 50.12 where a specific praise of the sons of Zadok appears. See also P. Höffken's conclusion in "Warum schwieg Jesus Sirach über Ezra"? *ZAW* 87 (1975) 184-202 cited by Olyan, "Ben Sira's Relationship to the Priesthood", 275 note 40.

16 Olyan, "Ben Sira's Relationship to the Priesthood", 270, remarks that even Simon's Zadokite lineage is ignored by Ben Sira.

him are called "sons of Aaron" (50,13.16).[17] By deliberately choosing one particular priestly ideology over other possible ones, like those in Deuteronomy and Jeremiah or in the work of the Chronicler, Olyan concludes that Ben Sira rejects the exclusivistic claims to the high priesthood made by Zadokites.[18]

The Temple itself also finds approbation in Sirach. In the famous Praise of Wisdom found in Chapter 24, God sends wisdom to dwell in Israel where she ministers in "the holy tent" (24,10). He then establishes her in Jerusalem, but specifically in Zion, that is, in the Temple.[19] In 49,12 Joshua and Zerubbabel are remembered as having "raised the holy temple destined for everlasting glory".[20]

Apart from the textual affirmations of the priests, cult and Temple given by Ben Sira, Patrick Tiller and Richard Horsley suggest that Ben Sira's position in Jerusalem society provides strong motivation for him to support the Jerusalem Temple establishment. In their paper, "Ben Sira and the Sociology of the Second Temple" (SBL 1992), they utilize the insights of the sociologist Gerhard Lenski in an attempt to sketch the contours of Judean society in the time of Ben Sira and to understand where he fits in the network of social relations revealed in his book.[21] They conclude that the first-person descriptions given by Ben Sira reveal him to belong to what they call the "scribe-sage" class, a class categorized by Lenski as a retainer class.[22] They argue that Ben Sira would have belonged to a retainer class that acted as mediators between the rulers, primarily priests in ancient Judea, and ordinary Jews. Some of the functions of this class would necessarily overlap with those of the priests, especially teaching the law (a responsibility given to Aaron in 45,17), which would have been delegated by priests to the scribe-sage class. Horsley and Tiller remark, "In Ben Sira's Judea, the sages

---

17 Ben Sira probably had personal experience of Simon officiating in the Temple, even though the book was probably written after the high priest's death. See Skehan and Di Lella, *The Wisdom of Ben Sira*, 9.

18 Olyan, "Ben Sira's Relationship to the Priesthood", 272, 275-276.

19 Skehan and Di Lella, *The Wisdom of Ben Sira*, 333.

20 This translation reflects MS B from the Geniza which is missing "to the Lord" found in the Greek.

21 Presented to the Sociology of the Second Temple Group, San Francisco, 1992. My thanks to the authors for making available to me a copy of their paper. They rely on Gerhard Lenski, *Power and Privilege* (New York 1966).

22 Horsley and Tiller, "Ben Sira and the Sociology of the Second Temple", 29.

performed the functions that Lenski ascribes to 'the clergy' in societies of limited literacy: officials and diplomats as well as educators".[23]

Consequently, this scribe-sage class would be heavily dependent on the priests for its livelihoood and social status; it would be both politically and economically vulnerable to the priests. Horsley and Tiller argue that such a social position would account well for Ben Sira's admonitions about how to deal with the ruling class. But, in addition, scribes would have some independence from the priests and retain some authority as those who guard, teach and interpret the divine commandments. Their presumed authority might even bring them into conflict with their priestly superiors. "The sages had a clear sense of their own, independent of their patrons, of how the temple-state should operate in accordance with (their interpretation of) the covenantal laws. Their high priestly superiors, however, had regular dealings with the Hellenistic imperial officials and were susceptible to greater influence from the wider Hellenistic culture".[24]

Thus, whatever Ben Sira's precise social position was, priest, scribe-sage or priest *and* scribe, he shows himself to be thoroughly on the side of the Jerusalem priestly establishment. He enjoins his charges to honor the priests, to give them their proper portions of the sacrifices, to offer the proper sacrifices at the right time. If he were actually a priest as Stadelmann argues, he would have a deep investment in viewing the Temple priesthood in this manner. Yet even if he were not a priest, but a member of a social group retained by the priests, as Horsley and Tiller claim, he would have cause as well to stand behind the legitimacy of the Jerusalem priests. These views on the priesthood did not take shape in some esoteric realm of theological detachment, but they were formed as a response to those whose views on the Jerusalem establishment were quite opposite Ben Sira's.

---

23   Horsley and Tiller, "Ben Sira and the Sociology of the Second Temple", 30.
24   Horsley and Tiller, "Ben Sira and the Sociology of the Second Temple", 32. This might also explain to a degree Ben Sira's support of the priests, on the one hand, and some of his apparently negative attitudes towards Hellenistic culture, on the other.

2. *Criticisms of the Priests in* 1 Enoch *and* Aramaic Levi

Two sections of *1 Enoch*, viz. the *Book of the Watchers* and the *Astronomical Book*, together with the *Aramaic Levi Document* are roughly contemporary with our Jerusalemite sage. Even if these third century BCE works slightly predate Ben Sira, they were clearly prized and in use in communities at his time.[25] Thus, the way that they view the priests in Jerusalem provides an excellent window through which to see Ben Sira's antagonists. Two questions surface regarding these works: what is the nature of the criticism and out of what kinds of groups do they arise?

Both David Suter and George Nickelsburg have argued that the *Book of the Watchers* contains veiled criticism of the Jerusalem priesthood, and by extension the legitimacy of the Temple cult, over the issue of improper marriages.[26] Suter examines *1 Enoch* 6-16. Chapters 6-11 have as a central part of the myth of the fallen Watchers a concern that they have been defiled by contact with women and blood and that the offspring of the unions between the women and the Watchers are *mamzerim*. Chapters 12-16, a commentary on the preceding chapters, demonstrate interest in the same problem, but also here there is the implication that the sexual contact "is defiling *per se* since it represents an illegitimate degree of family relationship...The incongruity of marriages of angels and women is underlined by 1 En. 15,4-12...". The giants are "hybrids" just as the offspring of the illicit priestly marriages are. For the *Book of the Watchers* "the concern for the purity of the angels in both sections [6-11 and 12-16], taken with the treatment of the giants as *mamzerim*, suggests that the myth needs to be examined in light of rules concerning family purity in Second Temple Judaism".[27] This preoccupation with family purity in *1 Enoch*, according to Suter's analysis, is about priestly purity, which was a primary concern for Jews in the Second Temple period. He concludes, "There is a parallel between the separation that the myth seeks to draw between the angelic

---

25 The *Book of the Watchers* was known to the author of *Jubilees*, and of course, portions of all three works were found among the Qumran manuscripts.
26 Suter, "Fallen Angel" and Nickelsburg, "Enoch, Levi and Peter". See also Martha Himmelfarb, *Ascent to Heaven in Jewish & Christian Apocalypses* (New York 1993) 9-29.
27 Suter, "Fallen Angel", 118-119.

and human realms and the tendency toward endogamy in priestly marriages".[28]

In addition other clues point to the priesthood as the critical problem in *1 Enoch* 6-16. In these chapters the Watchers pervert priestly responsibilities. The priest's role as teacher is subverted by the Watchers because they teach forbidden knowledge. The illegitimate marriages of the Watchers further result in their expulsion from heaven, which is depicted as a Temple. For the author of these chapters, like the Watchers expelled from the heavenly Temple, the priests in Jerusalem who contract illegitimate marriages should be prevented from serving in the earthly Temple.[29]

This interest in and concern for priestly purity may well indicate that the *Book of the Watchers* originated in circles of priests who were convinced that the Jerusalem priests had violated purity rules, were defiled as a result, and should be expelled from the Temple service. Several pieces of evidence indicate a priestly origin for this work. Michael Stone argues that the "scientific" speculations contained in the early parts of *1 Enoch* must have originated in groups of "educated men and may possibly have been associated with the traditional intellectuals, the wise and the priests". He notes in addition that the calendrical interests so notable in both the *Book of the Watchers* and the *Astronomical Book* are traditionally matters dealt with by priests.[30]

In his SBL paper, "The Priesthood and Apocalyptic", Suter looks to the sociological analysis of Edward Shils, who studied the roles of intellectuals in society, for indications as to who might have produced the *Book of the Watchers*. Shils's analysis shows that the center of society is made up of two systems, "a *central institutional system*, which wields power, and a *central cultural system*, which develops the myths legitimating the exercise of power". Suter combines this insight with the connection made by Stone between apocalyptic and Jewish intellectual traditions. He concludes, "Since the interests of the central institutional system are not completely identical with those of the central cultural system, it is possible to account for friction within the

---

28 Suter, "Fallen Angel", 122.

29 Suter, "Fallen Angel", 123-124. On heaven as a Temple in *1 Enoch*, see Nickelsburg, *Jewish Literature*, 53 and Himmelfarb, *Ascent to Heaven*, 14-16.

30 Michael Stone, "The Book of Enoch and Judaism in the Third Century B.C.E.", *CBQ* 40 (1978) 489. See below for a more detailed treatment of the calendar.

priesthood itself within Judean society, since priests are undoubtedly in the forefront of both systems".[31] That is, the criticisms in evidence in *1 Enoch* are not simply *about* the priesthood, they originate *within* priestly groups.

The roles ascribed to Enoch, the protagonist of this mythic drama and likely representative of the community, also provide evidence of the group that produced the work. Enoch is called "scribe of righteousness" (15,1), and in drawing up the petition of the Watchers he acts as a scribe. But, Enoch also plays the role of priest when he intercedes for the Watchers before God, intercession being a priestly function. Enoch has extraordinary access to the heavenly Temple, the Temple being a place that is the absolute domain of the priests.[32] As Suter notes regarding the role of scribe and priest, "a scribal role need not preclude a priestly one, and may even point in that direction".[33]

Nickelsburg concentrates specifically on the cultic language contained in *1 Enoch* 15,2-4, where Enoch is to tell the Watchers that their plea to God has been rejected. Rather than someone petitioning God for them, they should be interceding for humankind. The indictment of the Watchers follows in verses 3-4, "Why have you [the Watchers] left the high heaven and the eternal holy one and lain with women and defiled yourselves with the daughters of men and taken to yourselves wives and acted like the children of earth ...yet you defiled yourselves with the blood of women ...". The description of heaven in this work as a Temple and the angels as priests has prompted Nickelsburg, like Suter, to identify the Watchers as priests who have fallen and united themselves with women by marrying illegitimately. As a result, God has banned the Watchers from the heavenly Temple, and, those priests who have married women forbidden to them should be barred from the earthly Temple. This kind of anti-priestly polemic is consistent with several other Second Temple Jewish texts that report similar difficulties, and it demonstrates that the character of the

---

31 David Suter, "The Priesthood and Apocalyptic", 11. The paper was presented in the Worship/Cult in Ancient Israel Section of the 1981 Annual Meetings of the Society of Biblical Literature in San Francisco. My thanks to the author for making his paper available to me.

32 Himmelfarb, *Ascent to Heaven*, 23-25.

33 Suter, "The Priesthood", 9. Ezra is himself called scribe and priest. As one can see above in Section 1, scholars have attributed both offices to Ben Sira as well.

priesthood is a fundamental concern for many Jews in this period.[34] Nickelsburg concludes that "the easiest explanation [of the myth in *1 Enoch* 12-16] appears to be that the mythmaker has a grievance against the priesthood in his own time ... we have here in *1 Enoch* 12-16 an apocalyptic tradition emanating from circles in upper Galilee who view the Jerusalem priesthood as defiled and therefore under the irrevocable judgment of God".[35]

The situation in *Aramaic Levi* is very similar to that of *1 Enoch*. This work also contains elements of polemic against exogamous marriages. The specific comments of the fragmentary passage in 4Q213 2 about virgins ruining their names and bringing shame on their brothers, which Levi apparently sees in a vision, would seem to indicate that priestly exogamy in particular is the problem.[36] Later in *Aramaic Levi* 82-106, Levi's testamentary speech to his children predicts that in later generations they will cease to follow his instructions. The section begins with an admonishment by Levi that his children learn and teach wisdom. In 102-106 Levi makes clear that his descendents will abandon this wisdom and will "walk in the darkness of satan ... will become fools". They will turn to wickedness and evil (106).[37]

A number of other characteristics of the work also point to a priestly milieu for its origins. Levi's position as the ancestor of priests sets up a glorification of the priesthood as an institution while at the same time there is a condemnation of particular groups of priests; the polemic concerning illegitimate marriages and the wickedness of some priests recalls *1 Enoch*. The centrality of the figure of Levi also points in this direction. Several of the emphases of *Aramaic Levi* reflect priestly interests. *Aramaic Levi* is interested in the calendar and seems to use a solar year. The work includes detailed sacrificial instructions (13-60), and it emphasizes the levitical line.[38] Indeed the levitical line is so important that *Aramaic Levi* transferred to Levi the biblical verses

---

34 Nickelsburg, "Enoch, Levi and Peter", 584-585.
35 Nickelsburg, "Enoch, Levi and Peter", 586. Nickelsburg identifies the upper Galilee as the place where these groups live, primarily on the basis of descriptions of the places of revelation in *1 Enoch*, *Aramaic Levi* and the New Testament gospels.
36 Kugler, *From Patriarch to Priest*, 36, 77.
37 See Kugler, *From Patriarch to Priest*, 120, 122 for the text and translation.
38 In contrast to Ben Sira who emphasized a pan-Aaronid priesthood. See above.

referring to Judah that later took on messianic interpretations.[39] The *Testament of Levi*, which used *Aramaic Levi* as a source, attributes scribal characteristics to Levi (8,17; Chap. 13; 14,4).[40] Stone assesses *Aramaic Levi* this way, "[T]he circles responsible for *Aramaic Levi* laid a very strong emphasis on the instructional function of the priesthood and this aspect of the priesthood attracted sapiential motifs".[41] As in the case of Enoch in the *Book of the Watchers*, the two roles, scribe and priest, are subsumed under one figure, here Levi.

Thus, we find in roughly contemporaneous Jewish works quite opposite views of the priesthood. Ben Sira takes a positive stance toward the priests and encourages their support through the cultic performance in the Temple. He may even, in his pan-Aaronid views, be implicitly opposing levitical or Zadokite claims. *1 Enoch* and *Aramaic Levi* are quite harsh in their critical stance vis-a-vis the priests who are in control in Jerusalem, precisely the people whom Ben Sira honors.[42] These views are certainly enough to establish that the priesthood in the late third to early second century is a contentious issue in Second Temple Judaism. Is there evidence that Ben Sira and the groups who produced and used *1 Enoch* and *Aramaic Levi* may have been aware of each other? To this problem I now turn.

---

[39] M. E. Stone, "Ideal Figures and Social Context: Priest and Sage in the Early Second Temple Age", in Patrick D. Miller, Jr., Paul D. Hanson and S. Dean McBride, eds., *Ancient Israelite Religions: F. M. Cross Festschrift* (Philadelphia 1988) 580.

[40] Himmelfarb, *Ascent to Heaven*, 30.

[41] Stone, "Ideal Figures", 580.

[42] Ithamar Gruenwald, *From Apocalypticism to Gnosticism: Studies in Apocalypticism, Merkavah Mysticism and Gnosticism* (BEAT 14; Frankfurt am Main 1988) 139, expresses a similar view about works like *1 Enoch* and *Aramaic Levi*, "Moreover, if we take into consideration that Apocalypticism was to a large extent the product of levitic, or priestly circles, then the polemical tones struck therein do not merely have an anti-priestly orientation, but they do in fact echo an inner-priestly struggle for hegemony and authority".

3. The Relationship Between Sirach, 1 Enoch and Aramaic Levi

Several recent studies have shown that Sirach and *1 Enoch* have important literary similarities, and these similarities have suggested to some a possible social relationship. George Nickelsburg, on the basis of Sirach's and the *Epistle of Enoch's* treatments of the rich and poor, has speculated that perhaps "the *poor* of Ben Sira's time" produced the Epistle.[43] The two most detailed treatments of the issue come from Randal Argall in his study *1 Enoch and Sirach* and from Gabriele Boccaccini in his *Middle Judaism*.[44] Argall's book is concerned with the literary themes and forms in common between Sirach and *1 Enoch*. He demonstrates that these two Second Temple Jewish works treat identical themes) revelation, creation, judgment) and articulate them similarly. At the end of his book he ventures several possibilities about a social connection between the works. He remarks about their differing views, "Such differences are the stuff of conflict ... it is enough to make the case that each tradition views the other among its rivals".[45]

---

[43] George W. E. Nickelsburg, "Social Aspects of Palestinian Jewish Apocalypticism," in D. Hellholm, ed. *Apocalypticism in the Mediterranean World and the Near East* (Tübingen [2]1989) 651.

[44] Randal A. Argall, *1 Enoch and Sirach: A Comparative Literary and Conceptual Analysis of the Themes of Revelation, Creation and Judgment* (Early Judaism and Its Literature 8; Atlanta 1995); Gabriele Boccaccini, *Middle Judaism: Jewish Thought 300 B.C.E to 200 C.E.* (Minneapolis 1991). Argall's assessment of the dates of the different portions of *1 Enoch* relies on that of Nickelsburg. He uses those portions of *1 Enoch* that are contemporary with Sirach, as I do here. Primarily for reasons of space, I have limited this paper to the *Book of the Watchers* and the *Astronomical Book* while Argall has included in his study the *Epistle of Enoch* (*1 Enoch* 92-105). On the *Epistle of Enoch* see also, George W. E. Nickelsburg, "Revealed Wisdom as a Criterion for Inclusion and Exclusion: From Jewish Sectarianism to Early Christianity", in Jacob Neusner and Ernest S. Frerichs, eds., *"To See Ourselves as Other See Us:" Christians, Jews, "Others" in Late Antiquity* (Chico 1985) 74-77. A connection between Sirach and the *Epistle of Enoch* was originally suggested by Victor Tcherikover *Hellenistic Civilization and the Jews* (New York 1982 [reprint of 1959 edition]) 151. See also, Nickelsburg, "Social Aspects", 651.

[45] Argall, *1 Enoch and Sirach*, 250.

Boccaccini also examines the theological similarities and differences between Sirach, the *Book of the Watchers* and the *Astronomical Book*.[46] He claims that this literary relationship reveals that Ben Sira is aware of apocalyptic theologies and that he is writing against them. His literary analysis of the theologies of these works makes him think that there might be some direct literary confrontation between Ben Sira and these apocalyptic groups. Commenting on the theme of covenant in Sirach, Boccaccini writes,

> Ben Sira is intent on reaffirming the centrality of the covenant and the retributive principle, overcoming the aporias and doubts of Job and Qohelet. At the same time he *directly* [emphasis mine] confronts the suggestions of the apocalyptic movement. The calm and systematic style of this wisdom book should not lead us to lose sight of the terms of a bitter debate, addressing such precise referents and urgent questioning.[47]

Finally, in two brief but suggestive remarks, Saul Olyan links the polemics of the *Testament of Levi* and *1 Enoch* with Sirach. Olyan believes that both the *Testament of Levi* and *1 Enoch* witness to claims of the Levites to the priesthood against what they consider to be the pretensions of the Aaronids/Zadokites.[48] This position contrasts with Ben Sira's "refusal to recognize the Levites as a group", and Olyan further notes that "we may have evidence here [in *1 Enoch* 89,73] of a contemporary Levitic theology opposed to Ben Sira's pan-Aaronid exclusivism".[49]

Several passages in Sirach seem to me to treat very specifically issues found in *1 Enoch* and *Aramaic Levi*, and the way that Ben Sira addresses these problems shows his awareness of apocalyptic groups and their ideas. Four, in particular, the calendar, the inner workings of the universe, dreams and visions and the person of Enoch, suggest to me that Ben Sira in his instruction to his students is voicing his concern about the claims of these people.

---

[46] Boccaccini, *Middle Judaism*, chapter 2, "Ben Sira, Qohelet and Apocalyptic".
[47] Boccaccini, *Middle Judaism*, 80.
[48] Olyan, "Ben Sira's Relationship to the Priesthood", 279-280.
[49] Olyan, "Ben Sira's Relationship to the Priesthood", 280.

a) Problems of the Calendar

43,6   It is the moon that marks the changing seasons,
        governing the times, their lasting sign.
43,7   By it we know the sacred seasons and pilgrimage feasts,
        a light which wanes in its course.
43,8   The new moon like its name renews itself;
        how wondrous it is when it changes!
        An army signal for the cloud vessels on high,
        it paves the firmament with its brilliance.

"It is difficult to overstress the importance of the calendar". So
Michael Stone concludes about the character of third century BCE
Judaism.[50] Calendrical concerns are certainly in evidence in the
documents under consideration here, and the problem of the calendar is
addressed polemically in some of them. The fundamental issue at stake
is whether one reckons the year on the basis of the sun alone or by the
moon (or, sun and moon together). Control of the calendar means
control of the setting of the Jewish festivals and observances, and
Jewish groups who reckoned the calendar differently would fix
different days for the same celebrations. The Qumran community, in a
period slightly later than I am considering here, used a solar calendar,
but the origins of that calendar are clearly much earlier than the
Qumran *yahad* itself.[51]

The *Astronomical Book*, the *Book of the Watchers* and *Aramaic Levi*
all evidence use of a solar calendar. The *Astronomical Book* preserves
the most extensive and detailed treatment of a 364 day solar year.[52] In
this section of *1 Enoch*, the angel Uriel shows Enoch a vision in which
he sees the intricacies of the movements of the sun, moon and stars
through the heavens. The revelation given to Enoch provides the basis
for the solar year, and thus the reckoning of seasons and festivals.

---

50   Stone, "Enoch, Aramaic Levi", 166.
51   On the Qumran calendar, see Shemaryahu Talmon, "The Calendar Reckoning of
     the Sect from the Judean Desert", *Scripta Hierosolymitana* 4 (1958) 162-199. See
     also, R. Beckwith, "The Earliest Enoch Literature and Its Calendar: Marks of
     Their Origin, Date and Motivation", *RevQ* 10 (1981) 365-403.
52   The Aramaic fragments of the *Astronomical Book* found at Qumran show that the
     version used by the Qumranites was more extensive than that preserved in the
     Ethiopic *1 Enoch*. See, Milik, *The Books of Enoch,* and Matthew Black, *The Book
     of Enoch or 1 Enoch: A New English Edition* (SVTP 7; Leiden 1985). The solar
     year constitutes an integral part of both forms of the book.

Although the *Astronomical Book* was apparently not originally intended to be a polemic, two passages in the present form of the book, 75,2 and 82,4-7 and one eschatological addition to the book, 80,2-8, seem to polemicize against those who do not use the Enochic solar calendar.[53] *1 Enoch* 75,2 and 82,4-7 decry those who do not reckon the four epagomenal days that bring the calendar to 364 days. Otto Neugebauer remarks that 75,2 "could refer to the lunar calendar of the Jews (which has no intercalary days)".[54] *1 Enoch* 82,4-7 blesses the righteous who "do not err in counting all their days in which the sun travels in the sky ... together with the four (days) that are added ...". *1 Enoch* 80,2 begins by saying that "in the days of the sinners years shall become shorter. And their seeds shall be late in their lands and fields". This is a prelude to various eschatological tribulations. The "sinners" may be those who do not abide by the solar calendar revealed to Enoch, but who use a lunar or soli-lunar calendar that rapidly falls out of sync with the solar year. The same 364 day calendar is utilized later in clearly polemical contexts by the book of *Jubilees* (which knows *1 Enoch*) and by the people of Qumran. Nickelsburg's comment on these texts is apt here. "Behind all this [the problems concerning calendar evidenced in these works] appears to have been a bitter calendrical dispute with the Jewish religious establishment".[55]

The *Book of the Watchers*, although lacking the detail about the calendar of the *Astronomical Book*, also preserves clues that this calendar was an important facet of the Enochic visionary tradition generally. The solar calendar is not even explicitly mentioned in the *Book of the Watchers*, but the work clearly assumes such a calendar.

---

53 On these passages, see Black, *The Book of Enoch*, 252, 411 and Nickelsburg, *Jewish Literature*, 48. On *1 Enoch* 80-81 see James C. VanderKam, *Enoch and the Growth of an Apocalyptic Tradition* (CBQMS 16; Washington, D. C. 1984) 106-109. On the date of Chapter 80, VanderKam (107) remarks, "When and why they [the passages in chap 80] were spliced in the AB remains an enigma".

54 Black, *The Book of Enoch*, 402. James VanderKam notes, however, that the polemic about the four epagomenal days does not necessarily oppose a lunar calendar. He argues that the original *Astronomical Book* presented a 364 day calendar apparently without any active opposition to the calendar governing the cult in Jerusalem. See, "The 364-Day Calendar in the Enochic Literature", in Kent Harold Richards, ed., *Society of Biblical Literature 1983 Seminar Papers* (Chico 1983) 164.

55 Nickelsburg, *Jewish Literature*, 48.

Chapters 33-36 appear to be a summary account intended to end the work, and 33,2-4 specifically look like a condensed version of the material in the *Astronomical Book*. As was the case there, here Uriel shows Enoch the "gates of the heavens" and the determination of the calendar.[56] Chapters 34-36 also refer to these gates, even though the astronomical scheme is slightly different from the *Astronomical Book*.[57]

The fragmentary condition of *Aramaic Levi* makes it difficult to determine exactly how the calendar functioned in that work, but a calendar like that used at Qumran is recognizable. This conclusion depends primarily on the reports about Levi's children in *Aramaic Levi* 65-72.[58] Michael Stone and Jonas Greenfield conclude that the data given about the births of Levi's children are consistent with the Qumran solar calendar. These include: (1) the numbering of months as opposed to naming them, (2) the births of the children exactly three months apart putting them on the same date and day of the week, (3) two cases, where dates are provided, in which the births fall on a Wednesday, an important day in the Qumran calendar, (4) Kohath's birth on the morning of the first day of the month, morning being the time that the day begins at Qumran.[59]

Ben Sira's comments about the heavenly bodies reveal a position directly in contrast to that found in the works just examined. In the large section about the works of God's creation that acts as a preface to the Praise of the Ancestors (42,15-43,33), several important verses treat the celestial bodies. What Ben Sira has to say about the sun and moon especially should be read, in my estimation, as a polemic against the solar year found in *1 Enoch* and *Aramaic Levi*. His interest in the sun is actually quite mundane—it is hot. Four of the five verses devoted to this heavenly orb describe its fiery nature. It "parches the earth and no one can endure its blazing heat" (43,3). It is hotter than a furnace, and it "breathes out fiery vapors" (43,4). Nowhere does Ben Sira attribute

---

56 Argall, *1 Enoch and Sirach*, 52. See the notes to these chapters in Black, *The Book of Enoch*, 180-181.

57 Argall, *1 Enoch and Sirach*, 52.

58 On the various Greek and Aramaic portions of *Aramaic Levi* see, Michael Stone and Jonas Greenfield, "Remarks on the Aramaic Testament of Levi from the Geniza", *RB* 86 (1979) 214-215 and Kugler, *From Patriarch to Priest*, chapter 2.

59 Stone and Greenfield, "Remarks", 224.

to the sun any calendrical function. In fact, he notes quite specifically how it speeds on its course "at his (the Lord's) command".[60]

In diametrical opposition is Ben Sira's discussion of the moon, which centers almost exclusively on its role as that body that establishes the seasons and festivals. The moon governs the changing seasons (עתות), the festivals (מועד) and the pilgrimages (הג). As its name indicates, the moon gives the month its name, and it serves as an "army beacon" (כלי צבא).

A second text, Sir 50:6, also displays the same contrast between sun and moon. In the description of Simon II, Ben Sira compares him to both sun and moon. Simon is "like the full moon in the festival season" (מועד וכירח מלא בימי).[61] The description of the sun is consistent with that of 43,2-5. Here Simon is "like the sun shining on the Temple of the king" (אל היכל המלך וכשמש משרקת). Although the shining of the sun connotes Simon's glory for Ben Sira, the disparity between the brightness of the sun and the calendrical function of the moon is striking.

What is particularly notable about these statements is that Ben Sira not only denies the sun its primary function in the Enochic scheme, he does so in contrast to the role it plays in the Priestly creation account, which he certainly knows. This is all the more remarkable when one remembers Ben Sira's reliance on the Priestly narrative for his theology of the priesthood. In Gen 1,14-15, the sun and the moon *cooperate* in governing the calendar. "God said, 'Let there be lights in the vault of the heavens to separate the day from the night, and let *them* serve as signs both for festivals and for seasons and for years'".[62] I take Ben Sira's ignoring of Genesis in this way to indicate a deliberate attempt on his part not to make even an apparent concession to the calendrical schemes used by those Jews who produced and used the *Astronomical*

---

60 This is the NRSV translation. Skehan and Di Lella, *The Wisdom of Ben Sira*, 485, 488, translate, "at whose orders it urges on its steeds". For the translation of אבירי as "his steeds" they refer to Jer 8,16; 47,3; 50,11.

61 This is a reconstructed Hebrew. Ms B has an additional מבין from v. 6a that overloads the present colon. See Skehan and Di Lella, *The Wisdom of Ben Sira*, 549. My thanks to Alon Goshen-Gottstein for alerting me to this passage.

62 Alexander Rofé, "The Onset of Sects in Postexilic Judaism: Neglected Evidence from the Septuagint, Trito-Isaiah, Ben Sira and Malachi", in: Jacob Neusner, et al. *The Social World of Formative Christianity and Judaism* (Philadelphia 1988) 43-44.

Book, the *Book of the Watchers* and *Aramaic Levi*, Jews who claimed
the priority and foundational character of the solar calendar.

b) The Secrets of God and Creation

For Ben Sira, the Law contains God's revelation and wisdom. Its
fulfillment is paramount (cf. 15,1; 32,15.24; 33,2-3). The polemic
against the use of a solar calendar in Chapter 43 reflects his more
overarching suspicions about inquiring into matters that go beyond
what is in the Law. One passage in particular, 3,21-24, reveals Ben
Sira's unwillingness to delve into things inscrutible, notably the secrets
of the created order and what will be in the future.

> 3,21   What is too marvelous for you, do not investigate
>   And what is too difficult/evil for you, do not research.
>
> 3,22   On what is authorized, give attention,
>   But you have no business with secret things
>
> 3,23   And into what is beyond you, do not meddle,
>   For that which is too great has been shown to you.
>
> 3,24   For many are the thoughts of the sons of men,
>   Evil and erring imaginations[63] .

This passage has often been understood as a polemic against Jewish
participation in Greek philosophical inquiry and discussion. Patrick
Skehan and Alexander Di Lella summarize the issue this way,

> Ben Sira cautions his readers about the futility of Greek learning, its goals
> and techniques, and also reminds them of what the Lord has bestowed on
> them ... Hence it is better for the enlightened Jew to follow the certainties

---

63   Except for 3,21, I have used the translation of Argall, *1 Enoch and Sirach*, 75.
     Argall argues for adopting the reading of MS C from the Geniza for 3,21b against
     Skehan and Di Lella, *The Wisdom of Ben Sira* who use MS A. To judge from the
     Greek translation, however, the situation is more complicated than simply
     following one manuscript or the other. I follow MS A for the verbs since
     elsewhere in Sirach ἐκετάζω (Gk. colon b) only translates Hebrew חקר (11,7;
     13,11), but I prefer the adjectives used in MS C where Greek χαλεπώτερα seems
     to reflect a *Vorlage* more like MS C's רעים. The Hebrew of Ben Sira (except for
     MS F) can be most conveniently found in The Historical Dictionary of the
     Hebrew Language, *The Book of Ben Sira: Text, Concordance and an Analysis of
     the Vocabulary* (Jerusalem 1973 [Hebrew]). For MS F from the Geniza, see
     Alexander A. Di Lella, "The Newly Discovered Sixth Manuscript of Ben Sira
     from the Cairo Geniza", *Bib* 69 (1988) 226-238.

and true wisdom of the Law revealed to Moses than to strive after the often
contradictory musings and uncertain opinions of the Greek thinkers.[64]

Of course, Ben Sira's ultimate desire is that his students adhere to the
Law of Moses, but I think that the passage ought to be understood as
well against the backdrop of the mysteries of the cosmos and the
eschaton revealed to Enoch and Levi.[65]

Sir 3,21-24 is both clear and ambiguous at the same time. Ben Sira
clearly wants his students to refrain from certain kinds of inquiry. The
subjects at issue are "too marvelous", "too difficult/evil" or "hidden",
and Ben Sira forbids investigation into them.[66] But the passage is also
characterized by a pervasive vagueness. What exactly are those things
that are "too marvelous" or "hidden"? Two Hebrew terms used in this
passage may indicate what these forbidden subjects are.

The first, the adjective פלאות (3,21; Gk. is probably ἰσχυρότερα),
seems to describe the "works of God" generally and the secrets of the
universe in particular.[67] The term appears two other places in Sirach. In
11,4 it modifies "the works of God" (מעשי יהוה) and refers to the way
that human fortunes can unexpectedly change. פלאות in 43,25, which is
part of the poem on the wonders of creation, also describes the "works
of God", but in this case these works are the marvelous/incredible sea
monsters. Elsewhere in the poem on creation, the related term פלאות
appears, which indicates the unfathomable wonders of God's creation.
At the outset of the poem (42,15), Ben Sira exclaims, "I shall recall the
works of God (מעשי יהוה) ... through the word of the Lord are his works
(מעשיו)". These works are filled with God's glory (v. 16), and are

---

64 Skehan and Di Lella, *The Wisdom of Ben Sira*, 160-161. See also, Martin Hengel,
    Judaism and Hellenism (Philadelphia 1974) 139-140.
65 Several scholars have noted that this passage might be directed against
    apocalyptic thought. Most notably see Gruenwald, *From Apocalypticism to
    Gnosticism*, 17-18.
66 On this passage, see Argall, *1 Enoch and Sirach*, 74-76, 250.
67 Elsewhere in Sirach the phrase "works of God" refers to God's creation. In a
    reference to Genesis, Sir 16,26 speaks of God who created his works from the
    beginning, using ברא as does Genesis 1,1. Sir 33,15 speaks of God's works
    coming in pairs, which probably includes the created order. Sir 39,33 follows a
    long section treating the reasons that God made various things, such as wind and
    fire. Ben Sira says, "All the works of the Lord are good ... ". Finally, in Sir 43,28
    in the poem on creation, it is said that God is greater than "his works", clearly
    meaning creation.

impenetrable; even the "holy ones of God" cannot adequately describe "the wonders of God (נפלאות יהוה)". The poem concludes with Ben Sira extolling God for his power and inscrutible nature. In 43,32-33 he reprises his praise of God's works, "Many more things than these are marvelous (נפלא ?) and powerful. Only a few of his works have I seen. It is the Lord who has made all things and to those who fear him he gives wisdom".[68]

In one passage where no Hebrew text has survived, Ben Sira appeals to God's role as creator of wondrous things to establish his position as judge. In 18,4-7, he again claims that God's creation cannot be fathomed. No one is able to describe "God's works" or to measure his power. One cannot penetrate the "wonders of the Lord" (καὶ οὐκ ἔστιν ἐξιχνιάσαι τὰ θαυμάσια τοῦ κυρίου). This is a sentiment identical to that found in the poem on creation.

The second term, נסתרות (3,22; Gk. κρύπτα), probably refers to what the future holds. This word also occurs in the poem on creation that begins in Chapter 42. God plumbs the depths of the human heart and "he discloses the past and the future, and he reveals the deep secret things (נסתרות)" (42,19). The two verbs in this verse, מחוה and מגלה, connote revelatory activity, and נסתרות occurs in parallel with matters of the past and the future. This term, used as it is in the context of a poem on creation, connects both with revelation and with creation. The universe comprises not only the created order of visible and invisible things, but also the things that God has ordained to happen. These are all things that God has made, his works.

The poem culminates as I noted above in the claim that the creator gives wisdom to those who fear him. Is part of this wisdom the revelation of matters yet to happen, eschatology? Indeed, the same term, נסתרות, is used in 48,25, of those things revealed to the prophet Isaiah, "who foretold what should be till the end of time, hidden things (נסתרות) that were yet to be fulfilled". Here, Ben Sira believes that Isaiah has been shown eschatological realities. Thus, the most likely content of the נסתרות into which 3,22 prohibits inquiry is the

---

68 Skehan and Di Lella, *The Wisdom of Ben Sira*, 487, 490 follow the Greek here because of the fragmentary nature of Ms B, which only has the first word and part of the last word fully legible. On the basis of the traces on the manuscript, the Hebrew Language Academy edition of the Hebrew reconstructs the verse, רוב נ̇פ̇ל̇יא וחזק]מ[אלה. I have translated on the basis of this reconstruction.

eschatological future. Does Ben Sira's apparent distrust of looking for revelation of the future reflect an awareness on his part of the eschatological focus found in works like the *Book of the Watchers* or *Aramaic Levi*?

For his part, even though he understands himself to have a prophet-like inspiration, Ben Sira admits that he has seen only a small portion of God's works (43,32), and he does not make any pretensions about knowing the future. It is not that God completely withholds such revelation; he has, for example, revealed such things to Isaiah. What God has already given, however, is for Ben Sira's students plenty to contemplate, and these are the only things "authorized".

I do not think it entirely coincidental that the secrets of creation and revelation of the future are precisely two of the more conspicuous elements found in the *Astronomical Book*, the *Book of the Watchers* and *Aramaic Levi*. Certainly the foundation of the solar calendar in *1 Enoch* depends on the revelation to Enoch about the workings of the celestial bodies. In 1 Enoch 14, Enoch's encounter with God in the heavenly Temple, God reveals to Enoch the impending judgment of the Watchers, that is, the Jerusalem priesthood.[69]

The eponymous hero of *Aramaic Levi* also knows the future. If Robert Kugler's arrangement of the Qumran fragments is correct, 4Q213 2 constitutes Levi's heavenly vision which was initially reported in 4Q213 1 ii in which Levi sees the gates of heaven.[70] The extant text breaks off with mention of an angel. 4Q213 2, which may follow, concerns matters of priestly exogamy. Levi is thus shown in a vision that priests will enter into illegitimate marriages.[71] Later in the work Levi predicts the disobedience of his descendents in the text cited above (Section 1).

Thus, the admonitions given by Ben Sira in 3,21-24 to his students forbid them to investigate the inner workings of the universe, which

---

69   On this interpretation of the *Book of the Watchers*, see Nickelsburg, "Enoch, Levi and Peter"; Suter, "The Priesthood" and "Fallen Angel". The eschatology found in the *Astronomical Book* is in Chapters 80-81, which are probably not original to the book. See VanderKam, *Enoch and the Growth*, 106.

70   Kugler, *From Patriarch to Priest*, 77.

71   A major aspect of Kugler's analysis of the fragment has to do with its similarity to *Jub* 30,5-17. For the complete argument, see Kugler, *From Patriarch to Priest*, 83-84.

cannot be fathomed, or to try to divine future events, probably
eschatological happenings. By contrast, he directs their attention to
what is authorized, almost certainly a reference to the Law. He intends
to keep his charges grounded, to confine their study to the Law, in
which is contained the only acceptable revelation of God. Rather than a
polemic against Greek philosophy, this passage confronts unauthorized
interest in things that God has decided to withhold from human
understanding. Ben Sira is worried about what he considers to be an
unhealthy concern for matters too difficult, too great and perhaps even
too dangerous to investigate, the secrets of God's created order and the
revelation of the future.[72]

c) Dream Visions and Ascents

At the same time that Ben Sira forbids delving into certain subjects he
attacks the mechanisms by which this knowledge is acquired. In 34,1-8,
Ben Sira takes on dreams and visions.

34,1   Empty and false are the hopes of the senseless,
       and fools are sent winging by dreams.
34,2   Like one grasping at shadows or chasing the wind
       is whoever puts his trust in dreams.
34,3   What is seen in dreams is a reflection
       that mirrors the vision of the onlooker.
34,4   Can the clean produce the unclean?
       Can the liar ever speak the truth?
34,5   Divination, omens and dreams are unreal;
       what you already expect, the mind depicts.
34,6   Unless it be a vision specially sent from the Most High,
       fix not your heart on it.
34,7   For dreams have led many astray,
       and those who base their hopes on them have perished.

---

72 If Argall's translation of 3,23 is accepted, Ben Sira is even aware that these
    matters have "been shown" to some of his students or are being promulgated in
    rival wisdom schools. See, Argall, *1 Enoch and Sirach*, 76. It should be noted
    here that b. Hag 13a understands Sir 3,21-24 as referring to the secrets of
    creation.

34,8   Without deceit the Law is fulfilled,
        and well-rounded wisdom is the discourse of the faithful.[73]

Although the target in this passage is reliance on dreams and visions, Ben Sira says little about what is revealed in them. Martin Hengel thinks that the passage is concerned with mantic traditions or magical practices, and Skehan and Di Lella refer to the prohibition of divination and paying heed to omens as "pagan and untrustworthy".[74] The passage could very well be read as a general admonition about the uncertainty of understanding dreams and their meanings, a widespread concern throughout antiquity.[75] Since Ben Sira appears to have in his sights various matters connected with Jewish apocalyptic traditions, like differing calendars and unlawful revelation, the question arises as to whether this passage has a more focused concern on the specific vehicles by which that forbidden revelation is obtained.

The mention of "divination" and "omens" most likely indicates Ben Sira's use of the Mosaic proscriptions against such practices, but they are not the central theme of the passage. Since they are mentioned in verses 1, 2, 3, 5 and 7, dreams would appear to be the intended target.[76] Those who depend on these vehicles are "senseless" and "fools". Ben Sira recognizes the self- fulfilling nature of dreams; they simply mirror the one dreaming (vv. 3.5).

When we move from Ben Sira's anti-visionary remarks to the Enoch and Levi materials, we notice that dreams play a central role in how these patriarchal figures get their revelations. Three times in *1 Enoch* 13 and 14 Enoch says that his visions come in his sleep, and Ben Sira's caustic remark that "fools are sent winging by dreams" may even directly attack heavenly ascents in dreams, like Enoch's ascent and

---

73   The only Hebrew extant for this section is MS E, which only perserves portions of v. 1. The Greek constitutes the major witness for the remainder of the passage.

74   Hengel, *Judaism and Hellenism*, 240; Skehan and Di Lella, *The Wisdom of Ben Sira*, 409.

75   On dreams and dream interpretation generally, see Naphtali Lewis, *The Interpretation of Dreams and Portents* (Toronto 1976) and Patricia Cox Miller, *Dreams in Late Antiquity: Studies in the Imagination of a Culture* (Princeton 1994).

76   Argall, *1 Enoch and Sirach*, 82, notes that by linking dreams with divination and omen reading, Ben Sira connects these practices with those of the nations found in Deut 18,10-11. He also wonders whether the rhetorical question of 34,4 about purity indicates that the dreamers have separated themselves from the Temple.

heavenly tour.[77] Although *Aramaic Levi* is fragmentary, in 4Q213 1 Levi lies down and, after a lacuna in the text, he has a vision. It seems likely that some mention of sleep and/or a dream belongs in this unpreserved section. If so, Levi's vision, like Enoch's, also comes in a dream.[78]

Whatever the object of Ben Sira's scorn here, whether it is specifically apocalyptic dream visions or a more general distrust of nocturnal sights, he paints himself into something of a corner. Dreams and dream visions are frequent occurrences in the Hebrew scriptures, and most of the major biblical characters have them. The exception that he carves out for dreams, those sent from the Most High, seems to me to refer to these biblical events, but he nowhere says how one can tell a divinely inspired dream from one that simply "mirrors the vision of the onlooker". The passage does, however, end in verse 8 with the antithesis of "grasping at shadows", the fulfillment of the Law. The Law is placed together with "well-rounded wisdom", probably the kind that Ben Sira dispenses. Thus his rhetorical strategy here is like we have seen in other cases, the Law and its wisdom are the concern of his students, not the flights of fancy and fleeting visions found in the dreams of people like Enoch and Levi.

d) The Person of Enoch

Sirach contains within the Praise of the Ancestors two mentions of the patriarch Enoch (44,16; 49,14). What Ben Sira has to say about Enoch is clearly important in the context of other passages that may indicate his awareness of groups who appeal to traditions that have Enoch as their legitimator.

Sir 44,16 is a very well-known problem since the Masada scroll and the Syriac are missing this reference to Enoch, and its presence in MS B from the Cairo Geniza is certainly corrupt as it stands. Despite arguments contesting its authenticity, I contend that some mention of

---

77 Argall, *1 Enoch and Sirach*, 81.
78 On 4QTLevi[a] see, Michael E. Stone and Jonas C. Greenfield, "The Prayer of Levi", *JBL* 112 (1993) 247-266.

Enoch at the head of the Praise of the Ancestors is called for.[79] It is present in the Greek translation and although the Greek translator at times used a Hebrew that was apparently corrupt, an appeal to a corrupt text here does not seem a sufficient explanation.

The fact that the text is missing in the Masada scroll is often seen as conclusive evidence of the inauthenticity of the verse. One could easily posit, however, that its absence from the scroll found by Yigael Yadin can be accounted for by parablepsis on the part of the scroll's copyist. The scribe's eye would only have to skip from חנוך in 44,16 to נוח (as it is spelled in the Masada scroll) in 44,17 for the verse to drop out of the text.[80] Without the negative evidence of the Masada scroll, the presence of the verse in Greek and Ms B from the Geniza and the literary use of Enoch as an inclusio for the entire section up until Simon II would seem to be strong reason to consider 44,16 original.[81] The Greek translation used in conjunction with MS B would seem, then, to constitute the best basis from which to work. As almost all commentators recognize, the phrase נמצא תמים, which appears in MS B, is an intrusion from the reference to Noah in verse 17. Based on the Greek and MS B, the resulting passage should probably be reconstructed something like:

חנוך התהלך עם ייי ונלקח   אות דעת לדור ודור [82]

If the passage is original to Sirach, what does it tell us about Ben Sira's view of Enoch? Both verbs in the first colon clearly derive from

---

79 For arguments against the authenticity of 44,16 see Th. Middendorp, *Die Stellung Jesu ben Siras zwischen Judentum und Hellenismus* (Leiden 1973) 53-54, 109, 112, 134 and Skehan and Di Lella, *The Wisdom of Ben Sira*, 499. Several scholars, most notably Burton Mack, *Wisdom and the Hebrew Epic: Ben Sira's Hymn in Praise of the Fathers* (Chicago 1985) follow Middendorp.

80 I am grateful to Michael Stone for this suggestion.

81 J. Marböck, "Henoch - Adam - der Thronwagen: Zu frühjüdischen pseudepigraphischen Traditionen bei *Ben Sira*", *BZ* NF 25 (1981) 104 argues that 44,16 is authentic because it forms an inclusio to the Praise of the Ancestors and because, since David is mentioned twice, two mentions of Enoch do not disqualify it.

82 Argall, *1 Enoch and Sirach*, 9. My reconstruction is similar to Argall's. He has וילקח at the end of the first colon and omits the *waw* before דור in the second colon. I now agree with those commentators who see Yadin's reconstruction of 44,16 originally belonging with 49,14 (*The Ben Sira Scroll from Masada* [Jerusalem 1965] 38) as incorrect, despite my acceptance of this scheme previously (*No Small Difference: Sirach's Relationship to its Hebrew Parent Text* [SBLSCS 26; Atlanta 1989] 289-290).

Gen 5,24 and represent no more than the reporting of that tradition.[83] The second colon, however, is a different story. Several scholars argue that the phrase אות דעת betrays an awareness of extrabiblical tradition about Enoch. The strongest argument is made by Argall, who argues that the use of "the complete sign of wisdom" in *1 Enoch* 92,1, the beginning of the *Epistle of Enoch*, is essentially the same phrase. Argall also contends that this phrase "implies that Enoch has returned from heaven with revelation".[84] This phrase might simply be an elaboration on the first colon, however, and indicate that Enoch was the prime example of what it means to know God and to walk with him.[85] Nevertheless, even if the phrase reveals that Ben Sira was aware of Enochic lore) part of the central argument of this paper) it represents little more than a tipping of the hat to Enoch, a somewhat veiled acknowledgment of these traditions. It certainly does not constitute approbation of the extensive tradition that has built up around this biblical figure.[86]

---

83 The first verb in the Greek of Sirach, εὐηρέστησεν, also reflects the LXX translation. The second, μετετέθη, does not, probably because, although the Hebrew of Sirach is the same root as the Hebrew of Genesis, Genesis is *qal* and Sirach is *niphal*. On the Greek translator's use of the Jewish-Greek Scriptures for his translation of Sirach see Wright, *No Small Difference*, chapter 3.

84 Argall, *1 Enoch and Sirach*, 11. This latter claim seems to me to be based on *1 Enoch* 92,1, and I am not sure that a return from heaven is implied in Sirach. Marböck, "Henoch - Adam", 105-108 and P. Grelot, "La légende d'Henoch dans les apocryphes et dans la Bible: origine et signification", *RSR* 46 (1958) 181-183 also argue that this phrase reveals knowledge of Enochic tradition. Based on the dates of the Qumran Enoch fragments, Marböck (106) notes, "Ben Sira konnte also bereits Henoch*literatur* vor sich haben". He concludes, "So kann Sir 44,16 ebenfalls als zusammenfassende Aussage über Henochs umfassendes Wissen verstanden werden; noch dazu begegnet an beiden Stellen das Wort vom 'Zeichen,' für die künftigen Generationen".

85 This seems to be part of the point of M. H. Segal, *The Complete Book of Ben Sira* (Jerusalem 1958 [Hebrew]) 307.

86 The interpretive translation of the grandson, ὑπόδειγμα μετανοίας, is another problem altogether. Devorah Dimant thinks that the Hebrew phrase refers to Enoch's role as a witness against humankind (cf. *Jub* 4,24), but the Greek translator understood אות to mean "example". ("The Angels that Sinned' in the Scrolls from the Judean Desert and in the Apocryphal Books Related to Them" Ph.D. Dissertation, Hebrew University, 1974 [Hebrew], 120 note 332). On the Greek phrase, see also Friedrich Vinzenz Reiterer, *"Urtext" und Übersetzungen:*

The second passage, 49,14, also depends on Gen 5,24. Ben Sira notes that "few have been created like Enoch", since Enoch is not the only person to have been taken by God. Elijah was as well, and this recognition is made clear by Ben Sira's use of the verb הנלקח of Elijah in 48,9. So the fact that Enoch was not alone in being taken by God is consistent with the biblical testimony. The end of verse 19, however, does present a bit of a dilemma. The Hebrew of this colon, הוא נלקח פנים וגם is not altogether clear about where Enoch was taken. Argall maintains that פנים is a reference to the heavenly Temple that *1 Enoch* says that the patriarch visited and thus shows "some appreciation" for Enochic lore.[87] I think that this is overstating the case. The natural curiosity would, of course, be about where it was that Enoch was taken, but פנים here more likely means "into the presence [of God]", a less specific reference to Enoch's final destination.[88] The colon again says little more than the biblical notice in Genesis 5.

Thus, I think that what Ben Sira is doing in these verses is domesticating the image of Enoch. Almost the entirety of Ben Sira's remarks about Enoch reflect the biblical notice of this enigmatic figure. If 44,16 betrays any knowledge by Ben Sira of extra biblical tradition, he almost downplays it by its brevity. Enoch was for Ben Sira an extraordinary figure, who, because of his "walking" with God, was considered worthy to be taken into his presence.[89]

Sprachstudie über Sir 44,16-45,26 als Beitrag zur Siraforschung (ATSAT 12; St. Ottilien 1980) 84-85.

87 Argall, *1 Enoch and Sirach*, 12-13.

88 Steven D. Fraade, *Enosh and His Generation: Pre-Israelite Hero and History in Postbiblical Interpretation* (SBLMS 30; Chico 1984) 12 note 21.

89 Thomas R. Lee, *Studies in the Form of Sirach 44-50* (SBLDS 75; Atlanta 1986) 231-232, argues that Enoch and Joseph are being compared here, but he uses Yadin's reconstruction of the Enoch reference in 49,14, which brings 44,16 back to Chapter 49. Lee concludes that "it is stated that he [Enoch] was such a remarkable figure that even if he had died like other men, his corpse would have received the exceptional treatment given to Joseph's bones".

4. Ben Sira and His Opponents: The Social Situation

The pieces of evidence adduced above show that where criticisms of
the Jerusalem priests are concerned, Ben Sira takes both a positive and
a negative tack. On the positive side, he directly and unequivocally
maintains his support of the Temple priesthood and provides a strong
theological case for that position. On the negative, he attempts to
discredit several ways in which the groups who mount these attacks
legitimize them. If one reads these two different tacks as two sides of
the same coin, then several aspects of Jewish society in the late third to
early second century BCE begin to take shape. In general, Sirach, *1
Enoch* and *Aramaic Levi* reflect people and communities that care
about the priesthood primarily because all apparently were priests or
were closely connected with them. The most contentious issues seem to
be the legitimacy of marriages contracted by the priestly class in
Jerusalem and the use of varying calendars. We are presented then in
these works with competing groups/communities who most likely know
about each other, who don't really like one another and who actively
polemicize against one another.

More specifically, as I reconstruct the social situation reflected in
these works, it seems probable that the people who stand behind the
Astronomical Book, the *Book of the Watchers* and *Aramaic Levi*
represent groups of priests and scribes who feel marginalized and even
disenfranchised vis-à-vis the ruling priests in Jerusalem. They contend
that the repurcussions of transgressions of family purity, specifically
the contracting of illegitimate marriages by the Jerusalem priests and
the use of an incorrect calendar, have rendered the ritual conducted in
the Temple corrupt and defiled. In *1 Enoch* part of the attack on those
in power is veiled in the myth of the fallen Watchers in *1 Enoch* 6-16.
This group, like Ben Sira himself, legitimizes its understanding by a
particular concept of wisdom. The wisdom of those competing with
Ben Sira, however, depends on a different authority from his, namely
the ascent vision where the seer obtains his wisdom directly from God,
unmediated. These visions provide the foundation for the critical stance

taken by these groups, just as Ben Sira's concept of wisdom embodied in Torah grounds his position.[90]

The wisdom granted to Enoch is handed down as a sort of counter-wisdom to that offered by teachers like Ben Sira. For the authors of *1 Enoch* this wisdom has chronological precedence to that given to Moses in the Sinaitic Law. It is apparently even transmitted in written form that is legitimated by a prophetic inspiration. The "account" of Enoch's transmission of this knowledge to his son Methuselah in *1 Enoch* 82,1-3 makes this clear.

> And now, my son Methuselah, all these things I am recounting to you and writing down for you; and I have revealed to you everything, and given you writings of all these things. Keep, my son, Methuselah, the writings of your father's hand, that you may deliver them to the generations of eternity. Wisdom I have given to you and to your children, and to those who will be your children, that they may transmit it to their children, and to generations of generations forever, to whoever is endowed with wisdom; and they shall celebrate all the wise. Wisdom shall slumber, (but) in their mind those who have understanding shall not slumber, but they shall hearken with their ears that they may learn this wisdom, and it shall be better for those that partake of it than rich food.[91]

Ben Sira is aware of the attacks and the methods for legitimating them, and he returns the polemic. His wholehearted support of the priests and his treatment of the calendar, dreams and visions and inquiring into the workings of the universe are all intended to counteract these critical attacks. Ben Sira is a scribe, perhaps even a priest, who imparts *his* wisdom in *his* school (51,23). But his wisdom is different, being based on fulfillment of God's Torah through disciplined study.[92] Ben Sira expects his students to be thoroughly established in the study of the Law, where the only legitimate wisdom is found. If Argall's translation of 3,23b is correct ("for that which is too great for you was shown

---

90   The connection of Law and Wisdom is thoroughgoing in Sirach and the amount of scholarly literature on this subject is immense. For bibliography on these subjects see Skehan and Di Lella, *The Wisdom of Ben Sira*. See also, J. Marböck, *Weisheit im Wandel: Untersuchungen zur Weisheitstheologie bei Ben Sira* (BBS 37; Bonn 1971). For a view different from the usual identification of Law and Wisdom in Sirach, see Boccaccini, *Middle Judaism*, 88-98.

91   Translation taken from Black, *The Book of Enoch*, 70-71.

92   On the importance of discipline in Ben Sira, see Wright, "Putting the Puzzle Together".

you"), then Ben Sira's students may even have come from some of these other groups and told him their teachings.[93]

A major difficulty, however, is the nature of the polemic involved in these works; it is mostly indirect. That is, it is contained in literature that is not supposed to be read by the targets of the criticism, but by those inside the group that produced and used the literature. Rather than changing the minds of outsiders, this literature more probably promotes the stability and cohesion of the group's insiders and confirms their belief systems. The wisdom that Enoch transmits to Methuselah is for those who have not "slumbered", presumably the members of the Enochic community. The fragmentary condition of *Aramaic Levi* makes conclusions more difficult, but the emphasis on Levi as the primary actor may indicate its intended audience as dissaffected priests. Ben Sira intended his teachings for his students, the scions of Jerusalem society.

This, then, raises the question that if these books were so intended, how would the antagonists become aware of each other's criticisms and responses? I can only offer some informed speculations. It is certainly possible that, since the traditions seem to have been transmitted in writing, these people somehow acquired and read each other's literature. Priests, perhaps more so than other Jews, were required to be in Jerusalem, and criticism of other priestly groups did not necessarily preclude going to the city. No doubt these people came into direct contact and debate with each other within the city itself.[94] Finally, there was almost certainly some mobility of students among wisdom groups, and 'new students might communicate the teachings of previous teachers.[95] Without any substantial clues, however, the ways in which these groups knew about each other remains obscure.

But the polemic probably worked well internally. Ben Sira was certainly trying to inculcate certain views in his disciples. In order to

---

93 Argall, *1 Enoch and Sirach*, 75. Argall's book is an extended and detailed argument that Sirach and *1 Enoch* engage each other over the problem of competing wisdoms.

94 This, of course, assumes that some of these groups came from outside of Jerusalem as seems likely. For example, Nickelsburg, "Enoch, Levi and Peter", 586, argues for a Galilean provenance for *1 Enoch* 12-16.

95 Josephus, for instance, in *Life* 2 narrates his peripatetic youth, moving between different Jewish philosophies.

accomplish that he did not have to resort to direct social or even direct literary confrontation. He may not have wanted to draw what he considered unnecessary and unwarranted attention to the teachings of others. He had his own divinely inspired wisdom to pass on. Those students who received warnings to pay no heed to fleeting dreams or admonitions against seeking the secrets of the universe were less likely to do such things later. Ben Sira was a student of the Jewish scriptures, and Solomon's wisdom does counsel after all to "train up a child in the way he should go, and when he is old he will not depart from it" (Prov 22,6).

Ben Sira's social world was one in which differing and competing notions of scribal wisdom and priestly legitimacy were hotly contested. Jews lived in a complicated world where foreign cultural influences clamored for attention, where international politics intimately affected Jews in Palestine and where groups of priests battled each other for control of the political and religious establishment. Ben Sira was not isolated from that world, and in this complex book he addressed the pressing issues of the world around him. He could apparently view Hellenistic ideas with favor, at times enlisting Hellenistic philosophy in his service.[96] He also saw the dangers of those who criticized the Jerusalem religious establishment, and he confronted them.

Although some of the details will differ, this basic assessment of the situation generally complements and confirms the impressions of scholars like Boccaccini and Argall who have suggested some mutual awareness between *1 Enoch* and Sirach. Continued intertextual study of works that are contem-porary with each other such as those considered

---

[96] See for instance Jack T. Sanders, *Ben Sira and Demotic Wisdom* (SBLMS 28; Chico 1983) who describes Ben Sira's use of the Hellenistic philosopher Theognis or Reinhold Bohlen, *Die Ehrung der Eltern bei Ben Sira: Studien zur Motivation und Interpretation eines familien-ethischen Grundwertes in früh-hellenistischer Zeit* (TThSt 51; Trier 1991) who argues that Ben Sira used Hellenistic views about the family in conjunction with traditional Israelite morality. The most vigorous claims about Ben Sira's positive views toward Hellenism have been made by Middendorp, *Die Stellung Jesu ben Siras*. In contrast several studies have argued that Ben Sira had a more negative approach to Hellenism even if he enlisted some Hellenistic ideas in this argument. See, for example, Alexander A. Di Lella, "Conservative and Progressive Theology: Sirach and Wisdom", *CBQ* 28 (1966) 139-154 and Hengel, *Judaism and Hellenism*, 138-153.

here will continue to enrich our reconstructions of Judaism in the Second Temple period. Reading Sirach, *1 Enoch* and *Aramaic Levi* together sheds valuable additional light on a critical period in the history of ancient Judaism.

Abbreviations of Sigla

A	Hebrew Ben Sira Manuscript A
B	Hebrew Ben Sira Manuscript B
Bm	Marginal readings of B
C	Hebrew Ben Sira Manuscript C (Anthology)
D	Hebrew Ben Sira Manuscript D
E	Hebrew Ben Sira Manuscript E
F	Hebrew Ben Sira Manuscript F
Fs	Festschrift
G	Greek translation of the Book of Ben Sira
G I	Elder Greek translation of the Book of Ben Sira
G II	Revision of G I
H	Hebrew Text of the Book of Ben Sira
H I	First Hebrew Recension of the Book of Ben Sira
H II	Second Hebrew Recension of the Book of Ben Sira
J	Yahwist
LXX	Septuagint
Ma	Hebrew Ben Sira Scroll from Masada
MS(S)	Manuscript(s)
N.T.	New Testament
O.T.	Old Testament
P	Priestly Document
Syr	Syriac
V	Vulgate
2Q18	Two Hebrew Ben Sira Fragments from Qumran Cave 2
11QPs[a]	Psalms Scroll from Qumran Cave 11

Abbreviations of Periodicals, Reference Works and Series

AB	Anchor Bible
ABD	*Anchor Bible Dictionart* vol. 1-6 (ed. D.N. Freedman; New York 1992)
AnBib	Analecta Biblica
APOT	*Apocrypha and Pseudepigrapha of the Old Testament* (ed. R.H. Charles)
ATAbh	Alttestamentliche Abhandlungen
ATSAT	Arbeiten zu Text und Sprache im Alten Testament
BAC	Biblioteca de autores cristianos
BBB	Bonner Biblische Beiträge
BEAT	Beiträge zur Erforschung des Alten Testaments und des antiken Judentums
BEHE.R	Bibliothèque de l'École des Hautes Études, Sciences Religieuses
BET	Beiträge zur biblischen Exegese und Theologie
BETL	Bibliotheca ephemeridum theologicarum lovaniensium
BEvT	Beiträge zur evangelischen Theologie
Bib	*Biblica*
BiBa	Biblische Basis-Bücher
BR	*Biblical Research*
BTFT	Bijdragen Tijdschrift voor filosofie en theologie
BJSt	Brown Judaic Studies
BKAT	Biblischer Kommentar: Altes Testament
BN	*Biblische Notizen*
BOT	De Boeken van het Oude Testament
BR	*Biblical Research*
BWANT	Beiträge zur Wissenschaft vom Alten und Neuen Testament
BZ	*Biblische Zeitschrift*
BZAW	Beihefte zur *ZAW*
BZNW	Beihefte zur *ZNW*

CBQ	*Catholic Biblical Quarterly*
CBQMS	Catholic Biblical Quarterly Monograph Series
CRINT	Compendium Rerum Iudaicarum ad Novum Testamentum
DBS	*Dictionnaire de la Bible, Supplément*
DiKi	Dialog der Kirchen
DJD	Discoveries in the Judaean Desert
EHAT	Exegetisches Handbuch zum Alten Testament
EHS	Europäische Hochschulschriften
EncJud	*Encyclopedia Judaica*
EstBíb	*Estudios Bíblicos*
ExpTim	*Expository Times*
HAL	Hebräisches und Aramäisches Lexikon zum Alten Testament (Ed. W. Baumgartner) Leiden 1967-1996.
HBK	Herders Bibelkommentar
HBS	Herders Biblische Studien
HSAT	Die heilige Schrift des Alten Testaments
HTR	*Harvard Theological Review*
HUCA	*Hebrew Union College Annual*
IDB	*Interpreter's Dictionary of the Bible*
IEJ	*Israel Exploration Journal*
JAOS	*Journal of the American Oriental Society*
JBTh	Jahrbuch für Biblische Theologie
JE	The Jewish Encyclopedia
JQR	*Jewish Quarterly Review*
JSJ	*Journal for the Study of Judaism in the Persian, Hellenistic and Roman period*
JSOT.S	Journal for the Study of the Old Testament. Supplement Series
JSPE.S	Journal for the Study of the Pseudepigrapha. Supplement Series
JSS	*Journal of Semitic Studies*
JThS	*Journal of Theological Studies*
KEH	Kurzgefasstes exegetisches Handbuch
KStTh	Kohlhammer Studienbücher
LD	Lectio Divina
LiSa	Los Libros Sagrados
LoB	Leggere oggi la Bibbia
MoBi	Monde de la Bible

NRSV	New Revised Standard Version
OBO	Orbis Biblicus et Orientalis
PRR	*The Presbyterian and Reformed Review*
ParSpV	*Parola, Spirito e Vita*
PBS	Pamphlet Bible Series
PRR	*The Presbyterian and Reformed Review*
PWCJS	Proceedings of the Eighth World Congress of Jewish Studies (1981; Jerusalem 1982)
QD	Quaestiones Disputatae
RAC	*Reallexikon für Antike und Christentum*
RB	*Revue Biblique*
REJ	*Revue des études juives*
RevQ	*Revue de Qumran*
RivB	*Rivista Biblica*
RSR	*Recherches de science religieuse*
RSV	Revised Standard Version
RTL	*Revue théologique de Louvain*
SB	*La Sainte Bible* (ed. L. Pirot et A. Clamer; Paris 1951)
SBL	Society of Biblical Literature. Early Judaism and Its Literature
SBLDS	Society of Biblical Literature. Dissertation Series
SBLMS	Society of Biblical Literature. Monograph Series
SBLSCS	Society of Biblical Literature. Septuagint and Cognate Studies
SSS	Semitic Study Series
SVTP	Studia in Veteris Testamenti Pseudepigrapha
TRE	*Theologische Realenzyklopädie*
TThSt	Trierer theologische Studien
TTS	Tübinger theologische Studien
TU	Texte und Untersuchungen
TZ	*Theologische Zeitschrift*
VT	*Vetus Testamentum*
VTS	Vetus Testamentum, Supplements
WUNT	Wissenschaftliche Untersuchungen zum Neuen Testament
ZAW	*Zeitschrift für die alttestamentliche Wissenschaft*
ZNW	*Zeitschrift für die neutestamèntliche Wissenschaft*
ZKT	*Zeitschrift für katholische Theologie*

Index of references

Personalia

Pancratius C. Beentjes   Katholieke Theologische Universiteit
Utrecht, Netherlands

Claudia V. Camp   Department of Religion
Texas Christian University
Fort Worth, Texas (USA)

Núria Calduch-Benages   Pontifical Gregorian University
Rome, Italy

Alexander A. Di Lella   Catholic University of America
Washington DC (USA)

Maurice Gilbert   Facultés Universitaires Notre-Dame de la
Paix
Namur (Belgium)

Johannes Marböck   Karl-Franzens-University
Graz (Austria)

Corrado Martone   Dipartimento di Orientalistica
University of Turin (Italy)

Stefan C. Reif   Taylor-Schechter Genizah Research Unit
Cambridge University (UK)

Friedrich V. Reiterer   Paris-Lodron-University
Salzburg (Austria)

Benjamin G. Wright   Department of Religion Studies
Lehigh University, Bethlehem, Penn (USA)

Walter de Gruyter
Berlin • New York

Freundschaft bei Ben Sira
Beiträge des Symposions zu Ben Sira - Salzburg 1995

Herausgegeben von Friedrich V. Reiterer

1996. 23,0 x 15,5 cm. VIII, 265 Seiten. Ganzleinen. ISBN 3-11-015261-4
(Beihefte zur Zeitschrift für die alttestamentliche Wissenschaft, Band 244)

Exegetische Untersuchungen zu den wichtigsten Perikopen über Freundschaft unter Beibehaltung unterschiedlicher exegetischer Ansätze.

Zentrale Stellen zum Thema Freundschaft. - "Freundschaft" ist in keinem anderen biblischen Buch so umfassend behandelt wie in Ben Sira.

Hintergrund: Seit der Zeit der griechischen Oberherrschaft erfolgte der Anschluß der jungen Oberschicht (politische und wirtschaftliche Emporkömmlinge) an die Machthaber.

Gegengewicht: Betonung der spätisraelitischen Tradition und Bildung von kleineren gesellschaftlichen Strukturen (Freundeskreis) zur Erhaltung der Identität.

Der Herausgeber ist Professor für Alttestamentliche Bibelwissenschaft an der Universität Salzburg.

Siegfried Wagner
Ausgewählte Aufsätze zum Alten Testament

Herausgegeben von Dietmar Mathias

23,0 x 15,5 cm. VIII, 294 Seiten. 1996. Ganzleinen. ISBN 3-11-014833-1
(Beihefte zur Zeitschrift für die alttestamentliche Wissenschaft, Band 240)

Der Band enthält Studien zu den Problemen biblischer Theologie im allgemeinen und speziell zu Fragen der Offenbarung, Sündenlehre, Theologie der Psalmen und des Buches Hiob, zur Exegese der Bücher Amos und Nehemia sowie zur Biographie von Ludwig Diestel

Der Autor ist Ordinarius für Altes Testament an der Universität Leipzig. - Der Herausgeber ist apl. Professor für Altes Testament an derselben Universität.

Walter de Gruyter & Co • Berlin • New York • Genthiner Straße 13 • D-10785 Berlin
Telefon: (030) 2 60 05-0 • Telefax: (030) 2 60 05-2 22
Unser Programm finden Sie im World Wide Web unter http://www.deGruyter.de